The Amish Cookbook

Favorite recipes
collected and received
by
Alvin and Sallie Lapp

Double Pen Foundation
C/O/ P.O. Box 111
East Earl, Pennsylvania PZ 17519

Publisher, Double Pen Foundation
Illustrations by Helen Edgell

ISBN # 0-96 372 75-0-8

Introduction

This book contains over one thousand tried recipes from fourteen different states. We wish to say "Thank You" in a special way to each and every one who shared their recipes with us. We needed you to make this book complete.

This can be your opportunity to get all these different delights right inside your door and turn them into treats on your own kitchen table.

We put this book together for your enjoyment. Your family being a few or many in number, we pass this great pleasure onto you.

May all these selected recipes coming from far and wide prove to be special to you, and fill your house with love. While working hard, have faith in the Lord, and Happy Cookin!

My Kitchen Prayer

Bless my little kitchen
Lord I love its every nook
Bless me as I do my work
Wash pots and pans and cook.

May the meals that I prepare
Be seasoned from Above
With Thy Blessings and Thy Grace
But most of all Thy Love.

As we partake of Earthly food
The table thou hast spread
We'll not forget to thank Thee
Lord for all our daily bread.

So Bless my little kitchen
Lord and those who enter in
May they find naught but joy and peace
And happiness there in.

AMEN

Contents

Recipes came from
these fourteen states

Beverages

A kind heart is a fountain of gladness
Making everything in its vacinity
Freshen into smiles

RHUBARB DRINK

3 cups rhubarb scant
1 1/2 cups sugar
4 cups water

Cook these ingredients together for 5 min. and strain in sieve. Add juice of 1 lemon and 1 1/4 cups frozen orange juice. Add ginger ale and water to suit taste.

Esther Fisher
Millersburg, PA

ROOT BEER

2 cups white sugar
2 T. or more root beer
1/2 t. yeast
3 raisins

Put all in a gallon jug and fill with warm water.
Set out in sun for 1 day and cool.

Mrs. Raymond S. Miller
Millersburg, Ohio

FRIENDSHIP TEA

9 oz. Tang (small jar)
3/4 oz. Lipton iced tea
12 oz. Wylers Presweetener Lemonade mix
2 cups sugar
2 t. cinnamon

Mix well and put in tight container. Put 2 heaping t. in cup, add hot water or cold water.

Treva Lichty
Arshbold, Ohio

ORANGE-RHUBARB DRINK

Cook 12 cups rhubarb in 3 cups water. Pour into a cloth bag to drip. To the juice add 4 cups sugar and 1 pk. orange flavored Kool-aid. This concentrate can be canned. Add water until it is desired for a refreshing drink. Approx. 3 gal. to the total above concentrate. We also like to mix pineapple juice to it when opening a can of concentrate.

Mary A. Kinsinger
Meyersdale, PA

If your wife doesn't treat you as you deserve be thankful

PUNCH

3 large cans frozen orange juice 2 large cans frozen lemonade
2 - 1 qt. cans pineapple juice 4 qt. 7-Up
1/2 cup sugar (optional)

Add water as directed in frozen juices. Add 7-Up and ice. Serves 100.

Mrs. Wilma Mast
S. Hutchinson, KS

INSTANT HOT CHOCOLATE

8 cups instant milk 1 1/2 cups sugar
8 oz. creamer 3/4 cup baking cocoa
1 lb. Nestle's Quick cocoa

Mix and sift in large bowl. Store in dry place.
Use 1/2 cup of mix for 1 cup hot water.

Cathryn Schmucker
Litchfield, Michigan

QUICK ROOT BEER

2 cups white sugar 1 T. root beer extract
1 t. yeast

Melt sugar with hot water and pour in gallon jug. Put in water to fill till lukewarm. Add extract and yeast.
Let set in warm sun for 1/2 day, then turn cap loose and put in cold place.
Ready to drink the next day.

Mrs. Henry Stutzman
Conewango Valley, NY

The person who never makes a mistake
Must get tired of doing nothing

GRAPE JUICE

In a qt. jar put:

1 cup Concord grapes 3/4 cup sugar

Fill with boiling water and process for 30 min.

Mrs. Ray J. Gingerich
Fillmore, NY

SLUSH

Fill 8 qt. bowl with fluffy snow. Sprinkle 1 pkg. of dry Kool-Aid and 1 cup sugar over snow, then add 1½ cups hot water. Stir and put in glass. Then it is ready to drink.

Mrs. Ray J. Gingerich
Fillmore, NY

He who says he understands women
has a misunderstanding right there

Breads Doughnuts Rolls

It takes masonry and timber to build a house
But it takes love to build a home

RICH DINNER BUNS

1 cup sugar
1/2 cup shortening
2 cups milk or warm water
2 eggs
1 T. salt
1 cup mashed potatoes
1 T. yeast dissolved in water
8 cups flour

Mrs. Vernon E. Bontrager
Iowa City, Iowa

HILLBILLY BREAD

2 eggs
1 cup honey
6 T. yeast in warm water
1 1/2 cups oil
4 T. salt
2 sticks oleo or butter melted
3 cups milk heated to boiling point
Add other ingredients and yeast, then add:
3 cups cold water
12 cups white flour
10 cups wheat flour

Knead dough 15 min. Rise till double, then knead real good. Let rise again, then put in pans. Do not overrise in pans before baking. Bake at 375 deg. for 30 min. Makes around 8-9 big loaves. It does not rise much in oven.

Mrs. Vernon E. Bontager
Iowa City, Iowa

Every man must do his own growing
No matter who his grandfather was

FAMOUS CINNAMON ROLLS

5 cups warm water
1 1/2 cups. soft lard or oil
4 eggs beaten
4 T. yeast
7 t. salt
2 cups sugar
Approx. 12-13 cups flour (all purpose)

Let rise till double, punch down and let rise again. Roll out and spread with melted butter or oleo, sprinkle with cinnamon, then put a generous layer of brown sugar on. Roll up, cut and put in pans, let rise and bake at 350 deg. for approximately 30 min. I use 8 in. foil pans and put 6 or 7 in a pan. Makes 10-12 pans. Make a thin icing of powdered sugar and milk or water and frost.

Mrs. Ray J. Gingerich
Fillmore, NY

WHOLE WHEAT BREAD

1 stick margarine (melted) Scald;
2 2/3 cups milk then cool
Dissolve 2 T. dry yeast in 2 cups warm water
2 beaten eggs 1 scant cup sugar
2 t. salt

Mix all the ingredients together. Add 5 cups whole wheat flour and white flour to finish.

Catherine Swarey
Belleville, PA

MOLASSES OATMEAL BREAD

1/4 cup vegetable oil 1/3 cup molasses (scant)
2 cups warm water 2 eggs
1 1/2 cups oatmeal 2 pkg. yeast
5-6 cups flour

Mix in order given. Knead till smooth and elastic. Place in a greased bowl, let rise till double in bulk. Punch down. Let rise 10 min. Shape into loaves - 2 large or 4 small. Let rise until double in bulk and bake at 350 deg. for 20-30 min.

Joni H. Shrock
Middlefield, Ohio

DOUGHNUT GLAZE

1 cup butter - melted 2 t. vanilla
3 cups powdered sugar Enough milk for dipping consistancy
Keep warm in top of double boiler.
Dip doughnuts hot and drain a bit.
Wooden spoon handle works nicely.

Lydiann J. Bricker
Panama, NY

Enough is what would satisfy most of us
If the neighbors didn't have more

OATMEAL BREAD

3 1/2 cups boiling water
2 cups oatmeal
1 cup honey or 1/2 cup sugar
2 T salt
2 T yeast
1 cup warm water
4 eggs
1-3 cups whole wheat flour
Bread flour to finish

Pour boiling water over oatmeal. Let stand 1/2 hr. Add honey (or sugar) and salt. Dissolve yeast in warm water. Add eggs. Combine the two mixtures. Add whole wheat flour. Finish with bread flour. Makes 4 loaves.

Catherine Swarey, Belleville, PA
Saloma Petersheim, Mifflintown, PA

DOUGHNUTS PLAIN AND SIMPLE

2 eggs
1 cup white sugar
1 cup milk
4 cups flour
5 t. salt
1 1/2 t. vanilla
4 t. baking powder

Beat the eggs and sugar together until light, then add milk and vanilla. Soft flour, baking powder and salt together and add to wet mix. Roll this big doughy mess out to 1/4 in. thickness on a floured board. Cut into shape and fry in 380 deg. deep oil on each side for about 3 min. or until nicely browned. Remove from oil and drain on paper towels. Good eating plain, sprinkled with powdered sugar or white sugar and cinnamon.

Joni H. Shrock
Middlefield, Ohio

If men speak ill of thee
Live so that nobody will believe it

ORANGE DROP DOUGHNUTS

About 1 qt. cooking oil
2 cups flour
1/2 cup sugar
1/2 cup light cream
1/2 cup orange juice
2 eggs
2 t. baking powder
1/4 t.soda
2 t. orange peel
powdered sugar (optional)

Heat oil in saucepan to about 375 deg.. Mix flour, baking powder and soda and sift 3 times. Beat eggs well, add sugar gradually and mix. Add dry ingredients to egg mixture alternately with cream and juice mix. Drop by tablespoons into hot oil and fry about 2 1/2 min. Turn them as soon as they come to the top of the oil, then turn frequently until they are as brown as desired. Drain. Sprinkle with sugar. Makes 2 1/2 doz.

Joni H. Shrock
Middlefield, Ohio

DOUGHNUT RECIPE

1 cup sugar
1 cup cream
1/2 cup milk
3 eggs
3 cups flour
2 t. baking powder

Roll out and cut doughnuts and fry in deep fat. I like to roll in sugar.

Miss Sara Shetter
Glasgow, KY

GINGERBREAD

1 cup molasses
1/2 cup lard
1 cup milk, sweet or sour
3 cups flour
2 t. soda
1 t. cream of tartar
1 t. ginger

Good with the following sauce poured over each serving.

GINGERBREAD SAUCE

1/2 cup brown sugar
2 T. cornstarch

Add 1 cup boiling water slowly, add 1/2 cup raisins. Cook slowly 5 min., add 1 T. butter.

Martha Hostetter
Fort Plain, NY

WHOLE WHEAT BREAD

3 1/2 cups warm water | 2 T. sugar
4 T. yeast | Let set at least 10 minutes.

In another bowl mix:

1 1/2 cups warm water | 1 cup butter or lard
1 cup honey | 2 T. salt

Combine the two mixtures and add:

5 beaten eggs | 12-14 cups whole wheat flour

Saloma Petersheim
Mifflintown, PA

STICKY BUNS

1 1/2 cups water | 1 1/2 cups milk
1/2 cup shortening | 1 heaping t. salt
3/4 cup sugar | 1 pkg. yeast
4 eggs | Flour as much as needed to handle dough

Sticky:

3 cups brown sugar | 2 sticks margarine
3 cups cream

Measure brown sugar and margarine into a saucepan. Bring to a boil and boil 5 min. Remove from heat and add cream.

Aaron Brubaker
Liverpool, PA

MOUNT MARYS COLLEGE DOUGHNUTS

1 cup Crisco | 1 cup sugar
1 cup mashed potatoes | 2 T. salt
1 qt. milk (scalded) | 6 egg yolks
3 T. yeast | 13 cups flour

Let rise 1 hr. Roll out, cut; let rise again to almost double. Then deep fry, glaze or frost.

Mrs. Leroy Stutzman
Sugar Creek, Ohio

SWEDISH RYE BREAD

2 pkg. active dry yeast 1/2 cup warm water (110 or 115 deg.)
1 tsp. sugar 3 cups hot water
1/2 cup melted vegetable shortening 3 t. salt
1/2 cup white sugar 1/2 cup molasses
1 1/2 cups rye flour 9 1/4 cups white flour

Dissolve yeast in warm water. Stir in 1 tsp. sugar, set aside. In large mixing bowl mix rye flour with 1/2 cup sugar and salt. Add hot water gradually, mixing to a smooth paste. Gradually add melted shortening and molasses. Beat well. Add yeast mixture and white flour. When dough becomes two still to work with spoon, knead in remaining flour until dough is smooth and elastic. Place in warm area until double in bulk. Divide into 3 loaves and place in greased 9x5x3 pans. Let rise until double. Bake at 325 deg. for 40 min. Remove from pans and rub tops and sides with melted shortening.

Mrs. Dan J. Troyer
Mercer, PA

Love, peace and happiness in the home
Is Infinitely more valuable than
Honor, fame and wealth

HONEY OATMEAL BREAD

2 1/2 cups boiling water 3/4 cup cooking oil
1 cup honey, karo or molasses 2 pkgs. dry yeast
2 T. salt 2 cups quick oatmeal
4 beaten eggs 2 cups whole wheat flour (or more)

Dissolve yeast in 1 cup warm water. Pour boiling water over oatmeal and set aside to cool till lukewarm. Mix all ingredients and beat well, then add yeast, being sure everything is just warm, before adding. Work in enough white flour (preferably unbleached) to make a nice spongy dough that is not sticky. Grease top and let rise. Knead and let rise again. Bake at 400 deg. for 10 min. Lower heat to 350 deg. for 25-30 min. A delicious nourishing bread. You may use as much wheat flour as you wish.

Mary Ann Hilty
Monroe, IN

DONUTS OR ROLLS

Melt in a large bowl:

2 sticks oleo
2 cups milk
2/3 cup sugar (scant)
4 1/2 t. salt

Then add 2 cups of cold water to melted mixture to cool to lukewarm.

Have ready 3 pkgs. or 3 round T. of dry yeast in 1/2 cup lukewarm water. Add to first mixture if cooled. Then add 6 cups flour. Beat and add 6 eggs. Beat again and add 6 more cups of flour. Never add more or less. Use big white cups for measuring and level full. Let rise, stir down, let rise again, then shape and let rise again. Then bake. Makes 80-90 donuts or 8-9 pans of rolls.

Ida Miller
Medford, Wisconsin

APPLE BREAD

3 cups flour
1 t. soda
2 t. cinnamon
1/2 t. baking powder
1/2 t. salt
1/2 t. oil
2 cups sugar
2 eggs (beaten)
1/2 t. vanilla
3 cups grated apples
1 cup nuts

Combine flour, cinnamon, soda, baking powder and salt. Combine oil, sugar, eggs, vanilla and apples. Stir into flour mixture. Add nuts. Divide into 2 bread pans. Bake at 350 deg. for 40 min. or until done.

Emma Hersberger
Dover, Delaware

BREAD

4 cups warm water — 4 T. yeast
1/2 cup sugar — 3 t. salt
1/2 cup oleo — 12-14 cups flour

Measure warm water into bowl. Sprinkle in yeast and stir till dissolved. Add sugar, salt, oleo and 6 cups flour to make a soft dough - stir well. Then add the rest of the flour. Let rise 1 hr.; knead, then rise 1 hr.; knead again. Let rise another hr. and make into 4 loaves. Bake at 375 deg. for 30 min. or until done.

Emma Hershberger
Dover, Delaware

OATMEAL BREAD

2 1/2 cups boiling water — 2 cups quick oats (uncooked)
1/2 cup honey or brown sugar — 2 T. salt
3/4 cup cooking oil — 4 eggs
2 pkg. yeast — 2 cups whole wheat flour or more

Dissolve yeast in 1/2 cup warm water with 1 t. brown sugar (unless you use instant yeast, then you don't need to dissolve it). Put boiling water in bowl, add oats, whole wheat flour, salt, cooking oil and honey. Cool to lukewarm. Add eggs, yeast and enough bread flour to finish. Knead twice. Makes 4 small loaves. Bake in 400 deg. oven for 10 min. Reduce heat to 350 deg. for another 25 min.

Emma Hershberger
Dover, Delaware

One thorn of experience is worth more
Than a wilderness of advice or warning

TO GLAZE DOUGHNUTS

1 pkg. gelatin soaked in 1/4 cup cold water — 1/4 cup cold water
1 box confectioners XXX sugar — 1/4 cup boiling water
2 T. melted Crisco — 1 t. vanilla

Put in double boiler and keep over hot water while glazing cooled doughnut; put on long stick and let drip.

Sue Wickey
Norfolk, NY

DOUGHNUTS

Mix together:

1 cup hot water
2 T. sugar
1 stick oleo
1 t. salt

Then add:

1 cup boiled milk
2 pkg. yeast
3 T. sugar
3 cups flour

Beat well. Add 3 eggs, beat well. Then add 3 more cups flour. This is a very soft doughnut. Let rise only once. Roll on floured board and cut, let rise 20 min. Fry in hot shortening until brown; cool and glaze.

Sue Wickey
Norfolk, NY

MY BEST GINGER BREAD

1/2 cup lard
1/2 cup sugar
1 cup molasses
1 egg
1 t. cinnamon
1 t. ginger
1/2 t. cloves
1 1/2 t. soda
1/2 t. salt
2 1/2 c. flour
1 cup hot water

Saloma J. Byler
Dewittville, NY

ZUCCHINI BREAD

1 cup sugar
1/2 cup salad oil
2 eggs
1 t. lemon peel
1/2 t. orange extract
2 t. baking powder
1/2 t. salt
1/8 t. ginger
1/2 t. soda
1/8 t. nutmeg (grated)
1 cup unpeeled zucchini
1/2 cup nuts, coarsely chopped
1 3/4 cups flour

Bake in greased loaf pans and bake at 375 deg. for approx. 55 min.

WHITE BREAD

1 T. or pkg. of dry yeast
3/4 cup sugar
2 qt. warm water of milk or potato water may be added, and just that much less water
1 T. salt

Soak yeast in a cup of warm water, mix in the rest of ingredients with warm liquid (not hot). Stir yeast in and enough flour, a little at a time, and knead good with plenty of grease until it gets elastic. Let rise in a greased bowl for 10-15 min. Punch down, let rise again for 10-15 min. Punch down, let rise till double in size; punch down and shape and divide into loaves. Makes 4 or 5 loaves depending on your size of pans. Let rise, then bake for 45 min. in 350 deg. oven. Secret is in letting it rise and punching down every 10-15 min.

Sue Wickey
Norfolk, NY

CORN BREAD

1 cup corn meal
1 cup flour
4 t. baking powder
1/2 t. salt
1/4 cup sugar
1 egg
1/2 cup shortening (melted)
1 cup milk

Mix together in order given. Mix real good. Pour in greased 9x12" pan. Bake at 325 deg. for 3/4 hr.

Sue Wickey, Norfolk, NY
Martha Hostetter, Fort Plain, NY

SWEET MILK DOUGHNUTS

3 eggs well beaten
1 cup sugar
3 T. melted butter
1 t. salt
1 cup milk
3 1/2 cups sifted flour
4 t. baking powder
1 t. vanilla
1/2 t. nutmeg

Beat eggs, add sugar, then milk. Add sifted dry ingredients. Add melted butter. Roll out to 1/4 in. thickness. Fry in deep fat 2 to 3 min. Drain on brown paper. Roll in sugar and cinnamon.

Fannie Gingrich
Ethridge, TN

EASY GINGERBREAD

1 cup sugar
1/2 cup shortening
2 cups flour
1 t. cinnamon
1/2 t. allspice
1/2 t. salt

Mix as for pie crust and save 1/2 cup for top.
Add:

2 T. molasses
1 egg
1 t. soda
1 t. baking powder
1 t. vanilla
1 cup sour milk

Mix well, put in loaf pan, put crumbs on top. Bake 3/4 hr. in 375 deg. oven.

Martha Hostetter
Fort Plain, NY

CREAM STICKS

2 pkg. dry yeast soaked in 1 cup warm water
1 cup milk
1/2 cup butter or oleo
2/3 cup sugar
2 eggs
6 cups flour
1 tsp. salt

Put butter, sugar, eggs and salt into the scalded milk; let cool. Then add to the yeast. Add the flour. Let rise once, roll out and cut. Let rise again. Fry in deep fat or veg. oil. Make a slit in side and fill with filling. Also spread on top.

CREAM STICK FILLING

2 1/3 cups powdered sugar
1/4 t. salt
1 egg white beaten

Mix together and set aside.
Boil 1 minute:

2 T. water
1/4 cup white sugar

Add to first mixture. Add:

1 t. flavor
1/2 cup Crisco oil or veg. oil

Mrs. Joe J. Yoder
Lawrenceburg, TN

One of the great arts of living
Is the art of forgetting

RAISIN BREAD

1/2 cup sugar
2 T. salt
1 cup lard or oil
1 1/2 cup hot milk
2 eggs beaten
2 T. yeast in 1 cup warm water
1 T. cinnamon
1 1/2-2 cups raisins cooked 5 min. in water to cover; add water if necessary to make 5 cups liquid.
10 or 12 cups flour (more if necessary)
Bake at 350 deg. for 40 min.
Makes 4 or 5 loaves.

Lydia Stoltzfus
Bloomsburg, PA

WHOLE WHEAT BREAD

Heat 6 cups buttermilk or fresh milk.
Add 3 T. molasses (or natural brown sugar)
3 T. honey
3/4 cup soy oil or veg. oil
2 T. salt (less can be used)
3 cups warm water

Soak 3 T. of yeast in the warm water, cool boiled milk to lukewarm. Add all ingredients together after yeast has soaked 15 min. Stir in a few cups of flour at a time, beating and stirring till all the flour is stirred in (25 cups more or less). Knead good to a sponge-shape and put into 6 greased pans. Let rise some (not double in size). Put in hot over 450 deg. for 15 min. Lower heat to 300 deg. for 45 min. or longer.

Sue Wickey
Norfolk, NY

BANANA BREAD

2/3 cup sugar
1/2 cup shortening
2 eggs
3 t. sour milk
1 cup mashed bananas
Mix this, then add:
2 cups flour
1 t. baking powder
1/2 t. baking soda
Pour into greased loaf pan and bake at 350 deg. for 45 min. to 1 hr.

Aaron Brubacker
Liverpool, PA

BREAD FOR ONE LOAF

1 cup warm water
1 t. salt
1 T. sugar
1 t. lard or cooking oil
1 t. dry yeast
3 cups flour

Combine first five ingredients in order given. Let stand until yeast dissolves. Stir in flour, beat until smooth, add remaining flour. Work dough in bowl for 5-10 min. Let stand until double. Put in bread pan. Let stand for 1/2 hr. Knead and prick deeply with fork. Let stand till ready to bake. Bake in hot oven.

Mrs. J. David Byler
Panxsutawney, IA

ITALIAN BREAD

Mix:
1 1/2 cups flour
2 pkg. yeast
1 1/2 t. Italian seasoning

Heat until just warm:
1 cup milk
2 t. garlic salt
2 T. butter
2 T. sugar
1/2 cup warm water

Add to flour mixture.

Then add:
2 eggs
3 1/2 cups flour
1/2 cup parmesan cheese

Let rise till doubled. Work down. Let set 10 min. Shape into balls. Dip in melted butter and parmesan chees. Let rise until double. Bake at 375 deg. for 20-25 min.

Saloma Petersheim
Mifflintown, PA

RAISIN BREAD

8 cups lukewarm water
1 cup white sugar
6 T. dry yeast
2 heaping cups raisins
4 T. vegetable oil
6 t. salt
2 heaping T. cinnamon

Proceed with flour as for white bread.

Naomi Peachy
Little Falls, NY

WHITE BREAD

3 cups warm water
1/2 cup sugar
2 T. salt (scant)
1 T. lard
1 T. or 1 pkg. dry yeast
9 cups bread flour

Water should be very warm but not hot when tested on inside of wrist. Combine water, sugar, salt, yeast and lard. Let stand until yeast dissolved. Stir in 5 cups flour. Beat until smooth. Add remaining flour until dough can be handled. Turn out onto a greased surface and knead vigorously with both hands 5-10 min. Cover. Set in warm place to rise for 30 min. Then knead lightly. Let rise for 1 hr. then divide dough and put into greased pans. Let set for 30 min., then knead each loaf a few seconds. Repeat in about 30 min. Then prick each loaf deeply with a fork. Let rise until double in size or until light. Bake for 20-30 min. at 350-400 deg. Turn twice while baking. Grease top of loaf when removing from oven. Makes 3 loaves.

Catherine Swarey
Belleville, PA

TROPICAL GINGERBREAD

1/2 cup veg. oil
1/2 cup sugar
2 1/2 cups all purpose flour
1 cup baking molasses
1 cup hot water
1/2 t. salt
1 egg
1 1/2 t. soda
1 1/2 t. ginger
1 1/2 t. cinnamon
1/2 t. cloves

Beat together shortening, sugar, and egg. Sift together flour, soda, salt, and spices. Combine molasses and water; add alternately with dry ingredients to first mixture. Pour in greased 9x13" pan and bake in moderate oven.

Mrs. Dan J. Troyer
Mercer, PA

People who get out and dig
Are seldom in the hole

FARMER KNEP

2 cups flour
1 t. baking powder
2 T. sugar
1 egg
1/2 t. salt

Milk and cream to mix for a thick dough. Drop in hot lard or oil to bake, then dip in frosting.

Frosting:
Cook till soft:
1 cup brown sugar
1 cup cream
1 T. butter

Joe Borntreger
Cashton, Wisconsin

BREAD DOUGHNUTS

Add: 2 pkg. yeast to 1/2 cup warm water. Let stand.

Scald 3/4 cup milk; pour into large bowl with 1/4 cup sugar and 1 t. salt.

Blend together and cool to lukewarm. Stir yeast mixture well and pour into bowl.

Mix in:
1/3 cup soft shortening
2 eggs
3 1/4 cups sifted flour

Beat until batter is smooth and cover. Let rise in warm place until doubled, about 30 min. Roll out and cut while fat is heating.

Joe Borntreger
Cashton, Wisconsin

Whenever you get into deep water
It is wise to keep your mouth shut

FRENCH BREAD

3 cups warm water — 3 T. yeast
3 T. sugar
Let set 10 min.
Add:
1/4 cup shortening (melted) — 1 T. salt
5 cups bread flour

Work in 3-4 more cups of flour. Let rise once. Work out in 3 long loaves. Place on cookie sheets. Slash with sharp knife. Let rise again.

Brush on top before baking:
1 egg beaten
1 T. water
Bake at 350 deg. for 30 min.

Mrs. Wilma Mast
South Hutchinson, KS

Most folks are about as happy
As they make up their minds to be

BANANA BREAD

1/2 cup lard or less — 1 cup sugar
2 eggs beaten — 3 ripe bananas, mashed
2 cups flour — 1 t. soda
1/2 t. salt or less — 1/2 cup chopped nuts

Mix and bake in well-greased loaf pan. Bake at 325 deg. for one hr. or till done.

Joe Borntreger
Cashton, Wisconsin

BUTTERHORNS

2 T. yeast
1 1/2 cups warm water
2 cups scalded milk
3/4 cup sugar
1 cup oil or shortening
4 eggs
3 t. salt
10 cups flour

Pour hot milk over salt, sugar and shortening in a large bowl. Dissolve yeast in warm water in a smaller bowl. Add eggs to yeast and beat well. When milk mixture is lukewarm, add yeast mixture and beat well. Add 6 cups of flour and beat again. Stir in last 4 cups. Let rise until double (1-2 hrs). Divide dough into 4 equal parts. Roll each part into a circle, brush melted butter on dough and cut into 12 pie wedges. Begin rolling up from wide ends and place on baking sheet. Let rise 1 hr. and then bake at 325 deg. for 15 min.

Mrs. Wilma Mast
South Hutchinson, KS

To be without friends
Is a serious form of poverty

PUMPKIN DATE NUT BREAD

2/3 cup butter
3 eggs
2 cups sugar
1/2 cup water
1 1/2 cups canned pumpkin
2 1/3 cups sifted flour
2 t. soda
1 t. cinnamon
1 t. salt or less
1/2 t. cloves
2/3 cup chopped pecans
2/3 cup cut up dates

Cream butter and sugar. Gradually add eggs, beat well. Blend in water, pumpkin and sifted dry ingredients. Fold in nuts and dates. Pour into 2 greased loaf pans. Bake at 350 deg. for about 1 hr. Makes 2 loaves.

Joe Borntreger
Cashton, Wisconsin

MOLLY'S WHOLE WHEAT BREAD

3 T. yeast
3 t. sugar
4 1/2 T. maple syrup or molasses
3 t. salt
2 1/2 cups melted lard
1 1/2 cups warm water
3 cups potato water
6 T. sugar
9 cups whole wheat flour

Dissolve yeast in warm water and 3 t. sugar. Mix potato water, maple syrup, sugar and salt. Add yeast and whole wheat flour. Add melted lard. Mix well and let stand 12 min., then mix enough white bread flour to make a soft but not sticky dough. Let rise to double. Punch down and leg rise again. When double in bulk, shape into loaves and let rise 1 hr. Bake at 350 deg. for 30-35 min.

Martha Esh
Newburg, PA

CINNAMON YEAST ROLLS

1 T. yeast
1/4 cup sugar
1 t. salt
1/4 cup salad oil or oleo
1 T. cinnamon
1/2 cup brown sugar
1/4 cup water
1 cup lukewarm milk
3 cups flour
2 beaten eggs
3 T. melted butter
1/2 cup raisins
1 T. butter

Dissolve yeast in milk. Add sugar, 1 1/2 cups flour. When bubbly, add salt, eggs, salad oil and 1 1/2 cups flour. Knead. Let rise until double size. Roll to 1/4 in. thick. Spread with melted butter and sprinkle with cinnamon and raisins. Roll like jelly rolls, cut a 1/2 in. slices. Place in greased pans. Let rise till double in size. Just before baking, pour caramel syrup over it (made by bringing to boil the brown sugar, 1 T. butter and water). Bake at 350 deg. for 35 min. Makes 18 rolls.

Mrs. Samuel D. Beachy
Clark, MO

The trouble with our past
Is that it refuses to stay past

CORN BREAD

1/2 cup sugar
3/4 cup corn meal
1 1/2 cups flour
2 t. baking powder
1 cup milk
1/4 cup cooking oil or lard
1 egg
salt

Mix dry ingredients, add the rest, stir and bake.

Mrs. Samuel D. Beachy
Clark, MO

PARKERHOUSE ROLLS

2 cups scalded milk
1/2 cup sugar
1/2 cup warm water
2 cups bread mix
6 cups bread flour (more or less)
2 t. salt
3 T. shortening
2 pkgs. yeast
2 beaten eggs

Scald milk, add sugar, salt and shortening. Dissolve yeast in warm water. When milk mixture has cooled to lukewarm, add dissolved yeast. Mix thoroughly and add enough flour to make a thin batter and beat until smooth. Cover and set in warm place until light and bubbly. Add beaten eggs and flour to make a stiff dough. Knead until smooth and pliable. Let stand in warm place until double in bulk. Shape into rolls and place in pans. Let rise. Bake at 350 deg. for about 20 min.

Elizabeth Mae Raber
Montgomery, IN

BRAN MUFFINS

3/4 cup whole wheat flour
1/2 cup white flour
3 t. baking powder
1/2 t. salt
1/4 cup brown sugar
1 1/2 cups bran
1 cup milk
2 eggs
1/4 cup cooking oil

Sift together dry ingredients. Add milk, eggs and oil. Beat well. Bake in 12 greased muffin cups in 350 deg. oven for about 25 min. or until done.

Elizabeth Mae Raber
Montgomery, IN

BASIC SWEET ROLLS

Stir:
1 stick oleo | 1 cup sugar
2 pt. hot milk
Add:
4 eggs (beaten) | 2 T. salt

Put 2 T. yeast in 1 cup warm water. Cool milk, then add yeast. Put in order given. Add flour till stiff—about 12 cups.

Martha I. Ghetler
Glasgow, KY

EMMA'S BISCUITS

2 cups flour | 4 t. baking powder
3 T. lard | 3/4-1 cup milk

Sift flour, baking powser and salt together, cup in lard. When the mixture is in lumps the size of peas, add the milk all at once. Mix well together and turn dough out onto a floured board. Rill 3/4 in. thick and cut with biscuit cutter. Bake at 450 deg. for 12 min. Makes 16-18 biscuits. Drop biscuits may be made by adding 1/4 cup milk preceding recipe and dropping dough from a spoon onto cookie sheet or into muffin pans.

Mrs. Amos W. Yoder
Jamesport, MO

When there is love in the heart
There are rainbows in the eyes

Those that most need advice
Are the ones who like it least

Cakes & Icings

FROSTING RECIPE FOR CAKES

1 cup sugar
1 cup water
Cook it till it's thick like molasses; then beat the whites of 2 eggs and mix it. Add a little cream of tartar and mix it again, but don't cook it after you put in cream of tartar and egg whites.

Joe Borntreger

Cashton, WI

DOCTOR BIRD CAKE

3 cups flour
1 t. baking soda
1 t. cinnamon
2 cups sugar
1 t. salt
1 1/2 cups oil
3 eggs
1 - 8 oz. can undrained pineapples
2 cups diced ripe bananas
1/2 cups nuts
1 1/2 t. vanilla
Bake at 350 deg. for 1 hr. 20 min. in greased and floured tube pan.

Fannie S. Miller
Bird-in-Hand, PA

CHEESE CAKE

Crumbs:
2 1/2 cups graham cracker crumbs
3 T. sugar
3/4 cup butter (melted)
Then cook together:
1 T. gelatin
1/2 cup water
1 cup sugar
1 cup milk
2 egg yolks
Add:
1/2 T. lemon juice
1/2 T. vanilla
Mix to: 3 cups cream cheese
Beat:
2 egg whites
1/4 cup Dream Whip
1/2 cup water
Add to the above mixture and beat together. Pour over crust.

Fannie S. Miller
Bird-in-Hand, PA

PUMPKIN CAKE ROLL

3 eggs
1 cup sugar
2/3 cup pumpkin
3/4 cup flour
1 cup finely chopped nuts
1 t. lemon juice
1 t. baking powder
2 t. cinnamon
1/2 t. nutmeg
1/2 t. salt

Beat eggs, gradually add sugar, beat till fluffy. Stir in pumpkin and lemon juice. Add flour, baking powder, cinnamon, nutmeg, salt. Spread in greased and floured 15x10x1 in. pan. Top with nuts. Bake at 375 deg. for 15 min. Turn out on towel sprinkled with powdered sugar; roll towel and cake together; cool. Unroll, spread filling over cake and roll.

Filling:
1 cup 10X sugar
6 oz. cream cheese
4 T. butter
1/2 t. vanilla

Fannie S. Miller
Bird-in-Hand, PA

Don't let your house get too dirty
It attracts company

SILVER WHITE CAKE

Sift together:
2 1/4 cups flour
4 t. baking powder
1 t. salt
1 1/2 cups sugar
Add:
1/2 cup shortening
2/3 cup milk
1 t. flavoring
Beat 2 minutes.
Add:
1/3 cup milk
4 large unbeaten egg whites
Beat 2 min.
Bake at 350 deg. 30-35 min. or till done.

Joe Borntreger
Cashton, WI

RED VELVET COCOA CAKE

1/2 cup butter or margarine
1 1/2 cups granulated sugar
1 t. vanilla
2 eggs
1 T. red food color
2 cups unsifted all-purpose flour
1 cup buttermilk or sour milk
1/4 cup Hershey's cocoa
1 t. salt
1 1/2 t. baking soda
1 T. vinegar

Cream butter or margarine, sugar and vanilla in large bowl. Add eggs and food color; blend thoroughly. In separate bowl combine flour, cocoa, and salt; add alternately with buttermilk or sour milk to creamed mixture. Stir baking soda into vinegar; fold carefully into batter (do not beat). Pour into two greased and floured 9-inch round cake pans. Bake at 350 deg. for 30-35 min. or until cake tester comes out clean. Cool 10 min; remove from pans. Cool completely on wire racks.
*To sour milk: Use 1 T. vinegar plus milk to equal 1 cup.

Aaron Brubacker
Liverpool, PA

Some people seem to think they are big shots
Because they are always exploding

BEST GINGER BREAD CAKE

1/2 cup butter or lard
1/2 cup sugar
1 egg beaten
2 1/2 cups flour (sifted)
1 cup sorghum or molasses
1 cup hot water
1 1/2 t. soda
1 t. cinnamon
1 t. cloves
1/2 t. salt

Cream shortening and sugar; add beaten egg. Measure and sift dry ingredients. Mix molasses with hot water, add dry ingredients alternately with liquid a little at a time; beat after each addition. Bake at 350 deg. for 45 min.

Joe Borntreger
Cashton, WI

CREAM ALMOND CAKE

3/4 cup shortening 1 1/2 cup sugar
3 cups cake flour 1 cup milk
1/2 t. salt 2 t. baking powder
5 egg whites 1 t. almond extract
2 T. cornstarch in cup, fill up with flour. 1 cup cake flour.

Cream shortening, add sugar gradually and beat until fluffy, sift flour, measure and add salt, baking powder, sift again. Add dry ingredients alternately with milk and flavoring. Beat thoroughly after each addition. Fold in stiffly beaten egg whites. Pour into greased layer pans. Bake at 350 deg. for 30 min.

Joe Borntreger
Cashton, WI

SUN SHINE CAKE

7 eggs 1 1/4 cup sugar
1 cup flour 1/8 t. cream of tartar

Separate eggs. Beat the yolks. Put a little salt in the whites. Beat to foam and add the cream of tartar. Beat very stiff, add sugar, flavor, and beat again. Add the yolks and mix well. Last of all flour, beat in lightly.

Joe Borntreger

Cashton, WI

WHIPPED CREAM CAKE

1 cup thick cream 1 cup sugar
1 3/4 cups flour 2 eggs
1/4 t. salt 2 1/2 t. baking powder
1 t. vanilla

Whip the cream, then add beaten egg yolks and vanilla. Mix sugar, flour, salt and baking powder, add stiffly beaten egg whites last. Bake at 325 deg. or 350 deg.

Joe Borntreger
Cashton, WI

MOLASSES CAKE

1 cup cane molasses
1 t. soda
Stir until light color.
3 T. lard
1 egg
1 cup milk and cream
1/4 t. cinnamon
1/4 t. allspice
2 1/2 cups flour.
Bake at 325 deg.

Joe Borntreger
Cashton, WI

Happy Hearts Make
Happy Homes

SUGAR PLUM SPICE CAKE

Measure into sifter:
2 1/2 cups flour
1 t. baking powder
1 t. soda
3/4 t. salt
3/4 t. cinnamon
3/4 t. cloves
1 cup sugar
Measure into mixing bowl:
1/2 cup shortening
Measure into small bowl:
Sour milk or buttermilk
Have ready:
2/3 cup brown sugar firmly packed
2 eggs unbeaten

With butter, oleo, or lard, use 1 cup plus 2 T. sour milk or buttermilk. With vegetable oil or any other shortening use 1 1/4 cut sour milk or buttermilk.

1. Stir shortening just to soften. Sift dry ingredients in, add brown sugar. Add 1 cup of milk and mix until all flour is dampened. Then beat 2 min.
2. Add eggs and remaining milk and beat well.

Joe Bornteger
Cashton, WI

GOLDEN SPONGE CAKE

First Part:
Beat 6 egg whites; when foamy add pinch of salt and 1/2 t. cream of tartar. Beat until stiff; slowly add 3/4 cup sugar; fold in 1/2 cup flour sifted 3 times. Add 1/2 t. vanilla. Pour mixture in bottom of an ungreased angel food pan. Let stand while mixing second part.
Second Part:
6 egg yolks, well beaten
1/2 cup sugar
2 T. cold water
1/2 t. vanilla or lemon
3/4 cup sifted flour (scant)
3/4 t. baking powder; sift with flour 3 times.
Blend all ingredients, pour over first part. Bake about 50 min. or till finished.

Joe Borntreger
Cashton, WI

SPONGE CAKE

4 eggs beaten well
2 cups sugar, beat again.
2 cups flour with 2 t. baking powder.
Now add slowly 1 cup boiling water. Bake at 350 deg. till done.

Joe Borntreger
Cashton, WI

CHIFFON CAKE

1 cup egg whites (7 or 8 eggs)
1/2 t. cream of tartar
2 cups sifted flour
1 1/2 cups sugar
1/2 cup cooking oil
3/4 cup water
3 t. baking powder
1/2 t. salt
1 t. vanilla
2 t. grated lemon rind
7 unbeaten egg yolks

1. Preheat oven to 325 deg.
2. Whip egg whites and cream of tartar until very stiff peaks are formed (must be stiffer than for angel food cake)
3. Sift flour, sugar, salt and baking powder into a large mixing bowl.
4. Make a well in the center of the flour, add the oil, egg yolks, water, vanilla and lemon rind.
5. Beat with a wooden spoon until smooth.
6. Gradually pou egg yolks mixture over whipped egg whites folding generally with a rubber scraper just until blended. Do not stir.
7. Pour into an ungreased angel food cake pan. Bake at 325 deg.

Joe Borntreger
Cashton, WI

Lots of people know how to make a living
But few know how to live

BLUEBERRY BUCKLE CAKE

2 cups all-purpose flour
3/4 cup sugar
2 1/2 t. baking powder
3/4 t. salt
1/4 cup shortening
3/4 cup milk
1 egg

Carefully stir 2 cups well-drained blueberries into batter.

Topping:

1/2 cup sugar
1/2 tsp. cinnamon
1/3 cup all-purpose flour
1/4 cup soft butter

Sprinkle over batter in pans. Bake 45-50 min.

Aaron Brubacker
Liverpool, PA

CREAM CAKE

1 egg
1 cup sugar
1 t. baking powder
flavoring
1 cup sweet cream
1 cup flour
1 t. soda

Enos Yoders
Park City, KY

1, 2, 3, 4 CAKE

1 cup cream
3 cups flour
1 t. soda
flavoring
2 cups sugar
4 eggs
1 t. baking powder

Enos Yoders
Park City, KY

TASTY CAKE

2 cups flour
2 T. butter
4 eggs
1/4 t. salt
2 cups sugar
2 t. baking powder
1 cup milk
1 T. vanilla

Mix and pour in greased baking sheet 18"x21"x1". Bake at 350 deg. for 15 min. When done, spread an 8 oz. jar of peanut butter over cake. (For best results, warm peanut butter first to prevent tearing cake.) Let cool. Melt an 8 oz. Hershey Chocolate bar. Spread over peanut butter. Cut in bars and wrap each in plastic wrap. You can also use the recipe below instead of the peanut butter and chocolate.

GOOD TANDY CAKE ICING

3/4 cup sugar
1/4 cup milk
1/2 stick margarine

Boil steadily 1 minute, stirring constantly. Remove from heat and add 1 cup chocolate chips. Beat until thick and shiny.

Saloma Petersheim
Mifflintown, PA

MY CHOCOLATE CAKE

2 cups brown sugar
1/2 cup shortening
2 eggs
1 cup hot water
1/2 cup sour milk or cream
4 T. cocoa (Hershey's)
2 1/4 cup flour
2 t. soda
1/2 t. salt
1 t. vanilla

Mix in order given. Bake at 350 deg. for 35 minutes.

Enos Yoders
Park City, KY

CARAMEL FROSTING

1 1/2 cups brown sugar
1/2 T. butter
3/4 cup thin cream

Cook until soft ball is formed in cold water. Remove from heat and beat till thick enough to spread.

Enos Yoder
Park City, KY

MIDNIGHT CAKE

1 cup shortening
2 1/2 cups sugar
3 cups flour
6 T. cocoa
4 eggs
2 t. soda
2 t. baking powder
1 t. salt
2 t. vanilla
2 cups hot water

Enos Yoders
Park City, KY

CHOCOLATE CAKE WITH COFFEE

2 cups sugar 2 cups flour
3/4 cups cocoa
1 T. soda
3/4 cups oil
1 cup milk
1 cup hot strong coffee
vanilla
pinch of salt

Bake at 350 deg. for 35 to 40 min.

Esther Marie Fisher
Conneautville, PA

Before asking for another talent
Be sure you make use of the ones you have

NUT CAKE

2 cups flour
1 1/2 cups sugar
3 t. baking powder
1/2 t. salt
3/4 cup milk
1/2 cup butter or oleo
1 cup nut meats
1 cup coconut
1 t. vanilla
4 egg whites

Blend all ingredients; then add beaten egg whites. Bake either in loaf or 2 nine-inch pans.

Enos Yoders
Park City, KY

LOVELIGHT YELLOW CHIFFON CAKE

3 eggs, separated
1 1/2 cups sugar
2 1/4 cups sifted cake flour
3 t. baking powder
1 t. salt
1 cup cooking oil
1 cup milk
1 1/2 t. vanilla

Heat oven to 350 deg. Oil lightly and dust with 2 layer cake pans 9 x 1 1/2". Beat egg whites until frothy. Gradually beat in 1/2 cup sugar. Beat until stiff and glossy. In another bowl sift remaining sugar, flour, baking powder and salt. Add ccoking oil, 1/2 cup milk and vanilla. Beat 1 min. on mixer or 150 strokes by hand, add to remaining milk and egg yolks. Beat 1 min. Fold in beaten egg whites. Bake 30-35 min. Cool and frost.

Enos Yoders
Park City, KY

SPICY PUMPKIN SHEET CAKE

4 eggs
1 3/4 cups 16 oz. can pumpkin
1 cup sugar
3/4 cup firmly packed brown sugar
1 cup oil
2 cups flour
2 t. baking powder
1 t. baking soda
1 t. cinnamon
1/2 t. ginger
1/2 t. nutmeg

Esther Marie Fisher
Conneautville, PA

How to live in peace
Mind your own business

CREAM FILLED COFFEE CAKE

1 cup margarine
2 cups granulated sugar
2 eggs
2 t. soda
4 cups flour (scant)
1 t. salt
2 cups buttermilk or sour milk
2 t. baking powder

Topping:

1 cup brown sugar
4 T. margarine
4 T. flour
2 T. cinnamon

Put in 4 pie pans. Bake at 350 deg. Let cool. Take out of pan and cut in half.

Filling:

4 beaten egg whites
4 cups powdered sugar
2 t. vanilla
2 cups Crisco

Esther Marie Fisher
Conneautville, PA

PINEAPPLE DUMPCAKE

2 cups flour
1/2 t. salt
2 t. soda
1 1/2 cups white sugar
1 t. vanilla
2 cups crushed pineapple

Bake at 350 deg. for 35 min. in an ungreased 9x13 in. pan.

Topping for this cake:

1 small can milnot
3/4 cup sugar
1/4 stick oleo

Boil 5 min. stirring constantly. Pour over hot cake.

Ella Hershberger
Oakland, MD

QUICK CREAMED FROSTING

Cream:

1/2 cup honey
1/2 cup butter

Add vanilla

Beat:

2 egg whites till form soft peaks. Add 1 cup confectioner's sugar, gradually beating after each addition. Fold egg white mixture gradually into honey mixture. Nuts or coconut can be added if desired.

Martha Hostetler
Fort Plain, NY

DAFFODIL CAKE

As light and fresh tasting as the first daffodils of Spring. And almost too pretty to eat until you taste the delicate orange flavor. A springtime treat you'll enjoy all year long.

1 cup sifted flour
1 1/2 cups egg whites (about 12)
1/2 t. salt
1/2 cup egg yolks (about 6)
1 t. cream of tartar
3/4 cup sugar
1/2 cup sugar
1/2 t. vanilla
1 t. orange extract

Sift flour and 3/4 cup sugar together. Beat egg whites, salt and cream of tartar until whites form soft peaks. Add remaining 1/2 cup sugar to whites 2 T. at a time, beating well after each addition until whites are stiff, but not dry. Carefully fold in dry ingredients, divide batter in two parts; to 1/2 of batter add vanilla. Beat egg yolks until very thick and lemon color. To remaining batter fold in thick yolks and orange extract, spoon yellow and white batter alternately into ungreased 10" tube pan. Bake in a 350 deg (moderate oven for 50 min. Invert pan to cool before removing from pan. Makes 10-12 servings.

Mrs. Ammon A. Troyer
Ashland, OH

A lie may take care of the present
But it has no future

WALNUT BROWNIE BUTTER CAKE

2/3 cup butter
2 eggs
1 1/4 cups milk
3 cups cake flour
1 t. salt
1 3/4 cups sugar
1 1/4 t. vanilla
1/4 t. maple flavor
2 1/2 t. baking powder
1 cup nuts

Cream butter, sugar, vanilla, and maple flavor together until fluffy. Add cake flour, baking powder and salt. Add milk, then fold in nuts. Pour batter into 3 x 8 in. greased floured pans. Bake 350 deg. for 35 to 50 min. or until done.

Mrs. Ammon A. Troyer
Ashland, OH

SUSAN COFFEE CAKE

3/4 cup sugar
1 1/2 cups flour
1/4 cup oleo
1 1/2 t. baking powder
1 egg
1/2 t. salt
1/2 cup milk

Mix well the sugar, oleo, eggs. Sift flour, baking powder, and salt. Add to egg mixture alternately with milk. Spread half of batter in greased pan.

Mix remaining

1/2 cup brown sugar
2 T. water
1/2 cup nuts
2 T. flour
1 t. melted oleo
2 t. cinnamon

Spread half over batter in pan and circle in with fork for marble effect. Repeat with remaining batter and cinnamon topping. Bake at 375 deg. for about 30 min.

Mrs. Ammon A. Troyer
Ashland, OH

FRUIT CAKE

2 cups sifted flour
12 oz. (1 1/2 cups) red glace cherries
1 1/4 cups chopped dried figs
1 3/4 cups coarsely chopped pecans
1/4 cup dark molasses
1/2 t. each of cloves, mace and nutmeg
4 oz. (1/2 cup) diced candied citron
1/2 lb. butter
1/4 cup 80 proof brandy or brandy extract
1 t. cinnamon
1 1/3 cups raisins
1 cup sugar
1 t. soda
1 1/4 cups dates
5 lg. eggs

Grease a 9" angel food cake pan. Line bottom and sides with greased foil. Sift together 1 cup flour, soda, and spices. In another bowl mix the remaining 1 cup flour with the cherries, citron, raisins, dates, figs and pecans, using fingers to separate fruit. In a large bowl, cream butter and sugar. Beat in eggs, one at a time. (Mixture will look curdled.) Beat in molasses and brandy. Add flour mixture. Stir until blended. Add fruit and nut mixture. Mix well. Pour into prepared pan. Bake at 300 deg. approx. 2 hr. 15 min. or until top of cake is very brown and crusty. If cake browns too quickly, cover top loosely with aluminum foil. Cool cake on wire rack for 30 min. Remove cake from pan. Remove foil and turn cake right side up. Wrap in plastic wrap, then in foil.

Saloma Petersheim
Mifflintown, PA

DAFFODIL CAKE

Mix and set aside:

1 cup cake flour
3/4 cup plus 2 T. sugar

12 egg whites (1 1/2 cups)
1 1/2 t. cream of tartar
1/4 t. salt
3/4 cup sugar
6 egg yolks
1 1/2 t. vanilla
1/2 t. almond extract
lemon extract (opt.) to egg yolks

In large mixing bowl beat egg whites, cream of tartar and salt until foamy. Add remaining 3/4 cup sugar, 2 T at a time, beating on high speed until meringue holds stiff peaks. In smaller bowl, beat egg yolks about 5 min. or until very thick and lemon-colored. Gently fold flavoring into meringue. Sprinkle flour-sugar mixture, 1/4 at a time, over meringue, folding in gently, just until flour-sugar mixture disappears. Pour half the batter into another bowl. Gently fold in egg yolks. Spoon yellow and white batters alternately into ungreased tube pan. Bake on bottom of oven for 40 min. at 375 deg. or until top springs back when lightly touched. Invert pan on funnel; let hang until completely cool. Spread with one of the following glazes:

—Lemon Glaze: Mix until smooth:

1 cup confectioner's sugar
1/2 t. grated lemon peel
1 t. lemon juice
2 T. milk (approx.)
1 drop yellow food color

—Creamy Glaze: Mix until smooth:

1 1/2 cups confectioner's sugar
2 T. soft butter
1/2 t. almond extract
1-2 T. hot water

Saloma Petersheim
Mifflintown, PA

Everyone of us lives in two tents
Content or discontent

MOZNYS CAKE

1 cup lard or butter — 3 cups sugar
2 eggs, beat and add to mixture — 1 cup buttermilk or sour milk
2 t. baking powder — 4 t. vanilla
2 cups boiling water in which 4 t. soda is added.
Add 4 cups flour. Add to 1 cup cocoa. Use a large cake pan.

Mrs. Ammon A. Troyer
Ashland, OH

TURTLE CAKE

1 box German Chocolate Cake Mix — 14 oz. caramels
6 oz. chopped walnuts — 1/4 lb. oleo
1 can Eagle brand condensed milk — chocolate chip bits

Mix cake as on pkg. Bake half the mixture in greased 13x9" pan at 350 deg. for 15 min. In top of double boiler melt together butter, caramels and Eagle brand mix. Remove from heat and cool slightly. Pour over baked cake. Pour remaining batter over caramel mixture. Sprinkle with walnuts and chocolate chips. Bake for 25 min. at 350 deg.

Barbara Shrock
Spartansburg, PA

SPEEDY SHORT CAKE

1 cup sifted flour — 1/2 cup sugar
1 heaping T. lard — 1/4 t. salt
2 t. baking powder — 1/2 cup milk
1 egg — flavor

Have ingredients all at room temperature. Put all together in a bowl and stir 2 min. Put in pans and bake

Mary Swartzentruber
Apple Creek, Ohio

Worry is like a rocking chair
It gives you something to do
But gets you no where

CINNAMON BUTTERMILK COFFEE CAKE

2 cups sifted flour
2 cups brown sugar
1/2 cup butter (1 stick)
1/3 cup sifter flour
1 egg
1 cup buttermilk
1 t. baking powder
1 t. cinnamon
1/2 cup chopped nuts

Mix flour, brown sugar and butter; take out 3/4 cup for topping. To the rest add: 3 cups flour. Mix well, then add egg, buttermilk, baking powder and cinnamon. Mix only until dry ingredients are well-moistened. Pour in pan. Mix 3/4 cup crumbs and nuts. Sprinkle on top and bake.

Mary Swartzentruber
Apple Creek, Ohio

FUNNY CAKE

1 1/2 cup flour
1 cup sugar
1/4 cup cocoa
1/2 t. salt
1 t. soda
1 t. vinegar
1 t. vanilla
1/3 cup vegetable oil
1 cup cold water

Sift dry ingredients and make 3 holes in it. Put vanilla in one hole, vinegar in another and shortening in the last one. Pour cold water over all and mix till smooth. Bake in a 9x9" pan (or similar) at 350 deg. till toothpick comes out clean when inserted.

Mary Swartzentruber
Apple Creek, Ohio

CHOCOLATE EGGLESS CAKE

2 cups brown sugar
1/2 cup cocoa
1/4 cup lard
1 cup buttermilk
2 1/2 cups flour

Last add 1 t. soda in 1/2 cup hot water, vanilla, and bake.

Mary Swartzentruber
Apple Creek, Ohio

ECLAIR CAKE

1 box crushed graham crackers
2 small boxes instant French vanilla pudding
3 cups milk
8 oz. Cool Whip

Butter a 13x9" pan. Line with crackers. Mix pudding and milk Blend in Cool Whip. Pour half of mixture over crackers. Place second layer crackers over pudding. Pour remaining on top. Top with crackers. Refrigerate and prepare topping:

2 oz. unsweetened chocolate, melted
2 t. white corn syrup
3 T. butter
3 T. milk
2 t. vanilla
1 1/2 cups powdered sugar

Beat and spread over crackers.
Refrigerate 24 hrs. before serving.

Barbara Schrock
Spartansburg, PA

PINEAPPLE SHEET CAKE

2 eggs beaten
1/2 t. salt
2 cups flour
1 t. baking soda
2 cups sugar
1 t. vanilla
1 1/2 cups crushed pineapple (don't drain)

Mix all together. Bake for 20 min. at 350 deg.

Icing:

4 oz. cream cheese (room temperature)
1 t. vanilla
2 cups powdered sugar
1 stick oleo
1/2 cups chopped pecans

Mix till smooth. Ice while cake is warm.

Barbara Schrock
Spartansburg, PA

CARAMEL FROSTING

3 T. boiling water
1/2 cup brown sugar
2 T. butter (level)
Powdered sugar

Mix first 3 ingredients together being sure water is boiling hot. Then stir in powdered sugar until of the right consistency to spread. Vanilla and nuts may be added.

Ida Miller
Medford, WI

FROSTING

3 T. melted butter
1 T. table cream
1/4 cup sugar

Sprinkle 1/2 cup shredded coconut. Place under the broiler until top is a golden brown. Watch it closely as coconut browns quickly. Takes just 2-3 minutes.

Ida Miller
Medford, WI

TWO EGG HOT WATER SPONGE CAKE

2 eggs
3/4 cup sugar
1 cup flour
2 t. baking powder
1/2 t. salt
1/2 cup boiling water

Beat eggs until lemon colored. Add sugar gradually, beating until light. Sift flour, baking powder and salt together; then add to egg mixture and mix until well blended. Add 1/4 cup boiling water (a little at a time), then add remaining 1/4 cup boiling water (all at once) and flavor with vanilla or lemon. Bake in 8-9 in. square pan at 350 deg. until cake springs back lightly. Batter will be very thin, but bakes into delicious tender cake. Serve with crushed berries either fresh or frozen and whipped cream. Cake may be frosted if desired.

Ida Miller
Medford, WI

Most people can't stand prosperity
But then most people don't have to

$300.00 CAKE

Cream together:

1/2 cup butter or margarine
1 1/2 cups white sugar
2 eggs

In a small bowl make a paste of 2 oz. red food coloring and 2 T. cocoa; mix with sugar and egg mixture.

Add:

2 1/2 cups sifted cake flour
1 cup buttermilk
1 t. vanilla
1 t. salt

Mix together in a small dish 1 t. soda and 1 T. vinegar. Blend in with above mixture with a spoon. Bake in two 9 in. layer pans or in angel food pan at 350 deg. oven for 35 min.

Cake Frosting:

Cook 3 T. flour and 1 cup milk until thick like a thick white sauce. Let cool. cream 1 cup white sugar and 1 cup margarine or butter, then add the cold flour and mix mixture and 1 t. vanilla and mix well. Add gradually 1/2 box powdered sugar and cream until of spreading consistency.

Mrs. Joe J. Yoder
Lawrenceburg, TN

People do not lack strength
They lack will

DARK AMISH CHOCOLATE CAKE

1 1/2 cups white sugar
1/2 cup lard
1/2 cup cocoa
2 eggs
1 cup hot water
1/2 cup milk (dissolve 2 t. soda in milk)
1 2/3 cups bread flour
1 t. vanilla
1/2 t. salt

Mix sugar and lard well. Then add the milk and eggs and the flour. Add cocoa in hot water mixture before adding.
Bake at 350 deg.

Mrs. Joe J. Yoder
Lawrenceburg, TN

TOASTED SPICE CAKE

1/2 cup shortening
2 cups brown sugar
2 egg yolks
2 1/2 cups cake flour
1/2 t. salt
1 t. soda
1 t. baking powder
1 1/2 t. cinnamon
1 t. cloves
1 1/4 cups sour milk
1 t. vanilla

Cream together shortening and sugar; add egg yolks and beat well. Sift flour once. Measure and add salt, soda, baking powder and spices. Sift again. Add dry ingredients to first mixture alternately with milk and flavoring. Beat well after each addition. (Pour in flat pan 8x12x1 1/4 in.) Spread the following meringue mixture over the batter before baking.

Beat egg whites till stiff enough to hold peaks. Slowly add 1 cup brown sugar to whites, beating until smooth. Spread over cake batter and sprinkle with 1/2 cup finely chopped nuts or shredded coconut. Bake at 350 deg. for 40 min.

Fannie Gingerich
Ethridge, TN

GINGERBREAD CAKE

2 eggs
3/4 cup brown sugar
3/4 cup molasses
3/4 cup melted shortening
2 1/2 cups flour
1 cup hot water
2 t. soda
2 t. cinnamon
1/2 t. cloves
1/2 c. nutmeg
1 t. ginger or to suit taste

Bake.

Sauce for cake:

1 cup sugar
1 1/2 cups water
1 T. butter
1 T. flour

Cook together. Put flour in to thicken. Then put a piece of cake in a dish and pour sauce over it and eat it warm.

Fannie Gingerich
Ethridge, TN

MOIST CHOCOLATE CAKE

In a bowl mix:

3 cups flour
2 cups sugar
1/2 cups cocoa
2 t. soda
1 t. salt

Make a well in this and add:

2 t. vanilla
2 cups water
1 cup Crisco oil

Mix well. Put in 9x13 in. ungreased pan. Bake at 350 deg. for 30-40 min.

Fannie Gingerich
Ethridge, TN

PINEAPPLE FROSTING

For angel food cake.

1 pkg. Cool Whip
1 box instant vanilla pudding
1 can crushed pineapple

Mix all together and spread on cake.

Mrs. Emma Stitzman
Bronson, MI

CREAM CHEESE FROSTING

3 oz. pkg. softened cream cheese
6 T. soft margarine
1 t. vanilla
1 T. milk, more if needed
3/4 lb. powdered sugar.

Mrs. Emma Stutzman
Bronson, MI

GERMAN RAW APPLE CAKE

1/2 cup shortening
1/2 cup brown sugar
1 cup white sugar
2 eggs
2 1/2 cups flour
1/4 t. salt
2 t. cinnamon
2 t. soda
1 cup milk
2 cups raw apples (diced)

Topping:

1/2 cup brown sugar
1/4 cup white sugar
1/2 t. cinnamon
1/2 cup chopped nuts

Cream shortening, sugar and eggs; add dry ingredients alternately with milk. Spread apples over batter after it is poured into 9x13 in. greased pan. Spread topping over entire cake and bake at 350 deg. 35 min. or until done.

Esther Fisher
Millersburg, PA

A COATING TO GREASE CAKE PANS

1 part Crisco
1 part flour
Mix like pie crumbs and add 1 part Crisco oil. Will be like heavy cream. Do not use sparingly. Gives a nice glaze to bread too.

Esther Fisher
Millersburg, PA

PINEAPPLE CHEESE CAKE

1 small pkg. lemon jello, dissolved in 1 cup boiling water and 1 cup sugar. Put in refrigerator till syrup, then beat.
1 can crushed pineapple and 1 8 oz. pkg. cream chees, and mix in juice of pineapple.
1 can Pet milk. Beat till stiff and add jello and rest of ingredients. Put graham crumbs mixed with butter and sugar in bottom. Pour in ingredients.

Esther Fisher
Millersburg, PA

WACKY CAKE

1 1/2 cups flour
1/2 t. salt
3 T. cocoa
1 cup sugar
1 t. soda

Sift this together 3 times and place in baking dish. Then make 3 holes. In one put 1 T. vinegar, in second put 1 T. vanilla, and in third put 5 T. melted shortening. Over all of this pour 1 cup of water. Mix well all the ingredients. Bake in 8x8 in. pan 35 min. at 350 deg.

Mrs. Emma Stutzman
Bronson, MI

The narrower the mind
The broader the statement

SUGAR PLUM SPICE CAKE

Sift together:

2 1/2 cups flour
1 t. soda
3/4 t. cinnamon
1 t. baking powder
3/4 t. salt
3/4 t. cloves

Cream together and mix with dry ingredients:

1 cup sugar
1/2 cup shortening

Add:

2/3 cup brown sugar
2 eggs beaten
1 1/4 cups sour milk

Pour into greased pan and bake at 375 deg. for 25-30 min.

Mrs. Emma Stutzman
Bronson, MI

ROMAN APPLE CAKE

2 cups sugar
3 cups flour
1/2 t. baking powder
2 t. soda
3/4 cup shortening
2 eggs
1 cup milk
1 t. vanilla

Beat until creamy; then add 4 cups raw apples. Sprinkle with sugar and cinnamon on top. Bake; serve with milk.

Fannie Gingerich
Ethridge, TN

CRUMB CAKE

2 cups brown sugar
3 cups flour
1 cup lard (scant)

Mix together. Take out 1 cup crumbs to put on top. Then add:

1 T. molasses
1 t. cinnamon
1 t. allspice
1 t. cloves
2 t. soda
1 cup buttermilk
1 egg

Fannie Gingerich
Ethridge, TN

SNOW FLAKE CAKE

2 1/8 cups flour
2 1/2 t. baking powder
1 1/2 cups sugar
1/2 cup lard
1 cup milk
1 t. salt
1 t. vanilla

Beat 2 min. Add 1/2 to 2/3 cup beaten egg whites or 4 unbeaten whole eggs.

Fannie Gingerich
Ethridge, TN

QUICK FROSTING

1 cup brown sugar
1 T. flour
1 t. vanilla

Mix with enough cream until nice for spreading. Pour on cake while still hot.

Fannie Gingerich
Ethridge, TN

GRANDMA'S MOLASSES CAKE

1/4 cup shortening
3/4 cup Grandma's molasses
1 t. vanilla
2 eggs, unbeaten
3/4 cup sifted flour
1/4 t. salt
1/4 t. soda
1 cup chopped walnut meats.

Bake at 350 deg. or 375 deg.

Joe Borntreger
Cashton, WI

WHITE CAKE

1 cup sugar
1 T. butter
4 egg whites
1 t. flavor
1/2-2 cups flour
3 t. baking powder level
1/4 t. salt
1/2 cup milk or cream

Mix sugar and butter; sift flour; mix baking powder and salt to flour. Add cream and milk to sugar and butter. Add flour mixture. Beat thoroughly. Carefully fold in stiffly beaten egg whites. Pour in well-oiled pan. Bake at 375 deg. about 20 min. or till done.

Joe Borntreger
Cashton, WI

ORANGE CHEESE CAKE

1 orange cake mix - white or lemon may be used
2 T. oil
1/2 cup sugar
3 T. lemon juice
4 eggs
2 - 8 oz. cream cheese
1 1/2 cup milk
3 t. vanilla

Reserve 1 cup cake mix. Set aside. In large bowl mix remaining cake mix, 1 egg + 2 T. oil. Mix with hands till crumbly. Press in bottom and 3/4 up sides in obling pan (greased). In same bowl blend cream cheese and 3 eggs. Beat well, then add 1 cup cake mix at low speed. Add milk, lemon juice and vanilla; beat till smooth and pour in crust. Bake at 300 deg. for 45-55 min. Don't overbake.

Joni H. Shrock
Middlefield, OH

CEREAL CAKE

4 cups oatmeal
1 1/2 cups sugar
1/2 t. salt
1/2 cup shortening
2 cups whole wheat flour
2 t. soda
1 1/2 cups milk (may use sour)
1 t. vanilla or maple flavor

Can also add coconut, raisins, and dates. Mix and bake.

Ida Miller
Medford, WI

WHITE MOUNTAIN FROSTING

Soft — Easy Spreading
In a saucepan mix:
1 cup granulated sugar
2 T. water
1/4 cup light corn syrum

Cover saucepan and bring to a rolling boil. Remove cover and cook to 245 deg. or until syrup spins a 6-8 in. thread. Meanwhile beat 2 egg whites stiff. Very slowly pour the sugar mixture into the egg whites in a thin steady stream, beating all the time with a rotary egg beater. Beat hard until frosting stands up in peaks. Add vanilla or flavor of your choice, cake color, etc. Leave cake uncovered until icing is set.

Miss Sara Shetler
Glasgow, KY

AIRWAYS SPONGE CAKE

6 eggs, separated
1 1/2 cups sugar
1 1/2 cups sifted cake flour
(If you don't have cake flour, use other flour and put 2 T. cornstarch in.)
1/4 t. salt
1 t. lemon rind
1 t. lemon extract
6 T. cold water
1 1/2 t. baking powder

1. Beat egg yolks until thick and lemon colored.
2. Beat in sugar gradually.
3. Sift flour and salt together and add alternately with water to first mixture. Add lemon extract and rind.
4. Beat egg whites until foamy. Add baking powder and continue beating until they hold a point. Fold into an ungreased angel cake pan. Bake at 375 deg.

Joe Borntreger
Cashton, WI

OATMEAL CAKE

Pour 1 1/4 cups boiling water over 1 cup oatmeal. Let stand 20 minutes. Cream and mix the oats with:

1/4 cup butter
1 cup brown sugar
1 cup white sugar

Add:

2 eggs
1 t. vanilla
1 t. soda
1 t. salt
1 tsp. cinnamon
1 1/3 cups flour (sifted)

Pour into greased pan; bake 350 deg. for 1 1/4 hrs.

Make topping:

1/3 cup melted butter
1/4 cup milk
1/2 cup chopped pecans
2/3 cup brown sugar
1 cup coconut
1/2 t. vanilla

Mix together and pour over cake; put into oven and brown.

Sue Wickey
Norfolk, NY

NEVER FAIL FROSTING

1 stick butter (1/4 lb.); oleo may be used
1 cup brown sugar 1/4 cup sweet milk

Melt butter; add brown sugar and milk. Boil together for 2 min. Remove from heat. Cool slight, add 1/2 cup XXX sugar, stir until smooth. If this mixture is too stiff, add a small amount of milk. Will never crack or be sticky. Enough for two 9 in. cakes or 1 big loaf cake.

Sue Wickey
Norfolk, NY

MILLIE'S CHOCOLATE CAKE

2 cups sugar 1/2 cup lard
2 eggs 3 heaping T. cocoa
2 cups flour 1/2 cup sour milk or buttermilk
1 t. vanilla

1 level t. soda stirred into 1 cup boiling water added last. Dough will be thin.

The best chocolate cake yet. Bake in 9 x 13 in. loaf pan. Bake in 350 deg. for 30 to 40 min. till done.

Sue Wickey
Norfolk, NY

CARAMEL CAKE

1/2 cup shortening 2 cups brown sugar
1 egg 1 t. vanilla
1 cup sour milk or buttermilk 1 t. soda
1 T. cocoa 2 cups flour

Mix shortening, sugar, egg and vanilla until creamy. Add sour milk mixed with baking soda. Add cocoa and flour. Bake in 9" cake pans at 375 deg. for 30 min.

Catherine Swarey
Belleville, PA

Those who bring sunshine to the lives of others
Cannot keep it from themselves

SHORT CAKE

2 cups sifted flour
4 t. baking powder
2 T. sugar
1 t. salt
1/2 cup shortening
1 egg (slightly beaten)
2/3 cup milk

Sift together flour, baking powder, sugar and salt. Cut in shortening until mixture resembles coarse corn meal. Add milk and slightly beaten egg. Stir with fork until well-blended.
Serve with fresh strawberries and milk.

Catherine Swarey
Belleville, PA

FUDGE CAKE

2 1/4 cups flour
1 t. soda
1 t. baking powder
1/2 t. salt
1/2 cup lard
3/4 cup cocoa
1 1/2 cups sugar
1 t. vanilla
3 eggs
1 cup sour milk
1/3 cup hot water

Mix cocoa and hot water. Sift flour. Add remaining dry ingredients. Sift again. Add vanilla, eggs, milk and lard. Beat well. Add cocoa and hot water mixture last. Bake at 350 deg. for 30-35 min.

Mrs. Daniel Borntreger
Riceville, IA

The tie that binds
Is a gift from a gay relative

CHOCOLATE CHIP FROSTING

1 cup sugar
1/4 cup milk
1/4 cup butter

Boil for 1 1/2 min. Remove from heat. Add 1/2 t. vanilla and 1/2 cup chocolate chips. Beat until mixture begins to shape. Spread quickly.

Mrs. Daniel C. Borntreger
Riceville, IA

JIFFY CHOCOLATE FEATHER CAKE

1 egg, beaten 1/2 cup cocoa
1 cup sugar 1/2 cup shortening
1 1/2 cups flour 1/2 cup sour milk
1 t. soda 1/2 cup hot water
1 t. vanilla 1/2 t. salt

Mix ingredients together in order given. Beat well. Bake at 350 deg. for approx. 30 min.

Mrs. Daniel Borntreger
Riceville, IA

CARMEL FROSTING

1 cup brown sugar 1/2 cup milk
1 T. butter

Bring mixture to a boil. Remove from heat and add enough powdered sugar to spread nicely. A quick and delicious frosting.

Mrs. Daniel C. Borntreger
Riceville, IA

HALF AND HALF CAKE

Part 1
6 egg whites Pinch of salt
1/2 t. cream of tartar 3/4 cup sugar
1/2 cup sifted cake flour 1/2 cup vanilla

Beat egg whites and salt; when foamy add cream of tartar; beat till stiff. Slowly add sugar. Fold in flour sifted 3 times; add vanilla; pour mixture into bottom of an ungreased angel food cake pan. Let stand while mixing 2nd part.

Part 2
6 egg yolks, well beaten 1/2 cup sugar
2 T. cold water 1/2 t. vanilla
3/4 cup sifted cake flour (scant)
3/4 t. baking powder sifted with flour

Blend all ingredients. Pour over first part. Bake about 50 min.

Mrs. Clarence Miller
Medford, WI

CAKE FLOUR RECIPE

Put 2 T. cornstarch in cup and fill cup with flour. Sift together 3 times. This equals to 1 cup sifted cake flour.

Mrs. Clarence Miller
Medford, WI

2 - 4 - 6 FROSTING

2 cups brown sugar
4 T. butter
6 T. cream

Combine and bring to a boil. Cool. Stir till thick. Add a little milk if too thick.

Lydianna J. Bricker
Panama, NY

PRINCE OF WALES CAKE

1 cup sugar
1 egg
1 t. nutmeg
2 cups flour
1 t. cinnamon
1/2 cup shortening
1 cup sour milk
1/2 cup maple syrup
1 t. soda
1 t. cloves

Mix as usual. Bake.

Lydiann J. Bricker
Panama, NY

BROWN STONE FRONT CAKE

6 T. cocoa
2 1/2 cups flour
2 level t. soda
1 3/4 cups cream (sweet or sour)
2 well-beaten eggs
2 cups sugar
pinch of salt
Sift twice before adding:
1/4 cup milk

Bake in loaf pan.

Mrs. Clarence Miller
Medford, WI

Pleasure is the flower
That fades remembrance
Is the lasting perfume

SALAD DRESSING CAKE

2 cups flour
1 cup sugar
1 1/2 t. soda

Mix together, then add 1 cup salad dressing and 4 T. cocoa dissolved in 1 cup boiling water. Stir until blended. Do not beat. Add 1 t. vanilla. Bake in loaf pan.

Mrs. Clarence Miller
Medford, WI

CREAMY CHOCOLATE FROSTING

2 egg yolks
1/2 cup butter
1/4 t. salt
4 3/4 cups confectioner's sugar
1/2 cup cocoa
1 t. vanilla
3 T. milk
2 egg whites (beaten and add last to ingredients)

Naomi Peachey
Little Falls, NY

OLD STANDBY CHOCOLATE CAKE

1 cup lard (scant)
2 cups sugar
2 eggs
1 cup cocoa
2 cups boiling water
3 cups flour
1 t. salt
2 t. soda
1 t. baking powder

Mix boiling water with cocoa. Sift flour, salt, soda, and baking powder. Cream lard, sugar and eggs. Mix alternately with other ingredients.

Naomi Peachey
Little Falls, NY

Give a man credit for anything today
And He'll buy it

CRAZY CAKE

1 cup flour
1/2 t. salt
1/2 cup milk
2 T. butter
1 sq. chocolate or 1 rounded T. cocoa
2 t. baking powder
3/4 cup granulated sugar
1 t. vanilla

Sift together dry ingredients. Melt butter and chocolate. Add milk and vanilla. Add dry ingredients to mixture and pour into greased baking pan.

Mix:
1/2 cup granulated sugar
1/2 cup brown sugar
2 T. cocoa

Sprinkle mixture over top of cake batter.
Slowly pour 1 cup hot water over crumbs. Bake.

Saloma Petersheim
Mifflintown, PA

SHORT CAKE

Make crumbs from:
2 cups flour
4 t. baking powder
3/4 t. salt
1 T. sugar
1/3 cup shortening

Add 2/3 cup milk and 1 beaten egg to crumbs. Pour into small cake pan. Make topping below and spread on top of batter. Bake at 350 deg. Serve with fresh fruit and milk. We like to use fresh strawberries.

Topping:
1 1/2 cup sugar
1/2 cup flour
3 T. butter or oleo

Saloma Petersheim
Mifflintown, PA

RICH CHOCOLATE CAKE

2 cups brown sugar
1/2 cup cocoa
2 t. soda
2/3 cup lard or oil
2 eggs
2 1/2 cups flour
2 t. baking powder
1 t. salt
2 cups boiling water
2 t. vanilla

Sift dry ingredients together, then add oil, eggs, vanilla and 1 cut water. Stir well and add another cut water!

Mrs. Noah Wengerd, Jr.
Conewango Valley, NY

SEVEN MINUTE FROSTING

2 egg whites unbeaten
5 T. water
1 t. vanilla
1 1/2 cups sugar
1 1/2 t. light corn syrup

Put egg whites, sugar, water, and syrup in upper part of double boiler. Beat with rotary egg beater until thoroughly mixed. Place over rapidly boiling water. Beat constantly with rotary egg beater 7 min. or until frosting will stand on peaks. Remove from heat. Add vanilla and beat until thick enough to spread.

Joe Borntreger
Cashton, WI

CARROT CAKE

2 cups sugar
1 1/2 cups cooking oil
1/2 cups chopped nuts
2 t. soda
1 t. salt
3 cups raw carrots (shredded)
2 1/4 cups flour
4 eggs
2 t. baking powder
2 t. cinnamon

Cream together sugar and cooking oil. Add eggs and beat well. Sift flour, soda, baking powder, salt and cinnamon together. Then add to creamed mixture. Fold in carrots and nuts. Bake in moderate oven.

Mrs. Jacob Stutzman
Jeromesville, OH

BUTTER WALNUT CAKE

3 cups sifted flour
2 cups white sugar
1 cup chopped nuts
1/2 t. salt
1 t. maple flavoring
1 cup softened shortening
1 cup milk
2 t. baking powder
4 eggs, separated

Sift together flour, baking powder and salt. Cream butter; gradually beat in sugar. Add egg yolks one at a time, beating well after each addition. Beat egg whites until stiff but not dry. Add dry ingredients to creamed mixture alternately with flavor and milk. Combine lightly after each addition. Fold in nuts and egg whites. Bake in moderate oven.

PEANUT BUTTER CAKE

1/2 cup butter
1 1/4 cups granulated sugar
1 1/2 cups milk
3 eggs
1/2 t. salt
1 cup peanut butter
3 cups flour
1 1/2 t. vanilla
1 1/2 t. baking powder

Cream together butter, peanut butter, sugar and vanilla. Add eggs one at a time, beating well after each addition. Sift together flour, baking soda and salt. Add alternately with milk to creamed mixture. Bake in 10 or 12 in. tube pan for 35-40 min. at 350 deg. Cool pan 10 min. Turn out on serving plate. Especially good with chocolate icing.

Mrs. Jacob Stutzman
Jeromesville, OH

GOOD FROSTING FOR CAKES

1 cup white sugar
1 cup brown sugar
1 cup sweet or sour cream

Put in some butter and cook till thick enough; stir a lot while cooling it.

Joe Borntreger
Cashton, WI

FRUIT COCKTAIL CAKE

1 can fruit cocktail
2 eggs
2 cups flour
2 t. soda
1 1/2 cups sugar
1 t. salt

Mix all together at same time. Pour into cake pan. Sprinkle 1/2 cup brown sugar and 1/2 cup nuts on top. Bake 40-45 min. in 350 deg. oven.

Then cook together 5 min.:

1 stick butter (1/2 cup)
3/4 cup white sugar
1/2 cup Pet milk or cream

Beat till foamy. Add 1/2 cup coconut if you wish after beating. Pour over hot cake slowly so it will soak into cake. Keeps well and gets more delicious the older it gets.

Joe Borntreger
Cashton, WI

DIP FOR CAKES

1 cup sugar
1 T. butter
1 1/2 T. cornstarch
1 T. butter
1 t. vanilla
1 cup boiling water

Joe Borntreger
Cashton, WI

JOHNNY CAKE

1 cup whole wheat flour
1 cup sifted white flour
1/2 t. salt
4 t. baking powder
1 egg
1 cup milk
1/4 cup oil or shortening

When using sour milk or buttermilk, use 1 t. soda and 3 t. baking powder. Mix and bake in a greased pan. Serve hot or cold with fruit and milk.

Ella Hershberger
Oakland, MD

Experience is something you think you have
Till you get more of it

APPLESAUCE CAKE

1/2 cup butter
1 cup sugar
2 cups all purpose flour sifted
1 1/2 cups canned applesauce
1 t. clove
1 t. cinnamon
2 t. soda
1 t. seedless raisins

Cream butter and sugar together. Beat in flour and applesauce alternately. Stir in clove and cinnamon. Dissolve soda in 1 T. hot water and combine with mixture. Mix in raisins thoroughly. Pour batter into 2 greased 9 in. layer pans and bake at 325 deg. for 35 min.

Ella Hershberger
Oakland, MD

CARROT CAKE

Stir this first, then add eggs and mix in dry ingredients:
2 cups sugar
1 1/2 cups oil
Add:
4 eggs
2 cups flour
2 t. baking powder
1 t. salt
3 t. soda
Fold in 3 cups shredded carrots last.
Bake.
Frosting:
1/2 of 8 oz. cream cheese
1/2 cup oleo
1 t. vanilla
1 lb. powdered sugar
You can add some milk or cream if it is too thick.

Mrs. Ray J. Gingerich
Fillmore, NY

TEXAS SHEET CAKE

Mix together in a saucepan and bring to a boil:

2 sticks oleo
4 T. cocoa
1 cup water

Take this off of heat and add:

2 cups sugar
1/2 cup sour milk
2 eggs
2 cups flour
1 t. soda
1 t. vanilla

Mix well and bake at 375 deg. for 20 min. or more.

Icing for above cake:

Melt 1 stick oleo, 3 T. cocoa, 6 T. milk. Bring to a boil, then cool a little, then add 3 cups powdered sugar. Spread on cake while still warm.

Ella Hershberger
Oakland, MD

PUMPKIN CAKE

3 1/2 cups flour
3 cups sugar
2 t. soda
1 t. cinnamon
1 t. nutmet
4 eggs
1 cup salad oil
2/3 cup water
1/2 t. salt
1 cup nuts
1 1/2 cups pumpkin

Put everything in before stirring. Bake at 350 deg.

Ella Hershberger
Oakland, MD

PEANUT BUTTER CAKE

1 stick oleo
1/2 cup cooking oil
1/2 cup peanut butter
1 cup water
Bring to a boil and add:
2 cups sugar
2 cups flour
1/2 cup milk
1 t. soda
1 t. vanilla
2 beaten eggs
Mix this all together. Bake at 400 deg.
Icing for cake:
1 stick oleo
1/2 cup peanut butter
1/3 cup milk
Bring to a boil and add 1 lb. 10X sugar.

Ella Hershberger
Oakland, MD

COCOA CAKE (WITHOUT EGGS)

2 1/2 cups flour
2 cups brown sugar
1/2 cup cocoa
1/2 cup shortening
1 cup sour or buttermilk
Last, put 1 level t. soda in 1/2 cup hot water. Makes 3 layer pans or a 9x12 loaf pan. Bake at 375 deg.

Ella Hershberger
Oakland, MD

ANGEL FOOD CAKE DELUXE

Measure and sift together four times:
1 cup cake flour
1 1/2 cups powdered sugar
Beat in a large bowl until foamy:
2 cups egg whites
1 1/2 t. cream of tartar
1/4 t. salt
Then gradually add 2 T. at a time: 1 cup granulated sugar
Continue beating until the meringue holds stiff peaks. Then fold in 1 1/2 t. vanilla and the flour mixture. Push batter in 10" tube pan. Gently cut through batter with a knife. Bake in 350 deg. oven 35 min. or till done. Invert to cool.

Mrs. Wilma Mast
S. Hutchinson, KS

WHITE CAKE WITH COCONUT

1 cup butter
1 1/2 cups sugar
3 1/2 cups flour
1/2 t. salt
1 cup milk
8 egg whites - beaten
1/2 t. almond extract
1/2 t. coconut
3 1/2 t. baking powder

Cream butter until soft; gradually add sugar and cream until smooth. Combine flour, baking powder and salt; add to creamed mixture alternately with milk. Beat egg whites until stiff but not dry. Fold into creamed mixture. Stir in extracts. Bake in 3 greased and floured 9" pans at 350 deg. for 30-35 minutes or until done. Coll and frost and sprinkle with coconut.

Emma Hershberger
Dover, DE

CAKE

One cake mix, preferably yellow or white!
One can crushed pineapple

Bake the cake mix according to the directions in a loaf pan. When cool, spread pineapple on top.

Make a small amount of your favorite vanilla pudding; when cool, mix 1 pkg. - 8 oz. - cream cheese in the pudding. Add 1 cup cream which has been whipped. Spread over the pineapple; top with nuts.

Emma Hershberger
Dover, DE

RAISIN NUT CAKE

1 1/2 cups white sugar
1 1/2 cups brown sugar
1/2 cup shortening
2 eggs
1 1/2 cups warm raisin juice
1/2 t. salt
1/2 t. nutmet
1/2 t. cinnamon
1 t. soda
3 cups flour
1 cup chopped nuts
1 cup cooked raisins

Cream shortening and sugar; add eggs and beat well. Add sifted dry ingredients and raisin juice. Stir in raisins and nuts. Bake at 350 deg. for 45 minutes or longer. Add enough water to cook the raisins to make 1 1/2 cups juice. Cook a few minutes.

Lydia Stoltzfus
Bloomsburg, PA

FRUIT CAKE

1 1/2 cups white sugar
2 eggs
1/2 cup Wesson oil
2 1/4 cups flour
1/2 t. salt
2 t. soda
2 cups mashed fruit (applesauce or other fruit)
1/2 t. vanilla

Mix all together and bake at 350 deg. 40 or 45 minutes

Lydia Stoltzfus
Bloomsburg, PA

CINNAMON SUPPER CAKE

2 1/2 cups sugar
1 cup shortening
4 eggs
2 cups milk
4 cups sifted flour
6 t. baking powder
1 t. salt
2 t. vanilla

This makes a large cake. Mix all together and bake at 375 deg. for 45 or 50 min. Remove from oven and spread with soft butter or margarine. Mix 3 T. 10X sugar and 1 t. cinnamon and spread over top of cake.

Lydia Stoltzfus
Bloomsburg, PA

Only a bus driver
Can tell a women where to get off

CARROT CAKE

3 eggs, beaten
1 1/4 cups oil
2 cups sugar
2 cups flour
2 t. soda
1 t. cinnamon
1 t. salt
2 t. vanilla
1 cup coconut
1 cup chopped nuts
2 cups freshly shredded carrots
1 can crushed pineapples and juice

Mix all together and bake at 350 deg. for 50 minutes in large pan, 9x13 in.

Lydia Stoltzfus
Bloomsburg, PA

PINEAPPLE UPSIDEDOWN CAKE

1 cup brown sugar
1 - 20 oz. can crushed drained pineapples
1 box yellow cake mix 1/2 cup margarine

Mix brown sugar and margarine and press evenly in bottom of loaf pan. Spoon pineapples over mixture. Mix cake mix according to directions on box. Pour batter over pineapples. Bake at 350 deg. for 30 min. Serve warm with pineapple side up.

Cathryn Schmucker
Litchfield, MI

CREAM CAKE

Beat together
1 cup sugar 1 cup cream
2 eggs
Add:
1 3/4 cup flour 3 t. baking powder
1/2 t. salt 1 t. vanilla

Pour in greased pans. Bake at 375 deg. for 30 min.

Cathryn Schmucker
Litchfield, MI

WATERGATE CAKE

1 box white cake mix 1 cup plus 1 T. vegetable oil
1 box pistachio instant pudding mix
1/2 cup chopped nuts or pecans
1 cup ginger ale 3 eggs

Put in 9x13 pan. Grease and flour pan. Bake at 350 deg. for 30 min. Cool, add topping when ready to serve.

Topping:
1 Cool Whip or Rich's topping - 2 cups
3/4 cup milk
1 pkg. pistachio instant pudding

Mix and pour over cake. Let set a little.

Mrs. Leroy J. Byler
Frederichtown, OH

HO HO CAKE

Mix and bake a chocolate cake mix; cool.

Topping #1:

5 T. flour
1 1/4 cups milk
1 cup Crisco
1 cup white sugar
1 stick oleo

Mix flour and milk together. Cook until thick, stirring constantly. Cool completely. Cream the last 3 ingredients and gradually add to flour mixture. Beat well. Spread over warm cake.

Topping #2:

1 stick oleo
1 egg
1 t. vanilla
3 pkg. pre-melted chocolate
2 1/2 T. hot water
3 cups powdered sugar

Mix oleo and combine with the remaining ingredients and beat well. Spread over cake.

Mrs. Leroy J. Byler
Fredericktown, OH

SUGARLESS CAKE

1 cup hot water
1/2 cup Crisco
1 cup molasses
2 1/2 cups flour
3/4 cup cocoa
2 eggs
2 t. soda
1/2 t. salt
1 t. vanilla

Mrs. Leroy J. Byler
Fredericktown, OH

BUTTER PECAN CAKE

2/3 cup white sugar
1 cup brown sugar
3 eggs
3/4 cup lard
3 t. baking powder
1 1/4 t. maple flavoring
3/4 cup chopped nuts
2 cups flour
1 t. salt
1 t. vanilla
1 cup milk

Mix and bake at 350 deg.

Mrs. Leroy J. Byler
Fredericktown, OH

ZUCCHINI SQUASH CAKE

1/4 cup soft oleo
1/2 cup veg. oil
1 3/4 cups white sugar
2 eggs
1 t. vanilla
1/2 cup sour milk
2 1/2 cups flour
1/4 cup chopped nuts
4 T. cocoa
1/2 t. baking powder
1 t. soda
1/2 t. cinnamon
1/2 t. cloves
2 cups finely chopped zucchini
1/4 cup chocolate chips

Cream oleo, oil, sugar; add eggs, vanilla, sour milk; last stir in zucchini. Put in greased pan; sprinkle with chocolate chips and nuts. Bake at 325 deg. for 40-50 min.

Mrs. Leroy J. Byler
Fredericktown, OH

EXTRA GOOD SOUR CREAM CHOCOLATE CAKE

2 eggs
2 cups sugar
1/4 cup shortening
3/4 cup sour cream
1 t. salt
1 t. vanilla
4 oz. unsweetened chocolate, melted and cooled
1 cup water
1 1/4 t. soda
1 1/2 t. baking powder
2 cups flour

Bake in 9x13 loaf pan, 30-40 min. at 350 deg.

Mrs. Joseph Schrock

Agusta, WI

YELLOW ANGEL FOOD CAKE

Separate 7 eggs; add 1/2 cup cold water to yolks and beat to a froth.
Add: 1 1/2 cups sugar and beat again.
Sift: 1 1/2 cups flour and 1/2 t. baking powder together and add to egg mixture and blend.
Add: 1 t. vanilla
Add: 1/4 t. salt to egg whites; beat till foamy.
Then add: 3/4 t. cream of tartar and beat till stiff. Fold into egg yolk mixture. Bake in angel food pan for 1 hr. in slow oven.

Mrs. Joseph Schrock
Agusta, WI

DATE CAKE

1 cup chopped dates
1 1/2 cups boiling water - with 1 t. soda. Pour over dates; let cool.
Cream: 1/2 cup shortening
Add: 1 cup white sugar, 2 eggs beaten
Add: 1 1/2 cups flour, 1 t. salt, 1 t. soda
Pour in a 9x13 in. pan or cooking sheet.
Put on top:
3/4 cup chocolate chips
1/2 cup brown sugar
1/2 cup nuts
A quick and easy cake. Don't overbake

Mrs. Leroy Stutzman
Sugar Creek, OH

Our business policy
That never needs changing
Is honesty

FUNNEL CAKES

2/3 cup milk
1 egg
1/2 t. salt
1 t. baking powder
1 1/4 cups flour
2 T. sugar

Combine egg and milk. Sift together sugar, flour, baking powder and salt. Add to egg mixture. Beat until smooth. Head lard or cooking oil to 360 deg. Cover the bottom of funnel with finger and pour 1/2 cup batter into funnel. Remove finger and release batter in round circular motion. Fry until golden. Turn cake carefully. Fry other side until brown. Drain on paper towel. Sprinkle with confestioner's sugar. Serve warm.

Catherine Swarey
Belleville, PA

EAST MIX COCOA CAKE

3 cups flour
2 cups sugar
2/3 cup cocoa
1 1/2 t. salt
2 t. soda, dissolved in 1 cup boiling water
1 cup sour milk
2 eggs
2 t. vanilla

Bake at 350 deg. for 25 min. or till done on sheet cake pan. Don't overbake.

Cream Filling:

1/2 cup cocoa
1/2 cup Crisco
1/2 cup butter
1 cup sugar
2 egg whites, beaten
1 t. vanilla 1/2 cup hot milk

Frosting:

2 sticks oleo
4 T. cocoa
2 t. vanilla

Bring to boil. Cool slightly; add powdered sugar.
Spread filling on cake. Cool till set. When real cold, then frost.

Mrs. Ray J. Gingerich
Fillmore, NY

LARGE CHOCOLATE CAKE

2 cups white sugar
3/4 cup lard or oleo
2 eggs
2 1/2 cups flour
pinch of salt
2 t. soda
1 cup boiling water
1 cup sour milk or buttermilk
1 t. vanilla
3/4 cup cocoa

Mix well and bake till done.

Martha I. Shetler
Glasgow, Kentucky

YUTZY CHOCOLATE CAKE

2 cups brown sugar
2 eggs
1 stick oleo
2 t. soda
1 T. cocoa
1 cup hot water
2 cups flour
1/2 cup sour cream

Mix in order and bake in loaf pan.

Martha I. Shetler
Glasgow, Kentucky

MY CHOCOLATE CAKE

2 cups brown sugar
1/2 cup shortening
2 eggs
1 cup hot water
1/2 cup sour milk or cream
4 T. cocoa
2 1/4 cups flour
2 t. soda
1/2 t. salt
1 t. vanilla

Mix in order given. Bake at 350 deg. for 35 min.

Martha I. Shetler
Glasgow, KY

BRIDE'S CAKE

3/4 cup butter
1 T. vanilla
1/4 t. almond flavor

Cream together until butter is softened. Add gradually, creaming till fluffy: 1 cup sugar

Combine: 1/2 cup milk and 1/2 cup water

Combine: 3 cups sifted cake flour, 1 t. soda, 1/2 t. salt.

Add dry ingredients and milk mixture alternately to creamed mixture. Beat till smooth.

Beat till frothy: 6 egg whites

Gradually add: 3/4 cup sugar

Continue to beat till rounded peaks form. Spread whites over batter and gently but thoroughly fold in. Bake at 350 deg. for 45-50 min. or till done.

Brost with Bride's Cake butter frosting or other as desired.

Mrs. Ray J. Gingerich
Fillmore, NY

CHOCOLATE MAYONNAISE CAKE

2 cups flour
1 cup sugar
1/2 cup cocoa
1 cup boiling water
1 cup salad dressing (mayonnaise)
2 t. soda
1 t. vanilla

Sift flour, sugar, cocoa and soda. Mix with rest of ingredients. Bake 325-350 deg. for 45 minutes.

Naomi Peachey
Little Falls, NY

SIX SPICE CAKE

4 cups flour
4 t. baking powder
1/2 t. salt
1/2 t. ginger
1/2 t. allspice
1 t. nutmet
1 1/2 t. cloves
1 1/2 t. cinnamon
2 cups sugar
2/3 cups shortening
1 1/2 cups milk
2 eggs and 2 yolks
4 T. molasses

Cream shortening and sugar, add eggs and beat well. Add molasses; then add dry ingredients alternately with milk.

Saloma J. Byler
Dewittville, NY

HAPPY VALLEY CHOCOLATE CAKE

3 cups flour
2 cups sugar
2 t. soda
1 t. salt
6 T. cocoa
2 T. vinegar
2 t. vanilla
2 cups cold water
2/3 cup melted shortening

Sift dry ingredients together; add remaining ingredients in order and beat well for 5 minutes.

Saloma J. Byler
Dewittville, NY

PINEAPPLE UPSIDE DOWN CAKE

1 can pineapple slices
1 1/4 cups flour
1 1/2 t. baking powder
1/2 cup brown sugar
1/4 cup milk
1 t. vanilla
1/4 cup butter
1/2 t. salt
1/2 cup white sugar
1/3 cup shortening
1 large egg

Thoroughly drain pineapple; reserve 1/4 cup juice. In a 9x9x2 in. pan over low heat melt butter; sprinkle with brown sugar, add pineapple slices in single layer; quarter remaining slices and fill in centers.

Into a bowl sift flour, baking powder, salt and sugar. Add shortening, 1/4 cup pineapple juice, milk, vanilla and egg. Beat until smooth. Pour batter over pineapple, spreading evenly. Bake in preheated oven until done. Remove from pan after it has cooled a little.

Emma Hershberger
Dover, DE

The best way to tell a women's age
Isn't a very good one

FAMILY NUT ICING FOR CARROT CAKE

1 cup sugar
3 T. flour
1 cup rich milk
3 T. butter

Cook until thick. Remove from heat.

Add: 1/2 t. vanilla
1 cup coconut
1/2 cup nuts

Spread over cake and return to oven on top rack or broiler until the icing gets bubbly.

Emma Hershberger
Dover, DE

CARROT CAKE

4 eggs
2 cups sugar
1 1/2 cups oil
3 cups flour
2 t. soda
2 t. cinnamon
1 t. salt
3 cups grated carrots

Mix oil, sugar and eggs. Add carrots, then the rest of the ingredients. This cake will turn out best in a loaf pan. Bake at 300 deg. until done.

Emma Hershberger
Dover, DE

COFFEE CAKE

2 cups brown sugar
2 cups flour
1/2 cup lard
1/2 t. nutmeg
1/2 t. salt

Mix ingredients together to form fine crumbs. Reserve 1/2 cup of crumbs for top. Then add the following ingredients to the remainder.

1 cup sour milk
1 egg
1 t. soda

Pour into baking pan. Sprinkle the reserved 1/2 cup crumbs over the batter. Bake at 425 deg. approx. 30 min.

Mrs. Daniel C. Borntreger
Riceville, IA

STRAWBERRY LANG CAKE

Sift together:

2 cups flour
6 T. sugar
4 t. baking powder
salt

Mix in:

1/2 cup shortening
2/3 cup milk
1 large egg

Spread in a baking dish and cream together:

1/4 cup oleo
1/4 cup brown sugar
3 T. flour

Put on first mixture. Serve with fresh strawberring and cream while still warm.

Mrs. Joseph Schrock
Agusta, WI

APPLE CAKE

4 cups chopped apples
2 cups sugar
Stir and let this form juice.
Then add:
1 cup oil
2 eggs, beaten
1 t. soda
3 cups flour
1/2 t. salt
2 t. vanilla
1 cup coconut
1 cup chopped nuts
Pour into a 9x13 in. pan.
Bake in 350 deg. oven for 1 hr.

Mrs. Amos W. Yoder
Jamesport, MO

FRUIT CAKE

2 cups sugar
1 cup lard
3 eggs
1 cup apple sauce
1 cup mashed peaches
Mix sugar, eggs and lard. Add peaches and applesauce; then add:
1 cup raisins
1 cup nutmeats
3 cups flour
2 t. soda
1/4 t. cloves
1/2 t. nutmet
1/2 t. salt
1/2 lb. candied cherries
This makes a large cake. Bake 1 hr.

Saloma J. Byler
Dewittville, NY

INDIAN SUMMER CAKE

2 cups sifted cake flour
1 1/2 t. baking powder
1/2 t. salt
1/2 t. soda
1/2 c. lard
3/4 cup milk
1 1/3 cup brown sugar
2 eggs unbeaten
1 1/2 t. vanilla
Bake in moderate oven.

Naomi Peachey
Little Falls, NY

KANSAS DESSERT CAKE

1 large package oreo chocolate cookies
1 - 8 oz. pkg. cream cheese (room temperature)
1/2 cup oleo 1 cup powdered sugar
1 tub of whipped topping (Cool Whip). Whipped cream may be used if you have cream
2 boxes instant vanilla pudding
3 cups milk 1 t. vanilla

Crush cookies. Put 1/2 of crumbs in a 9x13 in. pan. Mix cream cheese and oleo. Add powdered sugar. Fold in whipped cream. In a separate bowl mix milk, vanilla pudding. Fold 2 mixtures together, then pour over crumbs. Add remaining crumbs on top. Let set several hrs. or overnight. May be served frozen or chilled.

Ida Schrock
Haven, KS

COCOA CHIFFON CAKE

Stir until smooth; cool:
3/4 cup boiling water 1/2 cup cocoa

Step 1:
1 3/4 cups cake flour 1 3/4 cups sugar
3 t. baking powder 1 t. salt
1/2 cup Wesson oil 7 unbeaten egg yolks
Add to the cooled cocoa mixture:
1 t. vanilla 1/4 t. red food coloring
Stir with spoon until smooth
Step 2:
Measure into large bowl:
1 cup egg whites 1/2 t. cream of tartar

Beat until stiff. Gently fold into batter until blended. Pour into ungreased 10 in. tube pan. Bake at 325-350 deg. for 55-60 min. or until done (cake springs back when lightly touched). Invert cake over funnel or bottle until completely cool. Loosen cake with spatula. Invert on serving plate. Garnish as desired.

Aaron Brubacker
Liverpool, PA

REAL GOOD BLACK CHOCOLATE CAKE

4 cups granulated sugar
4 eggs
1 1/2 cups shortening or margarine
1 cup cocoa
4 bups boiling water
5 1/3 cups flour
4 t. baking powder
4 t. baking soda
4 t. vanilla

Bake at 350 deg. for 1/2 hr.

Aaron Brubaker
Liverpool, PA

One today
Is worth two tomorrows

APPLE WALNUT CAKE

3 eggs (well beaten)
1 cup cooking oil
2 cups sugar
2 t. vanilla
3 cups flour
1 t. baking soda
1 t. salt
1 t. cinnamon
1 cup chopped nuts
3 cups sliced apples

Bake in a greased floured 9x13" cake pan at 325 deg. for 45 minutes. While still warm, sprinkle with confectioner's sugar.

Naomi Peachey
Little Falls, NY

FEATHER CAKE

3 eggs
2 cups sugar
1/2 cup butter or shortening
1 cup sweet milk
3 cups flour
3 t. baking powder
1 t. vanilla

Naomi Peachey, Little Falls, NY
Saloma J. Byler, Dewittville, NY

COTTAGE CAKE

1 1/2 cups flour
1 1/2 t. baking powder
3/4 cup milk
1/4 cup salad oil
1 cup sugar
1 egg
pinch of salt

Bake and cut in squares and put in serving dishes.

Sauce for Cake:

1 cup sugar
1 pt. boiling water
2 t. vanilla
2 T. butter
2 T. flour

Cook till thick. Dip it over the cakes. Fresh fruit may be put on top, like bananas, sliced peaches or strawberries.

Ida Schrock
Haven, KS

The time to make friends
Is before you need them

MINUTE FUDGE FROSTING

1/4 cup butter
1/4 cup milk
1/8 t. salt
1/8 cup cocoa
1 cup sugar

Melt butter in saucepan. Add other ingredients, stirring until sugar is dissolved. Boil 1 minute. Remove from heat and stir until creamy enough to spread.

Saloma J. Byler
Dewittville, NY

BANANA CAKE

1/3 cup lard
1 cup mashed bananas
1 egg
4 T. milk
1 t. soda
1 cup sugar
2 cups sifted cake flour
1 t. salt
2 t. baking powder
1 t. vanilla

Cream together sugar and lard. Add eggs, milk and bananas, then add dry ingredients.

Mrs. Henry Stutzman
Conewango Valley, NY

SHORT CAKE

1 egg
1 cup cream or milk and batter
1 t. baking powder
1 cup sugar
1 1/2 cups flour
1/2 t. soda

Mrs. Noah Wengerd, Jr.
Conewango Valley, NY

SPICE CAKE

1/2 cup shortening
2 egg yolks
1 t. baking powder
1 t. cloves
1/2 t. salt
1 t. vanilla
2 cups brown sugar
2 1/2 cups flour
1 1/2 t. cinnamon
1 1/4 cup sour milk
1 t. soda

Cream together shortening and sugar. Add egg yolks and beat well. Add dry ingredients to first mixture, alternately with milk and flavoring. Beat well after each addition. Fold in beaten egg whites.

Mrs. Noah Wengerd, Jr.
Conewango Valley, NY

PANUCHE FROSTING

1/2 cup oleo
1/4 cup milk
1 cup packed brown sugar
2 cups powdered sugar

Put brown sugar, oleo and milk together and cook 2 min. Then cool a little and add powdered sugar. Rich and soft!

Mrs. Noah Wengerd, Jr.
Conewango Valley, NY

BANANA CAKE

Cream: 1/3 cup oleo
Gradually add 1 1/2 cups sugar; blend until light and creamy.
Add 3 beaten egg yolks
Mix:
1 cup mashed bananas 1/2 t. salt
1/2 cup sour cream 1 t. baking soda
Gradually stir to other mixture.
Now add:
2 cups flour (may use 1 cup whole wheat)
1 1/2 t. baking powder 1/2 cup chopped nuts
Beat stiff but not dry 3 egg whites and pinch of salt. Fold into batter.
Bake in moderate oven 350 deg. 30-40 min.

Martha Mast
Revere, MO

1 - 2 - 3 ICING

Mix: 1 T. cocoa, 2 T. flour,3 T. sugar, a little vanilla and salt, enough milk to make paste which spreads easily. Have ready to put on cake as soon as it is taken out of oven.

Martha Mast
Revere, MO

BUTTER SPONGE CAKE

Heat: 1 cup milk and 1 cup oleo till oleo milts. Cool slightly.
Add: 1 t. vanilla, 1/2 t. lemon extract.
In large bowl beat 12 egg yolks (1 cup) till thick and lemon colored; gradually add 2 cups sugar, beating till thick and glossy.
Gradually add milk mixture, mixing well.
Sift together: 2 1/2 cups flour, 2 t. baking powder, 1 t. salt. Fold in egg mixture. Pour batter into ungreased 10 in. tube pan. Bake in slow oven, 325 deg., about 1 hr. and 20 min. or till done. Invert pan to cool.

Martha Mast
Revere, MO

ANGEL FOOD CAKE

Sift 6 times: 2 1/4 cups sugar, 1 3/4 cups flour.
Beat 3 cups egg whites partly; add 1 1/2 t. cream of tartar, beat until stiff but not dry. Fold in sugar 3 T. at a time.
Add: 1 1/2 t. vanilla and 1 t. almond extract.
Lightly fold in flour, using sifter too, adding small amount at a time.
Add 3 T. cold water.
Rinse tube pan with cold water before pouring batter in. Bake in moderate oven 50-55 min.

Martha Mast
Revere, MO

LOVELIGHT 2-EGG CHIFFON CAKE

2 eggs, separated
1 t. salt
1 1/2 cups sugar
1/3 cup cooking oil
3 t. baking powder
1 1/2 t. flavoring
2 1/4 cups sifted cake flour
1 cup milk

Beat egg whites until frothy. Gradually beat in 1/2 cup sugar. Continue beating until very stiff and glossy. Sift remaining sugar, flour, baking powder and salt into another bowl. Add oil, half of milk, and flavoring. Beat 1 min. Add remaining milk, egg yolks, beat 1 min. Fold in meringue. Pour into 2 rounded layers and bake at 350 deg. for 30-35 min.

Elizabeth Mae Rober
Montgomery, IN

FEATHER LIGHT CAKE

2/3 cup shortening
3 1/2 cups sifted cake flour
4 egg whites, stiffly beaten
2 T. boiling water
4 t. baking powder
1 1/2 cups sugar
1 1/2 cups cold water
2 t. vanilla
1/2 t. salt

Cream together shortening and sugar until light and fluffy. Add flavoring. Blend thoroughly. Add boiling water. Beat 1 min. Sift flour and salt together 4 times. Add alternately with cold water to shortening mixture, beating well. Sift baking powder over top of batter and fold in with beaten egg whites. Bake in 3 rounded layers about 30 min. in moderate oven.

Elizabeth Mae Rober
Montgomery, IN

SOFT CREAM JUMBLES

1/2 cup lard
1 1/2 cups sugar
1/2 t. soda
1/2 t. baking powder
1 t. vanilla
2 eggs beaten
3 1/2 cups flour
1/2 t. salt
1 cup sour cream or milk

Cream lard and sugar; add beaten eggs. Sift dry ingredients. Add dry ingredients and cream to creamed mixture. Blend well. Drop by spoonfuls onto baking sheets. Bake at 350 deg.

Topping:
1/4 cup sugar
1 t. cinnamon

Mix above and sprinkle on top before baking.

Mrs. Amos W. Yoder
Jamesport, MO

CHERRY COFFEE CAKE

2 cups flour
2 t. baking powder
1 egg and milk to make 1 cup
1 cup sugar
1/2 cup butter
1 can cherry pie filling

Topping:
1 cup flour
1 cup sugar
1/2 cup butter

Mix together flour, sugar, and baking powder. Cut in butter as for pie dough. Break into cup and milk to make 1 cup of liquid. Beat. Add to first mixture. Put in pan; then add cherry pie filling. Bake at 375 deg. for 30-35 min. Mix topping and sprinkle over pie filling.

Mrs. Amos W. Yoder
Jamesport, MO

HONEY CAKE

1 cup sour cream
1 cup sugar
1 egg
1/2 t. soda
2 cups flour
favor to taste

Bake 1/2 hr. To be eaten while still warm.

Mrs. Amos W. Yoder
Jamesport,MO

CRAZY CHOCOLATE CAKE

3 cups flour | 2 cups sugar
6 T. cocoa | 2 t. soda
1 t. salt | 2 T. vinegar
2 t. vanilla | 3/4 cup salad oil
2 cups cold water | 1 t. instant coffee (optional)

Combine all ingredients, but 1 cup cold water, and mix. Add water and mix again. Don't overbeat. Bake at 350 deg. for 35-40 min. Makes 1 9x12 cake or 3 doz. cupcakes.

Mrs. Joe J. Miller
Apple Creek, OH

BUTTERMILK CAKE

Make into crumbs:
4 cups flour | 2 cups sugar
3/4 cup oleo

Take out 1 cup crumbs. To the rest mix:
1 1/2 cups buttermilk or sour cream | 4 eggs
1 t. vanilla | 1 t. soda

Pour batter in pan; spread crumbs on top; bake.

Martha Mast
Revere, MO

Carrying a grudge
Can wear a person out very quickly

CHOCOLATE FROSTING

1 cup sweet or sour cream | 1 cup sugar
1 t. cocoa

Mix and bring to a boil and add a pinch of soda and let boil until forms a soft ball in cold water. Remove from stove. Add vanilla and 1 t. butter. Beat till it holds its form.

Joe Borntreger
Cashton, WI

BLACK CAKE

2 cups sugar
1 cup sour or sweet milk
1 cup butter or cream
2 eggs
3 cups flour

To the flour add 4 T. cocoa; add 1 T. vanilla and beat well. Dissolve 2 t. soda in 1 cup hot water. Add last and don't beat, just fold in.

Joe Borntreger
Cashton, WI

WALNUT WONDER CAKE

2 1/2 cups sifted flour
3 t. baking powder
1 t. salt
1 1/2 cups sugar
1/2 cup shortening
1 cup milk
1 t. vanilla
2 eggs unbeaten

Sift flour and measure. Add baking powder, salt and sugar. Stir shortening just to soften. Sift in dry ingredients. Add 3/4 cup of the milk and vanilla and mix well. Then beat 2 min. Add eggs and remaining milk. Beat 1 min. longer.

Joe Borntreger
Cashton, WI

YELLOW LOVELIGHT CAKE

Sift:
2 1/4 cups flour
3 t. baking powder
1 t. salt
1 cup sugar

Add:
1 1/3 cups Mazola oil
1 cup water or milk
2 egg yolks
flavor

Beat 2 egg whites and 1/2 cup sugar and add last.

For maple nut cake, take 1 cup brown instead of 1 white sugar and add 1 t. maple nut flavor; also add 1/2 cup nuts (walnuts or pecans). Bake in layers. Bake at 350 deg. 30-35 min. for layers and loaf 40-45 min.

Joe Borntreger
Cashton, WI

VELVET CAKE

3 cups flour
2 cups white sugar
2/3 cup butter
3 t. baking powder
1 cup water
3 egg whites, beaten stiff

Cream butter and sugar. Sift flour, baking powder and salt 4 times. Add water and eggs. Bake at 350 deg. or 375 deg.

Joe Borntreger
Cashton, WI

GLORIFIED GINGERBREAD CAKE

1/2 cup shortening
1 cup sugar
2 cups flour
1/2 t. ginger and cinnamon

Sift flour, measure and add spices. Sift again. Rub shortening into dry ingredients to make fine crumbs. Take out 1/2 cup crumbs to sprinkle on top of mixture. To remaining crumbs, add:

1 egg, beaten
2 T. molasses
1 cup sour milk or buttermilk
1/2 t. salt
1 t. soda

Beat until smooth. Pour into a greased pan, sprinkle with crumbs. Bake at 350 deg. for 45 min.

Joe Borntreger
Cashton, WI

PLAIN WHITE CAKE

2 cups sugar
1 cup shortening
1 cup cold water
3 cups cake flour
3 t. baking powder
2 t. vanilla
1 t. salt
whites of 5 eggs

Cream sugar and shortening. Add vanilla. Sift flour, baking powder and salt. Add alternately with water to first mixture. Fold in beaten egg whites. Bake at 375 deg. for 30 min.

Mrs. Dan J. Troyer
Mercer, PA

Happiness depends upon ourselves

BROWN SUGAR ICING

1 cup brown sugar 2 T. butter
2 T. karo 3 T. water
Boil 4 min. and add flavoring. Add confectioner's sugar till right consistency.

Mary A. Kinsinger
Meyersdale, PA

SNOW CAKE

1 cup shortening 2 cups white sugar
1 cup milk 2 cups flour
1 cup cornstarch 5 t. baking powder
1/2 t. salt 1 t. vanilla
6 egg whites or 1 cup
Cream shortening, add sugar. Sift flour, cornstarch, baking powder and salt. Add alternately with milk. Fold in stiffly beaten egg whites.

Elizabeth Stutzman
Union City, PA

SOUR CREAM CAKE

2 eggs in a cup, fill with rich sour cream 1 cup sugar
1 cup flour 1/2 t. soda
1/2 t. vanilla
Mix in order given. Put soda in cream. Bake in moderate oven.

Cora Stutzman
Union City, PA

SNOW CAKE

2 1/4 cup flour 1/2 cup shortening
1 1/4 cup white sugar
2 t. vanilla
2 1/2 t. baking powder
1/2 t. lemon flavor & 1/2 t. almond flavor if desired
1 cup milk 1/4 t. salt
Combine and add 3 beaten egg whites last.
Bake at 350 deg. until toothpick when inserted comes out clean.

Mose E. Helmuth
Edgewood, IA

FRESH COCONUT POUND CAKE

1 cup butter
3 cups sugar
6 eggs
1 t. baking powder
3 cups all-purpose flour
1/4 t. baking soda
1/4 t. salt
1 carton (8 oz.) dairy sour cream
1 cup fresh coconut
1 t. vanilla extract
1 t. coconut extract

Mose E. Helmuth
Edgewood, IA

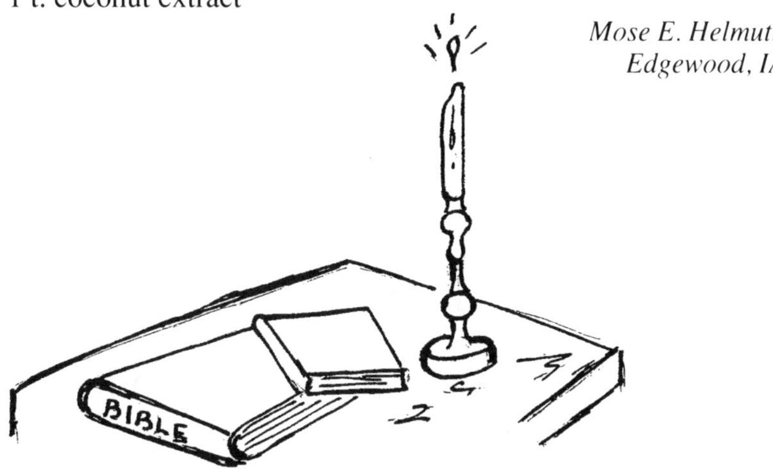

CHOCOLATE CUPCAKES

(No cholesterol)
Sift together:
1 1/2 cups sifted flour
2 t. baking powder
1/3 cup dry cocoa
Cream together:
3/4 cup corn oil margarine
1 cup sugar
1 t. vanilla
Beat until stiff:
3 egg whites
pinch of cream of tartar

Preheat oven to 350 deg. After the creamed mixture is well blended, add the sifted mixture alternately with 1/2 cup of water. Blend, then with a wire whisk blend in the beaten egg whites. Should make 18 cupcakes.

Mrs. Dan J. Troyer
Mercer, PA

NO BAKE FRUIT CAKE

2 cups miniature marshmallows
1/2 cup orange juice
2/3 cup evaporated milk
4 pks. Graham crackers (finely crushed)
1 lb. mixed fruits and peels
1 t. cinnamon
1/2 t. allspice
1 lb. dates (chopped)
1 cup raisins
1 cup nuts
1/2 t. cloves

Mix orange juice and evaporated milk, add marshmallows and let stand about 20 min. Mix rest of ingredients together in large bowl. Add first mixture and blend well. Press in foil-lined loaf pan. Best if made several weeks ahead.

Mrs. Dan J. Troyer
Mercer, PA

WHITE CAKE

1 1/4 cups lard
2 1/2 cups milk
2 1/2 t. vanilla
3 1/8 cups sugar
5 1/2 cups cake flour
2 1/2 T. baking powder
2 t. salt
5 eggs

Add 5 T. of the milk and the vanilla flavoring to the lard. Whip until light and fluffy or about 2 min. on electric mixer at medium speed. Sift dry ingredients together, add to lard along with 2/3 of the milk. Beat until smooth. Add remaining milk and eggs. Beat until smooth. Pour into greased and floured 12 1/2 x 18 in. pan. Bake in moderate 350 deg. oven 35-40 min. or until done.

Mrs. Dan J. Troyer
Mercer, PA

ORANGE CHIFFON CAKE

Preheat oven to 325 deg.
Measure and sift together:
2 1/4 cups cake flour
1 1/2 cups sugar
3 t. baking powder
1 t. salt
Make a well and add in order:
1/2 cup cooking oil
5 unbeaten egg yolks
2 T. grated orange rind
juice of 2 oranges, plus water to make 3/4 cup liquid
Beat with spoon until smooth
Whip very stiff:
1 cup egg whites
1/2 t. cream of tartar
Pour egg yolk mixture over whipped egg white mixture, folding it in—do not stir. Pour into ungreased 10 in. tube pan and bake 65-70 min. Let cool 1 hr.

Mrs. Dan J. Troyer
Mercer, PA

LOVELIGHT PEANUT BUTTER CAKE

2 eggs separated
1/2 cup sugar
2 1/4 cups cake flour
3 t. baking powder
1 t. salt
1/4 t. soda
1 cup brown sugar (packed)
1/3 cup chunk-style peanut butter
1/2 cup vegetable oil
1 1/4 cup milk
Blend brown sugar, flour, baking powder and salt in a bowl. Add oil, half of milk and peanut butter. Beat 150 strokes vigorously by hand. Scrape sides and bottom of bowl constantly. Add remaining milk and egg yolks. Beat 1 more min. Beat egg whites until frothy. Gradually beat in 1/2 cup sugar. Beat till stiff and glossy. Fold into batter and bake at 350 deg. about 40 min.

Mrs. Dan. J. Troyer
Mercer, PA

Your temper is one of the few things
That improves the longer you keep it

SUNDAY MORNING COFFEE CAKE

2 1/4 cups flour
1 cup raisins
3/4 cup white sugar
1 t. baking powder
1 egg
1 cup butter
1/3 cup lard
1 t. salt
1 t. soda

Mix:
1 T. butter
1 t. cinnamon
1/2 cup brown sugar

Sprinkle over batter and bake. Can also add nuts.

Mrs. Raymond S. Miller
Millersburg, OH

JIMMIE CARTER CAKE

1st Layer:
Mix:
1 cup flour
1 cup chopped peanuts
1 stick butter

Press in 9x13 in. ungreased pan. Bake at 250 deg. for 20 min. Cool.

2nd Layer:
Mix:
1 cup peanut butter
1 cup 10X sugar
1 - 8 oz. softened cream cheese

Fold in 1 cup Cool Whip by hand after mixing other ingredients. Spread over first layer.

3rd Layer:
Mix:
1 small box instant chocolate pudding
1 small box instant vanilla pudding
3 cups milk

Pour over 2nd layer. Top with Cool Whip and crushed peanuts. This freezes well. Take out 1 hr. before needed.

Frances Helm
Shippensburg, PA

ZUCCHINI CRAB CAKE

2 cups grated zucchini
2 eggs
1 cup chopped onions
salt and pepper to taste
1 t. old bay seasoning
enough cracker crumbs to make soft batter
Drop by T. in deep fat.
Serve with sour cream

Sarah Flaud
Newburg, PA

MARBLE CHIFFON CAKE

1/4 cup cocoa
1/4 cup white sugar
1/4 cup boiling water
Measure and sift into large bowl:
2 1/4 cups pastry flour
1 1/2 cups sugar
1 t. salt
3 t. baking powder
Make a well and add in order:
1/2 cup salad oil
7 unbeaten egg yolks
3/4 cup cold water
1 t. vanilla
Beat until smooth.
Measure into large bowl:
1 cup egg whites (7)
1/2 t. cream of tartar
Beat until whites form very stiff peaks, 3-5 min. Do not underbeat. Pour egg yolk mixture over egg whites, gently folding in. Divide batter in 2 parts. To 1/2 of the batter mix in the chocolate syrup. Spoon dark and light batter alternately in 10 in. tube pan. Bake at 375 deg. for 1 hr.

Mrs. Dan J. Troyer
Mercer, PA

If you lose your temper it is a sign
You have wrong on your side

PERFECT CHOCOLATE CAKE

1 cup unsifted unsweetened cocoa
2 cups boiling water
2 3/4 cups sifted all purpose flour
2 t. baking soda
1/2 t. salt
1/2 t. baking powder
1 cup butter or regular margarine, softened
2 1/2 cups granulated sugar
4 eggs

Filling:
1 cup heavy cream chilled
1/4 cup unsifted confectioner's sugar
1 t. vanilla extract

Frosting:
1 pkg. 6 oz. semisweet chocolate pieces
1/2 cup light cream
1 cup butter or regular margarine
2 1/2 cups unsifted confectioner's sugar

Do not overbeat. Preheat oven to 350 deg. Grease well and lightly flour 3 - 9x1 1/2 in. layer cake pans. Bake 25-30 min. or until surface springs back when gently pressed with fingertip. Cool in pans 10 min. Carefully loosen sides with spatula; remove from pans and cool on racks. Then put filling between layers and frost.

Joni H. Schrock
Middlefield, OH

When the outlook is not good
Try the up look

LAZY WOMEN'S CAKE

Sift together in a large bowl or greased 9x13 in. loaf pan:
3 cups flour
2 cups sugar
5 T. cocoa
2 t. soda
1 t. salt
Make 3 holes in mixture
Hole #1 - 1 cup cooking oil
Hole #2 - 2 T. vinegar
Hole #3 - 1 t. vanilla
Pour 2 cups water over this mess and stir with a fork until well blended. Bake at 350 deg.

Mary A. Kinsinger
Meyersdale, PA

CRAZY CAKE

3 cups flour
2 cups sugar
4 T. cocoa
2 t. soda
1 t. salt

Mix above ingredients well and make a hole in dry ingredients and add:

2 T. vinegar
2 t. vanilla
3/4 cup oil or melted shortening

Pour 2 cups cold water over all. Stir till well blended. Put in 9x14 in. pan and bake at 350 deg. till done.

Mrs. Neal Kauffman
La Plata, MO

COWBOY CAKE

2 cups brown sugar
2 cups flour
1/2 cup oleo

Mix well and take out 1/2 cup crumbs.

Add:

1 cup buttermilk
1 t. soda
1 egg
1 t. vanilla
1/2 t. salt

Stir till well blended, pour into 9x14 in. pan. Shake 1/2 cup crumbs over top of dough. Place in oven and bake at 350 deg. till done.

Mrs. Neal Kauffman
LaPlata, MO

PINEAPPLE PECAN CAKE

3/4 cup sugar 1/4 cup shortening
1 egg 1/2 cup milk
1 1/2 cup sifted flour 2 t. baking powder
1/2 t. salt
Pineapple topping:
2 T. softened butter 2 T. honey
1/2 cup well-drained, crushed pineapple
1/3 cup chopped pecans

Mix sugar, shortening and egg thoroughly. Stir in milk. Sift together dry ingredients and stir into shortening mixture. Spread batter in a greased and floured 9x9x2 in. square pan. Mix topping ingredients and spread over batter. Bake at 375 deg. for 25 or 35 min. or until done. Serve warm. Makes 9 - 2 1/2 in. squares.

Mose E. Helmuth
Edgewood, IA

CHERRY BURIED TREASURE CAKE

13 oz. pkg. cream cheese 1/2 cup butter
1 cup sifted all purpose flour 3 T. sugar
1/2 cup finely chopped almonds

---

1 cup sugar 1/4 cup cornstarch
1/2 t. salt 1 1/2 cups cherry juice
2 T. butter Few drops red color solution
2 No. 303 cans waterpack tart red cherries, drained

---

1 1/2 cups sifted all purpose flour 2 t. baking powder
1/2 cup sugar 1/2 t. salt
1/4 cup butter melted
1/2 cup warm water 1 t. vanilla
3 egg yolks, slightly beaten 3 egg whites 1/2 cup sugar
Confectioner's sugar

Beat cream cheese with 1/2 cup butter. Add 1 cup flour, 3 T. sugar and the almonds. Blend and spread evenly over bottom of 25x11 3/4x1 3/4 in. pan. Combine 1 cup sugar, cornstarch, salt and cherry juice. Cook, stirring constantly until thickened. Add drained cherries, butter and red color solution. When cool, pour over bottom cake layer in pan. Sift together flour, baking powder, 1/2 cup sugar and salt. Combine butter, water, vanilla and egg yolks, and stir into dry ingredients. Beat egg whites until stiff enough to form soft peaks, gradually adding 1/2 cup sugar. Fold cake mixture into beaten egg whites; pour over cherry filling. Bake at 350 deg. for 50-60 min. When cool, sprinkle generously with confectioner's sugar. Decorate with cherries if desired.

Mose E. Helmuth
Edgewood, IA

A friend is one who knows all about you
And still loves you

CHOCOLATE MACAROON BUNDT CAKE

2 cups flour — 1 3/4 cups sugar
1/2 cup cocoa — 1 t. salt
1 t. soda — 2 t. vanilla
3/4 cup cold water — 1/2 cup oleo
1/2 cup sour cream — 4 eggs

Mix well till blended for 3 min. at medium speed.

Macaroon Filling:

1 egg white, beaten stiff

Fold in:

1/4 cup sugar — 1 cup coconut
1 t. vanilla — 1 T. flour

Spray bundt pan with Pam. Put 1/2 of cake batter in, then the filling. Be sure the filling doesn't tough the outside of the pan. Then put in the other 1/2 of cake batter. Bake at 350 deg. for 55-60 min. Cool 10 min. before lifting.

Mose E. Helmuth
Edgewood, IA

DELICIOUS NUT CAKE

Cream together until fluffy:
2/3 cups shortening 2 egg yolks
1 1/2 cups sugar
Sift together:
3 cups flour 3 1/2 t. baking powder
3/4 t. salt
Add to creamed mixture alternately with:
1 1/3 cups thin milk (1/2 water) 2 t. vanilla
3/4 cup chopped nuts
Fold in 2 egg whites stiffly beaten. Pour into greased and floured pans. Bake.

Emma Hershberger
Dover, DE

FAIRY CAKE

6 egg yolks 7 T. water
Beat 5 min.
Add 1 1/3 cup sugar, beat 5 min. more.
1 1/3 cup flour - sifted 3 times 1 t. salt
1 t. vanilla
Add to creamed mixture.
Add 6 egg whites stiffly beaten
Bake in angel food pan for 1 hr. at 300 deg.

Emma Hershberger
Dover, DE

FRENCH CHOCOLATE CAKE

1 cup sugar 1/2 cup butter
1 cup sour milk 3 eggs
2 cups flour 1 t. soda
1 t. vanilla
Dissolve 2/3 cup cocoa and half cup sugar in a little hot water. Add this to the sugar, butter, milk and eggs, then add the flour and soda and bake at 350 deg. till done. Good with white fluffy frosting.

Mrs. Joe J. Miller
Apple Creek, OH

BRIDE'S FROSTING

Cream until butter is softened:
2/3 cup butter
1 1/2 t. vanilla
1/4 t. almond flavor
Add gradually 6 cups powdered sugar
Stir in 3-6 T. cream to spreading consistency.

Mrs. Ray J. Gingerich
Fillmore, NY

WEDDING CAKE FROSTING

2 lbs. powdered sugar
1 3/4 cups Crisco
2/3 cup cold water
pinch of salt
clear vanilla
Beat together till real fluffy, add a speck of blue food coloring to give it a whiter effect.

Mrs. Ray J. Gingerich
Fillmore, NY

CHOCOLATE CAKE

(A strong chocolate flavor)
2 cups brown sugar
1/4 cup oleo
1 cup buttermilk or sour milk
1 cup cocoa
2 cups flour (level)
salt
vanilla
1 t. soda
1/2 cup hot water
Frost with a good chocolate frosting.

Mrs. Ray J. Gingerich
Fillmore, NY

EASY SO EASY FRUIT CAKE

2 1/2 cups flour
1 t. soda
2 eggs slightly beaten
1 (28 oz. jar) mincemeat (I use homemade 3 1/2 cups)
1 - 14 oz. can Eaglebrand Condensed milk
2 cups mixed candied fruit
1 cup coarsely chopped nuts
Bake for 20-25 minutes

Mrs. Ray J. Gingerich
Fillmore, NY

CUP CAKE

(My Mother's Wedding Cake)

1 cup butter
2 cups sugar
4 eggs
1 cup sweet milk
3 cups flour
3 t. baking powder

Bake in loaf or layers. Mix like any other cak and bake at 350 deg. This must be almost 100 years old.

Mrs. Joe J. Miller
Apple Creek, OH

WHIPPED CREAM CAKE

1 cup whipping cream (whipped)
4 egg whites (beaten stiff)

Combine the two ingredients.

Mix well:

1 1/2 cups sifted white sugar
2 cups sifted cake flour
3 t. baking powder
1/2 t. salt
1/2 cup cold water

Add the sugar gradually to the cream and eggs. Sift baking powder and salt with flour. Add dry ingredients and cold water alternately to the cream and eggs and sugar mixture.

Use two well-greased 8 in. layer cake pans for baking. Bake at 350 deg. for 20 min. A supreme cake.

Mrs. Joe J. Miller
Apple Creek, OH

TOLL HOUSE CRUMB CAKE

Topping: Mix and set aside:

1 T. flour
1/2 cup brown sugar
1/2 cup chocolate chips
2 T. butter
1/2 cup nuts

Cake:

2 cups flour
1 t. baking powder
1 t. soda
1 t. vanilla
3 eggs
1/2 t. salt
1/2 cup butter
1 cup sugar
1 cup sour cream

Mix liquid ingredients and sugar. Gradually add flour, etc., alternately with sour cream. Fold in a 1/2 cup chocolate chips.

Sprinkle topping over batter. Bake at 350 deg. for 40-50 min.

Mose E. Helmuth
Edgewood, IA

NEVER FAIL CHOCOLATE CAKE

2 eggs
2 sticks oleo or 3/4 cup lard
2 cups sugar
3 T. cocoa
Make these real creamy and add:
1 cup sour milk
1 t. soda
1/2 cup cold water
2 1/2 cups flour
1 t. vanilla
pinch of salt
Bake in loaf pan in moderate oven.

Mrs. Philip Yoder
Fairbank, IA

RHUBARB CAKE

2 eggs
2 cups brown sugar
1 cup sour milk
1 stick oleo
1 t. soda
1 t. vanilla
dash of salt
2 cups fresh rhubarb, cut up
2 cups flour
Mix all together and pour in greased pan. Mix sugar and cinnamon and spread on top of batter. Bake.

Mrs. Philip Yoder
Fairbank, IA

MOTHER'S BEST ANGEL FOOD CAKE

Beat:
2 cups egg whites
1 t. vanilla
1/2 t. almond extract
1/2 t. salt
2 t. cream of tartar
Add:
1 1/2 cups sugar 2 T. at a time and beat until stiff.
Sift together and fold in:
1 1/2 cups flour
1 cup sugar
Bake 50-60 min. in tube pan in moderate oven.

Mrs. Philip Yoder
Fairbank, IA

EASY SHORTCAKE

Sift together:
2 cups flour
1/3 cup sugar
4 t. baking powder
1/2 t. salt
Cut in 1/2 cup oleo and a well beaten egg
1/3 cup milk (or a little more)
Mix until well blended.
Bake at 450 deg. for 15 min.
Serve with milk and your favorite fruit.

Mrs. Samuel D. Beachy
Clark, MO

HAPPY VALLEY CHOCOLATE CAKE

3 cups flour
2 cups sugar
2 t. baking powder
6 T. cocoa
1 t. salt
2 cups cold water
2 t. vanilla
2 t. vinegar
10 T. vegetable oil
Mix dry ingredients, add remaining ingredients. Bake at 375 deg. for 55 min. or until done.

Mrs. Amos W. Yoder
Jamesport, MO

ROMAN APPLE CAKE

1 cup sugar
1/2 cup brown sugar
1 cup shortening
2 eggs
2 1/2 cups flour
2 t. cinnamon
1 t. baking powder
1/2 t. salt
1 cup sour milk
1 t. soda
2 cups diced apples
Topping:
1/2 cup sugar
1/2 cup nuts
1 t. cinnamon
Mix and put on top. Bake 30-40 min.

Mrs. Vernon E. Bontreger
Iowa City, IA

RHUBARB SHORTCAKE

1 cup sugar
1 cup sour cream
1 t. soda
2 cups flour
2 cups rhubarb (cut fine)

Put soda in sour cream, add sugar and beat well. Stir in flour. Then add rhubarb. Sprinkle with nutmeg on top. Bake. Eat with milk.

Mrs. Samuel D. Beachy
Clark, MO

FRUIT CAKE

1 cup flour
1/2 cup sugar
1 t. soda
1 egg
salt
1 cup fruit

Mix and bake.

Mrs. Samuel D. Beachy
Clark, MO

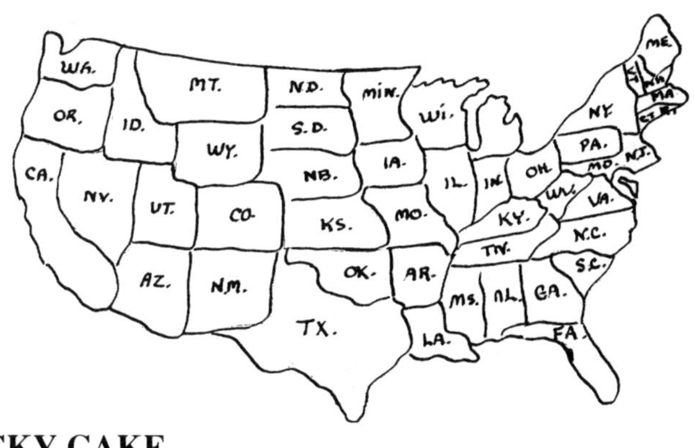

WACKY CAKE

Sift together:
3 cups flour
2 cups sugar
2 t. soda
1/2 t. salt
3 T. cocoa

Add:
3/4 cup cooking oil
2 T. vinegar
1 T. vanilla
2 cups cold water

Mix well. Bake at 350 deg. for 3/4 hr.

Mrs. Samuel D. Beachy
Clark, MO

AMISH CAKE

Cream together:
1 cup margarine
1 cup brown sugar
1 cup white sugar
Add 2 cups buttermilk or sour milk with 2 t. soda
Add 3 cups flour, vanilla, salt
Bake. Spread on top the following after cake is baked:
6 T. butter
4 T. milk
1 cup brown sugar
1/2 cup nuts
Return to oven and bake until bubbly—1 min.

Mrs. Samuel D. Beachy
Clark, MO

GERMAN COFFEE CAKE

3/4 cup oleo melted
3/4 cup brown sugar
3/4 cup white sugar
pinch of salt
2 1/2 cups flour
Blend all ingredients. Reserve 1 cup of the crumbs mixture for topping.
Add:
1 egg
1 t. baking powder and soda
1 cup sour milk or sweet milk to which 2 t. vinegar has been added
Blend ingredients and add to part 1. Spread mixture evenly in a thin layer and sprinkle with 1/2 cup nut meats. Put crumbs on top. Bake at 350 deg. for 35 min.

Mrs. Samuel D. Beachy
Clark, MO

SOUR CREAM RAISIN CAKE

1 cup sour cream
1 cup sugar
2 cups flour
1 cup raisins (chopped)
2 eggs
vanilla
1 t. salt, soda, cloves, cinnamon and nutmeg
Bake.

Mrs. Samuel D. Beachy
Clark, MO

COCONUT PINEAPPLE CAKE

1 1/2 cups sugar
1/2 cup butter
Add 4 eggs one at a time. Beat well after each egg.
1 cup crushed pineapple (don't drain)
2 1/2 cups flour, sift with 2 t. baking powder
1 cup full coconut
Bake in a moderate oven in a loaf pan.

Alma Yoder
Lovington, IL

Candy

CAROB CANDY

5 lb. carob or chocolate
1 - 3 oz. box rice krispies
2 cups crushed peanuts
2 cups coconut

Melt carob, add peanute, etc., and drop on wax paper; set in a cold place. For variation, you could use raisins, seeds, and cashews, etc.

Fannie S. Miller
Bird-in-Hand, PA

TURTLES

1 lb. brown sugar
1/2 lb. butter
a can Eagle Brand milk
1 cup white karo
1 t. cream of tartar

Put in pan and bring to a full boil. Boil 12. min. Cool without stirring. Drop on top of nuts and cover with chocolate.

Mrs. J. David Byler
Punxsutawney, PA

COCONUT CANDY

1 cup mashed unsalted potatoes. Add enough powdered sugar to hold together. Add 4 cups coconut and vanilla. Form into balls. Let set a while. Dip in chocolate.

Mrs. Clarence Miller
Medford, WI

BEST EVER CARAMEL

2 cups white sugar
1 cup light corn syrup
1 cup milk
1 cup brown sugar
1 cup heavy cream
1 cup butter

Cook slowly till firm ball stage, 248 deg. Remove from heat and add 1 1/4 T. vanilla (also nuts if desired). Cool slightly. Pour into greased pans. Cut in squares when cold.

Mrs. Clarence Miller
Medford, WI

You can go broke buying bargains

APRIL HORNS

1/2 cup margarine
1/2 cup creamed cottage cheese
1 cup flour

Blend together. Add more flour if necessary to form a soft dough. Shape into 1" balls—refrigerate overnight. Roll each ball into a 3" round on a well-floured board. Roll only 10 at a time; keep rest of dough cold. Place a t. of filling in center of each; fold into horn shape. Brush with egg whites and roll in nut mixture. Bake on greased sheet 375 deg. for 12-15 min. About 3 doz.

Filling:
1 cup dried apricots (grind before cooking)
Add 2/3 cup sugar to apricots. Cool. Add 1 beaten egg white.
Nut Mixture: 1/4 cup sugar
1/4 cup ground nuts

Fannie S. Miller
Bird-in-Hand, PA

CARMEL CANDY

1 lb. (2 2/3 cups) brown sugar
1 t. cream of tartar
1/3 lb. butter
1 can Eagle Brand milk
1 cup white Karo
1 cup nuts
1 t. vanilla

Put all together but nuts and boil 12 min, stirring all the time. Add nuts. Pour in greased pan. Cut and wrap.

Mrs. Dan J. Troyer
Mercer, PA

DELICIOUS FUDGE

4 cups white sugar
1 t. vinegar
2 T. light or dark karo
2 squares chocolate or 2 T. cocoa
1 cup evaporated milk

Bring to a rolling boil and boil 3 minutes. Remove from heat and add 1 pint peanut butter and 1 pint marshmallow cream. Spread in pan. Cool and cut in squares.

Lydia Stoltzfus
Bloomsburg, PA

PEANUT BRITTLE

1 1/3 cup white sugar
1/2 cup water
1 cup white syrup
2 t. soda
1 1/3 cup raw peanuts

Cook sugar syrup and water till almost hard ball stage. Add raw peanuts and continue cooking until golden brown. Remove from heat and add soda and vanilla. Stir quickly so soda is well mixed but candy still foaming. Pour on buttered cookie sheet and leave undisturbed till cold.

Fannie Gingerich
Ethridge, TN

NUT BALLS

1 cup soft oleo margarine
1/2 cup confectioners sugar
1 t. vanilla
2 1/4 cups plain flour
1/4 t. salt
3/4 cup chopped nuts

Cream butter, sugar and vanilla. Sift together flour and salt, stir into first mixture. Add nuts. Roll in balls about 1 inch. Place on ungreased sheet. Bake at 400 deg. for 10-12 min. Remove from oven; while still warm roll in powdered sugar. Makes about 4 doz.

Fannie Gingerich
Ethridge, TN

IRISH POTATO CANDY

1 small potato - boiled and peeled
1 or 2 boxes of powdered sugar
Peanut butter, crunchy or smooth (smooth preferred)

Mash your potato, start adding sugar. The mixture will become thin as you add sugar. The more you add, it will soon become stiff. Make it stiff so you can roll out on wax or freezer paper. Roll thin, smooth your peanut butter all over, roll up like jelly roll and slice in pinwheels.

Fannie Gingerich
Ethridge, TN

One talent that should be buried
Is finding fault

CHERRY DROP CANDY

1 cup powdered sugar
1 cup cream cheese

Mix together. Now roll up in small balls and press a sweet cherry in the balls. melt chocolate to dip the drops in.

Mrs. Joe J. Yoder
Lawrenceburg, TN

CHURCH WINDOWS

1 stick margarine
12 oz. chocolate chips
10 1/2 oz. pkg. miniature marshmallows (colored preferred)
1 cup chopped nuts
1 1/2 cups shredded coconut

Melt margarine and chocolate chips in double boiler. Cool. Add to marshmallows and nuts. Sprinkle coconut on a sheet of waxed paper. Pour mixture on this. Form into 1 or 2 rolls and cover with coconut. Refrigerate till hardened. Slice and serve.

Barbara Schrock
Spartansburg, PA

CANDY PEANUT BUTTER BALLS

2 T. butter
2 cups peanut butter
2 cups 10X sugar

Mix together and cool. Roll into small balls and dip in melted chocolate. Variation: add rice krispies.

Bertha Beiler
Loganton, PA

DATE FINGERS

1 stick margarine
1 cup sugar
1 cup chopped dates
1 egg beaten
1 cup walnuts, chopped
1 t. vanilla
2 1/2 cups Rice Krispies
1 cup shredded coconut

Combine oleo, sugar, dates, and egg in saucepan. Bring to a boil, stirring constantly. Cook for 5 min. Be careful not to burn. Reduce to medium heat and add nuts. Cook for 10 min. over low heat. Remove from heat and add vanilla and Rice Krispies. Drop by t. on wax paper and while still warm roll in coconut. Makes about 48.

Barbara Schrock
Spartansburg, PA

PEANUT BUTTER CUPS

2 cups peanut butter
2 cups powdered sugar
1/4 cup oleo or butter
vanilla

Mix together. Fill a layer of melted chocolate in baking cups; then put one t. of peanut butter mixture in center. Cover with melted chocolate. Can also put peanut butter mixture on balls and dip in chocolate.

Mrs. Ammon A. Troyer
Ashland, OH

SNOWY FUDGE

1 1/2 cups peanut butter
2 cups sugar
2/3 cup milk
1 cup marshmallow cream
1 t. vanilla

Cook sugar and milk to 234 deg. or until syrup forms a soft ball which flattens when removed from water. Add other ingredients. Mix well. Pour into 8x6x2 buttered pan.

Sadie Miller
Fort Plain, NY

He who always plans ahead
Never has to do anything right now

TURTLE CANDY

2 cups white sugar
3/4 cup light corn syrup
3/4 cup oleo
2 cups cream
1 T. vanilla

Put all of syrup, sugar and 1/2 of cream in pan and bring to a boil. Stir mixture constantly. Add rest of cream and oleo slowly so mixture does not stop boiling. Boil to soft ball on candy thermometer. Add vanilla and pour over pecans. Have pecans ready single layer on pan.

Mrs. Emma Stutzman
Bronson, MI

BUN BARS

1 can sweetened condensed milk
1/2 cup shortening
peanuts
melted chocolate
8 oz. cream cheese
powdered sugar
maple flavor

Combine all except nuts and chocolate, adding powdered sugar until right consistency. Drop by t. full on peanuts. Cover well with peanuts. Then dip in melted chocolate. Put on waxed paper. Makes a big batch.

Mrs. Ammon A. Troyer
Ashland, OH

PEANUT BUTTER PATTIES

2 lb. powdered sugar
4 cups crunchy peanut butter
pinch of salt
6 cups Rice Krispies
2 sticks melted oleo

Mix all ingredients together. Melt coating chocolate. Make mixture into small patties and dip in chocolate and let set. Makes a large batch.

Mary Swartzentruber
Apple Creek, OH

CHOCOLAGE COVERED CHERRIES

2 cups sugar
2 T. light karo
3/4 cup boiling water
1/8 t. salt
1/4 t. almond extract
maraschino cherries (drained several hours)
chocolate

Combine all ingredients, except extract in 2 qt. heavy saucepan and stir over low heat until sugar is dissolved and mixture comes to a boil. Cover and boil 1 min. Then remove lid and cook to the soft ball stage (238-240 deg.). If sugar crystals form on side of pan, wipe them off. Cool until lukewarm. Stir till fondant is white and creamy. Add almond extract. Knead until smooth. Put in plastic bag and close tightly. Place in refrigerator to mellow at least 24 hrs. or several weeks. Melt fondant in top of double boiler over warm not hot boiling water. You may add a little cherry juice to tint and to help melt it to desired consistency - that of a thick syrup. Dip cherry in fondant completely coating it. Place on waxed paper. The coating gets firm quickly. When all cherries are dipped and cooled, take them 1 by 1 in your hand and dip only the bottom in chocolate - return to waxed paper. Let harden, then dip in chocolate like any candy centers.

Joni H. Shrock
Middlefield, OH

A ship in harbor is safe
But that is not what ships are for

PEANUT BUTTER CANDY

2 cups peanut butter
2 oz. cream chees (soft)
1/2 cup soft or melted butter
2 1/2 cups 10X sugar
1 t. vanilla
1/2 cup brown sugar

Blend peanut butter with butter and cream cheese. Add brown sugar, vanilla and 10X sugar. Chocolate chips can be melted and poured on top if put in a pan. Or the peanut butter mixture can be made in balls or other shapes and coated with chocolate or carob coating.

Lydia Stoltzfus
Bloomsburg, PA

MARSHMALLOW CANDY

2 T. or 2 envelopes gelatin
1/2 c. cold water

Soften gelatin in cold water.

2 cups sugar
3/4 cup boiling water
1 t. vanilla
pinch salt

Boil sugar and water until thread forms when syrup drops from a spoon. Remove from heat. Add softened gelatin mixture. Let stand until partly cool. Add salt and vanilla. Beat until mixture becomes fluffy and soft. Pour into an 8x4 pan, thickly coated with 10X sugar. Let stand in refrigerator until thoroughly chilled. With a sharp, wet knife loosen around edges of pan. Turn out onto board lightly covered with 10X sugar. Cut into squares, roll in 10X sugar, finely chopped nuts or coconut.

Catherine Swarey
Belleville, PA

PEANUT BUTTER CUPS

1/2 lb. graham cracker crumbs
1/2 lb. butter or oleo
1 cup peanut butter
1 lb. powdered sugar
2 cups chocolate chips

Combine butter, crumbs, peanut butter and powdered sugar. Work until smooth. Press this mixture in a 9x9 pan or larger for thinner squares. Melt chocolate chips over hot water. Spread over mixture in pan. Refrigerate until firm. Cut in squares.

Mary A. Kinsinger
Meyersdale, PA

EASY AND DELICIOUS FUDGE

10 oz. marshmallows
2 T. butter or oleo
2 cups chocolate chips

Partially melt these ingredients. Stir in:

2 cups coconut
2 cups chopped nuts
2 cups rice krispies
1 t. vanilla

Pat into a greased pan and cut when cool.

Mary A. Kinsinger
Meyersdale, PA

MINTED WALNUTS

1 cup sugar
1/2 cup water
1/8 t. salt
1/4 cup light Karo

Cook to soft ball stage. Add 6 cups cut-up marshmallows. Stir till melted. Add 3 drops wintergreen oil, 2 1/2 cups walnuts. Stir till the shine dulls and it sets lightly. Quickly pour on waxed paper. Cut in squares.

Lydiann J. Bricker
Panama, NY

BUTTERSCOTCH CANDY

7 1/2 oz. marshmallow cream
2/3 cup rich cream
1/3 cup butter
1 3/4 cup sugar
1/4 t. salt
1 cup chopped nuts
6 oz. butterscotch bits

Combine all but bits in 4 qt. pan. Put over medium heat. Bring to a full rolling boil and boil 5 min. stirring constantly. Remove from heat. Add bits. Stir ttill smooth. Add nuts. Turn into buttered pan. chill and cut.

Lydiann J. Bricker
Panama, NY

TOFFEE BAR CANDY

Salted soda crackers to cover the bottom of cookie sheet or jelly roll pan
1 cup brown sugar (packed)
1 cup margarine
1 - 12 oz. bag of milk chocolate chips
1 cup chopped pecans or walnuts

Preheat oven to 375 deg. Line pan with foil and grease foil. Boil sugar and margarine for 3 min. Pour over crackers. Bake 5 min. at 375 deg. Remove from oven and spread melted chips on top. Add nuts on top. Refrigerate until firm. Before cutting, let stand out at room temperature. Cut into squares. Makes 50 squares.

Ida Miller
Medford, WI

MARAVIAN MINTS

1 lb. 10X sugar — 3 T. hot water
1/8 lb. melted butter — 4 drops peppermint

Mix sugar and butter real well. Add oil of peppermint and hot water. Knead the candy with hands till well mixed. Divide in 2 or 3 different bowls, add different food colorings. Make small balls, press down with fork and let set awhile.

Sara Esh
Paradise, PA

PEANUT BUTTER BARS

These taste almost like Butterfinger bars
2 cups crushed graham cracker crumbs
2 cups powdered sugar
2 cups peanut butter (chunky style)
1/4 cup butter or margarine

Mix together like pie crust mix. Chill at least 1 hr. Make into small bars. Dip in melted chocolate. While dipping keep chocolate on low heat. Place on waxed paper and chill overnight. Store in airtight container.

Mrs. Samuel D. Beachy
Clark, MO

EASY AND DELICIOUS FUDGE

Partially melt:
10 oz. marshmallows — 2 T. butter
2 cups chocolate chips

Stir in:
2 cups coconut — 2 cups chopped nuts
2 cups rice krispies — 1 t. vanilla

Pat into a greased pan and cut when cool.

Mrs. Samuel D. Beachy
Clark, MO

We are not really ready to live
Until we are ready to die

TURTLES

Cook the following to soft ball in winter, a few points above in summer:

1 pt. thick cream
2 cups brown sugar
2 cups white sugar
1/4 bar oleo
3/4 cup light karo
vanilla and salt to taste

Grease pans with oleo and put pecans or rice krispies in to cover the bottom; then pour the hot caramel in there. When cool, cut and dip in melted chocolate.

Mrs. Jacob Stutzman
Jeromesville, OH

ROCKY ROAD CANDY

2 lb. milk chocolage
3 lb. broken nuts
1/2 lb. soft butter
10 oz. miniature marshmallows

Melt chocolate, stir until smooth. Add butter and mix well (will be thick but warm). Set in a cold place while it thickens around edges. Stir occasionally while cooling. Bring to warm room and stir 5-10 min. until creamy and thinner. Add marshmallows and nuts. Pour into greased cookie sheet. Press 3/4 in. thick and cool; sut in squares at room temperature.

Mrs. Joseph Shrock
Agusta, WI

TURTLE CANDY

1 1/2 cups white sugar
1/2 t. salt
1/2 cup brown sugar
1/2 cup oleo
2 cups light cream
1 t. vanilla
1 cup light corn syrup
Pecans as desired

In a heavy saucepan heat cream to lukewarm. Pour out 1 cup and reserve. To remaining cream in saucepan add sugar, corn syrup and salt. Cook over moderate heat and stir till it boils. Very slowly stir in reserved cream (1 cup) so mixture does not stop boiling. Cook and stir constantly for 5 min. Stir in butter about 1 t. at a time. Turn heat low. Boil gently and stir part time until temp. reaches 248 deg. or until small amount dropped in cold water forms a firm ball that does not flatten when removed from water. Remove from heat. Gently stir in vanilla and cool slightly. Pour over pecans placed in a cake pan. When cold, cut in squares and dip in chocolate.

Mrs. Joseph Schrock
Agusta, WI

CASHEW CRUNCH

1 cup butter
1 cup white sugar
1 cup cashews

Mix together and stir and boil till caramel color. Pour in meat loaf pan and cool. Break up when cold.

Mrs. Jacob Stutzman
Jeromesville, OH

BUN BARS

1 can condensed milk
1/2 cup margarine
melted chocolate
8 oz. cream cheese
maple flavor
powdered sugar

Combine milk, cream cheese, margarine and flavoring, powdered sugar until right consistency. Drop by t. full on clusters of peanuts or just stir full of peanuts. Dip in chocolate. Put on waxed paper.

Mrs. Jacob Stutzman
Jeromesville, OH

ALMOND JOY CANDY

2/3 cup sugar
3 T. water
1 scant cup of karo

Bring to a boil, then add 3 cups coconut. Cook to soft boil, then drop on sprayed sheets by spoonful. Shape when cool. Chill and dip in melted coating chocolate. May put an almond on top if desired.

Mrs. Ray J. Gingerich
Fillmore, NY

BUCK EYE CANDY

1/4 cup oleo or butter
1 lb. powdered sugar
2 cups peanut butter
3 cups rice krispies
12 oz. pkg. chocolate chips
1/2 stick paraffin

Mix first 4 ingredients. Form into small balls. Chill, melt chocolate and paraffin in double boiler. Roll balls in chocolate mixture. Cool on wax paper. Makes about 4 doz.

Irene Wingard
Shipshewang, IN

Canning & Preserving

GRAPE JUICE

15 cups grapes
9 cups boiling water
Boil 5 min. Drain. Add 5 cups water, drain again. Add 3 1/2 cups sugar. Heat to boiling, then can.

Mrs. Leroy J. Byler
Fredericktown, OH

NO BLANCH SWEET CORN

15 cups corn, cut fresh from the cob
1/3 cup sugar
1/8 cup salt
2 1/4 cups water
Mix well. Put in plastic containers and freeze.

Mrs. Wilma Mast
South Hutchinson, KS

PIZZA SAUCE

4 qt. chopped tomatoes
1 sweet red pepper
1 t. oregano
2 t. salt
1 large onion
1 clove garlic
1/4 t. basil
Cook tomatoes, onion, and pepper together and put thru juicer. Then add oregano, salt and use 1 t. garlic powder. Also use 1/3 cup sugar. Cook this real good and make a thickening with a 3/4 cups cornstarch. Cook until thickened. Put in cans and process 10 min. at 5 lb. Some put in crushed red peppers.

Mary Ann Hilty
Monroe, IN

One talent that should be buried
Is finding fault

MEAT CANNING BRINE

For beef steak, tenderloin, or ham:
1 pt. brown sugar
1 cup salt
1 gal. water
Divide this in 14 qt. jars, fill with meat, put in pressure cooker at 10 lbs. pressure for 1 1/2 hrs.

Lucinda Hilty
Monroe, IN

WEINER BEANS

8 1/2 lb. navy beans
1 1/2 lb. weiners
salt to taste
5 qt. tomatoe sauce or more
1 lb. white sugar
3/4 cup brown sugar
1 t. dried mustard
1 t. cinnamon
2 qts. water
1/2 t. black pepper
1/2 cup flour and cornstarch (some of each)

Soak beans in water overnight. Cook beans till about soft (drain). Add the above. Mix: cold pack 3 hr.

Joe Borntreger
Cashton, WI

TO TENDERIZE BEEF CHUNKS FOR CANNING

2 T. salt petre
salt and pepper as you would to can
Mix to 6-7 gal. meat
Let stand 10 days, then can.

Mrs. Philip Yoder
Fairbank, IA

CANNING IN BRINE

1 gal. soft water
1 cup brown sugar
1 cup salt

Bring to a boil, then cool. Put 1 cup brine in jar first then steaks and cold pack 3 hrs. or pressure cook 1/2 hr. at 10 lb.

Mrs. Philip Yoder
Fairbank, IA

IOWA BOLOGNA

100 lb. meat (beef or deer)
Mix:
2 lb. tender quick 16 oz. salt
2 t. salt petre
Spread on meat and mix; grind fine and let stand 3 days, then grind again.
Mix:
2 oz. black 1 1/2 oz. ground coriander seed
4 t. mace 1 t. garlic
2 lb. cornstarch in approx. 4 1/2 qt. water depending on dryness of meat and pour over meat and mix; stuff in casings; smoke 4 hrs. at 125-150 degrees. Place in 150-160 degree water for 30 min. for 2 in. casings and 90 min. for 4 in. casings; then cool in cold water. Ready to eat.

Mrs. Philip Yoder
Fairbank, IA

If you had never tasted the bitter
You wouldn't know what is sweet

CHICKEN BOLOGNA

25 lb. fresh chicken meat
Add 1 lb. Morton's tender quick; grind twice
Let set 24 hrs., then add the following:
1 oz. black pepper
1/2 cup sugar 2 t. salt petre
2 t. powdered garlic 3 T. liquid smoke
Mix well, grind again. The process as for any fresh meat such as stuffed, cooked, and frozen. The recipe can also be used for hamburger. Do not cook the cut up meat or dressed chickens in water overnite or more than necessary.

Mrs. J. David Byler
Punxcutawney, PA

PORK AND BEANS

7 lb. dry beans - cook till nearly done
3 qt. tomatoe juice1 1/2 lb. sugar
1/3 lb. salt (or salt to taste)
1 cup molasses
1 qt. catsup
1 t. dry mustard
1 t. cinnamon
1/2 t. red pepper

Heat above ingredients and add to beans. Put in cans. Cold pack 1 1/2 hrs. Yield 12 qts.

Mrs. Neal Kauffman
La Plata, MO

WHOLE TOMATOES TO CAN

Peel and place tomatoes in cans. Cover with water. Add 1 t. salt per qt. Cold pack, start in cold water and heat to boil. Boil 2-3 min. Let set 10 min.

Mrs. Neal Kauffman
La Plata, MO

SPAGHETTI SAUCE

4 qts. tomato juice
2 cups chopped onions
6 green or red peppers, chopped
1 cup sugar
4 t. salt
2 cups ketchup
2 T. dry mustard
3 T. paprika
1 cup chopped celery or 2 T. celery seed

Combine all ingredients and simmer 1 1/2 hrs. Put in jars and seal.

Lydia Stoltzfus
Bloomsburg, PA

RED BEETS

1/4 t. salt
1 cup sugar
3 T. vinegar
Syrup for 1 qt.

Pack beets in jars and add syrup and fill with water. Cold pack 10 minutes.

Lydia Stoltzfus
Bloomsburg, PA

A cookbook is a volume of stirring

PICKLED CANTALOUPES

7 cups sugar
3 1/2 cups water
1 cup plus 4 T. vinegar
1 t. salt
Boil and cool
Pour over lopes - cold pack 30 min.

Bertha Beiler
Loganton, PA

VEGETABLE SOUP (TO CAN)

1 qt. potatoes
1 qt. sweet corn
1 qt. carrots
1 qt. peas
1 qt. celery
1 qt. cooked spaghetti
1 qt. navy beans
1 qt. onions
6 or 7 qts. tomato juice
1 lb. hamburger fried in butter

Cook all separate in as little water as possible. When soft, drain. Have all ready before adding 6-7 qt. tomato juice. Now add 1/2 cup white sugar, 1 t. chili powder, salt to taste. Cold pack 2 hrs. Makes 27 pt.

Ella Hershberger
Oakland, MD

CANNED BEEF STEAKS

3/4 pint salt
1 pint white or brown sugar
1 gal. water
Divide water in 14 qt. jars filled with beef steaks. Cold pack, boil 1 hr.

Joe Borntreger
Cashton, WI

Happiness is not perfected
Until it is shared

CHICKEN BOLOGNA

Cut the meat from bones (raw)
To 25 lb. fresh chicken meat add:
3/4 lb. Morton's tender quick (more or less as you wish)
Grind twice, let set 24 hrs., then add the follow. Mix well, grind again:

1 oz. black pepper or some red pepper
2 t. garlic powder
1/2 cup sugar
3 T. liquid smoke or less
2 t. salt peter
2 t. mace

Then process as for any fresh meat stuff or can in jars as a hamburger. Put in jars. Cold pack 3 hrs.

Joe Borntreger
Cashton, WI

KATIE'S GRAPE JUICE

15 cups grapes
9 cups hot water

Boil 5 min., then drain.
Add 5 cups water and drain again.
Add 3 1/2 cups sugar.
Heat to boiling point, then can.

Louella Borntrager
Sugar Creek, OH

MEATLOAF TO CAN

12 lbs. hamburger
4 large onions (chopped)
4 eggs beaten
6 t. salt
2 pkgs - 6 cups crackers (crushed)
pepper to taste
Soak 6 slices bread in 2 cups tomatoe juice
2 cups milk

Mix and can like you would hamburger, except don't make jars too full.

Emma Hershberger
Dover, DE

BAKED BEANS

8 lbs. navy beans
4 qts. tomato juice
2 qts. white sugar
2 cups molasses
1/2 cup cornstarch
1/3 cup salt
2 qts. water
1 1/2 cups brown sugar
1 t. mustard

Soak beans overnight. Cook until almost tender. Mix the rest of the ingredients. Boil for 1/2 hr., add corn starch (made in a smooth paste), cook 1/2 hr. longer. Pour over beans. Can, pressure for 15 min.

Emma Hershberger
Dover, DE

Dig your neighbor out of trouble
And you'll find a place to bury yours

CHICKEN BURGER

100 lbs. meat, ground
3 oz. salt petre
5 lbs. water
2 1/4 lbs. tender quick
1 lb. brown sugar

Let stand 4 days and grind again. Put in cans and pressure cook 1 hr. at 10 lb. pressure.

Elizabeth Mae Raber
Montgomery, IN

HOMEMADE BOLOGNA

100 lbs. beef
4 lbs. tenderquick
10 T. salt petre
5 T. garlic powder
2 1/2 T. cayenne
50 lbs. pork
10 T. black pepper
10 cups brown sugar
10 oz. liquid smoke

Let stand 2 days and grind twice. May be stuffed in casing or packed in jars and cold packed. Do not pack jars too full or they will burst.

Mrs. Jacob Stutzman
Jeromesville, OH

BOLOGNA

100 lb. meat
3 1/4 lb. salt
1 1/2 lb. white sugar
1 1/2 lb. brown sugar
4 t. salt petre
3 oz. pepper
1 gal. molasses

Mix dry ingredients thoroughly. Put a layer meat, then a layer of dry ingredients, followed by molasses till all is in container. Avoid having molasses on the very top to prevent spoilage. Let set 7-10 days before grinding and stuffing in bags. Smoke 3 days.

Bertha Beiler
Loganton, PA

HOT PEPPER RINGS

1 peck hot peppers
1 qt. vinegar
3/4 qt. water
1 pt. oil
1/2 cup oregano
1/4 box salt (2 hands full)
2 cloves garlic - chopped

Mix together first ingredients. Slice peppers 1/4" thick. Put in brine. let set 6-8 hours. Pack in jars. Cold pack and seal.

Naomi Peachy
Little Falls, NY

APPLE BUTTER

2 1/2 gal. cider - cook down to half

Add 2 gal. apples. When apples are cooked to a mush, add 5 lb. sugar (preferably less - depends on the kind of apples used) 1 t. cinnamon and 1/2 t. allspice may be added if desired (we prefer it without spices).

Catherine Swarey
Belleville, PA

BOLOGNA

25 lb. meat
1/2 lb. tender quick
2 T. pepper
2 cups brown sugar

Put on meat - grind and let stand 24 hrs.

Add:

2 T. liquid smoke
1/4 t. garlic powder
3/4 cup coriander

3 qt. water - more if you prefer softer bologna. We like to use about 5 lb. pork, instead of the full amount beef or venison. Cold pack 2 1/2 hrs.

Mrs. Noah Wengerd, Jr.
Conewango Valley, NY

TO CAN BEEF STEAK

1 pt. brown sugar
1 gal. water
1 cup salt

Divide this into 14 qt. jars. Fill jars with meat which has been cut in steak size pieces. Process 3 hrs.

Catherine Swarey
Belleville, PA

God puts us on our backs at times
So we may look up

REALLY RED CATSUP

2 gal. tomato juice
8 T. salt
2 onions, chopped fine
20 drops each cinnamon and clove oil
2 t. celery seed
3 cups vinegar

Mix and boil down to about 1/3 (cook tomatoes, make juice, drain a while before measuring for catsup).

When cooked down to 1/3 mix:

8 cups sugar
6 T. (heaping) of cornstarch

Mix together with a little water to make a paste, stir in almost last, and a little red pepper to taste; bring to a boil, bottle and seal.

Sue Sickey
Norfolk, NY

GRAPE JUICE TO CAN

(Without sugar or preservatives)
Put cleaned grapes in a stainless kettle about 3/4 full; add water to about an inch of grape level; cook until soft, 15 min. or more. Then strain through cloth and let drip until juice is out; pour juice in cans while boiling hot. Seal. You may add water to juice after opening cans, if desired, to suit taste.

Mrs. Amos W. Yoder
Jamesport, MO

TOMATOE DRINK

6 qts. tomatoe juice
1 T. garlic salt
2 T. salt
2 T. onion salt
2 T. celery salt
1 1/2 cups sugar

Boil all together; put in cans and seal.

Mrs. Amos W. Yoder
Jamesport, MO

TASTY KETCHUP

1 bu. tomatoes
3 onions
3 peppers (chopped)

Cooked until soft. Drain overnight.
Add:

3 cups vinegar
1/2 t. cinnamon
1 t. mustard
1/2 cup salt
6 cups sugar
bits of cloves, mace and red pepper

Cook 5-10 min. Pour into jars and seal.

Aaron Brubacher
Liverpool, PA

HOME MADE KETCHUP

9 qt riced tomato juice
4 1/2 cups sugar
4 cups vinegar
1/3 cup salt
Tie in a cloth:
1 1/2 t. celery seed
2 lg. onions, cut up
1/2 t. dry mustard
1/3 t. red pepper
1 1/2 t. cinnamon
1 1/2 t. allspice

Cook 3 hr. Remove cloth with onions. Thicken with clear jell to desired thickness.

Catherine Swarey
Belleville, PA

JERKY

1/4 cup soy sauce
3/4 cup water
1 t. ground pepper
2 t. garlic salt or 1 t. garlic powder
1 t. seasoned salt

Soak meat in brine overnite. Place in oven at 200 deg. for 2 hrs. Turn. Bake 2 more hours.

For very thin meat, 3 hrs. total baking time is enough.

Saloma Petersheim
Mifflintown, PA

HAM CURE

1 pint salt
3 T. brown sugar
2 T. black pepper
1 T. red pepper

Mrs. Noah Wengerd, Jr.
Conewango Valley, NY

HOMEMADE CHICKEN BOLOGNA

Cut off meat from chicken bones (as for hamburger). To 25 lbs. of fresh chicken add 1 lb. tender quick and grind twice. Let set 24 hrs.

Add the following:

1 oz. black pepper
1/2 cup sugar
2 T. liquid smoke
2 t. salt petre
2 t. garlic

Grind again. Mix well, put in cans and process as for any other meat (cold pack) 3 hrs. This can also be put in cloth bags, cooked and put in freezer. Hamburger can also be used.

Mrs. Emma Stutzman
Bronson, MI

SMOKED CHICKEN

1 lb. brown sugar
2 1/4 lb. salt
1/2 oz. salt petre
2 gal. water
1 oz. pepper

Bring to boil; cool. Soak whole chicken in this brine for 3 days, then smoke for 3 hours.

Saloma Petersheim
Mifflintown, PA

SUGAR CURE FOR 1 HOG

6 hands full salt
2 hands full sugar
2 T. salt
2 T. pepper
1 T. salt petre

Salt meat with common salt the first eve, rub sugar cure in the next eve.

Mrs. Joe J. Yoder
Lawrenceburg, TN

DELICIOUS CANNED STRAWBERRIES

7 qt. boxes of strawberries

Clean them and mash. Add sugar to taste.

1 box Danish Dessert Mix

Put in jars and cold pack 10 min. Let stand for a while before removing the jars. After canned, they taste like fresh berries out of the garden.

Mrs. Joe J. Yoder
Lawrenceburg, TN

CORN HOMINY

1 can lye — 4 gal. corn
4 gal. water or — 3 T. lye
1 gal. corn — 1 gal. water

Cook 1 hr. in a big iron kettle; put out of kettle; let stand 1/2 hr. longer in granite dish pans, then wash good in wash tubs. Use plenty of water. Then cook it till about soft, then chill overnight. Cold pack 3 hrs. 8 gal. dry shelled corn. Makes 60 qts. hominy.

Mattie Borntreger
Cashton, WI

TO CAN STEAKS

1 cup brown sugar — 1 cup salt
1 gal. water

Dissolve. Divide in 14 jars and cold pack 1 hr. Put this in jars before meat.

Elizabeth Stutzman
Union City, PA

CURING BEEF OR PORK

For 100 lb. meat
Cut steak in desired thickness. Mix well together:

6 qt. salt — 6 lb. brown sugar
6 oz. salt peter — 6 oz. baking soda

Place a springling of mixture in bottom of crock and a layer of meat alternately until container is full. Cover tightly or seal with melted lard. This can be kept a long time. To us, fry, then cook until tender; it makes good gravy.

Elizabeth Stutzman
Union City, PA

CANNING NUTS

Put nutmeats in dry glass jars, with 2 piece lids. Set jars on cookie sheets, heat oven to 250 deg., put on oven grate for 3/4 hr. Then turn off and let in oven overnite.

Mrs. Raymond S. Miller
Millersburg, OH

MEAT BRINE

2 lbs. brown sugar
6 lbs. salt
2 oz. black and red pepper
1 oz. salt peter

Put 4 gal. water in kettle, bring to a boil. Let cool, put in barrel, pack meat in, (ham and bacon), weight it down. Hams 4 weeks — Bacon 3 days.

Emma Hershberger
Dover, DE

BEAFSTEAK BRINE

1 cup coarse salt
1 cup brown sugar
1 gal. water

Boil together until sugar and salt are dissolved. Cool.
Put 1 cup liquid in a qt. jar before you put the steak in. Add steak to fill jar. Pressure 40 min. at 10 lb. pressure.

Emma Hersberger
Dover, DE

It isn't your position that makes you happy
It's your disposition

CHILI SAUCE TO CAN

1/2 bushel tomatoes
1 doz. onions
red and green peppers
2 bunches celery

Peel tomatoes and chop other vegetables fine. Put in 12 qt. kettle and add:

6 cups sugar
2 T. salt
1 t. cinnamon
1 1/2 t. red pepper
1/2 t. black pepper
1 cup vinegar

1 T. mixed spices (put in a bag and place in pot while boiling, then remove).
Cook together for 2 hrs., stirring once in a while so it won't burn. Hot pack and seal in jars.

Esther Fisher
Millersburg, PA

PIZZA SAUCE

10 qt. tomatoes
4 cups onions
4 cups sugar
2 T. salt
4 T. oregano
1 T. chili
10 T. salad oil
2 T. garlic salt
1 t. hot pepper

Cook 1 hr. and thicken with clear jell. This sauce is to can. Cook 15 min. after it is in jars.

Esther King
Millersburg, PA

BOLOGNA

40 lbs. beef
10 lbs. pork
2 lbs. tenderquick
1 t. salt petre

Let cure for 24 hrs.
Then mix rest of ingredients:

2 oz. coriander seed
1 T. garlic salt
1 T. black pepper
8 lb. cold water
5 T. liquid smoke
1 t. mace

Cold pack 3 hrs. or pressure cook for 1 hr. at 10 lb.

Mrs. Joseph Shrock
Agusta, WI

Cookies

DOUBLE CHOCOLATE CHIP COOKIES

2 cups butter
2 cups sugar
1 cup brown sugar, packed
6 1/2 cups flour
1/4 cup milk
2 cups chocolate chips
4 eggs
1 t. cream of tartar
2 t. baking powder
8 T. cocoa
1 cup chopped nuts

Combine butter, sugars, eggs, flour, cream of tartar, soda, cocoa and milk in order given. Add choc. chips and nuts. Drop by rounded t. on greased cookie sheet. Bake in 375 deg. oven 10-15 min. Don't overbake.

Mrs. Jacob Stutzman
Jeromesville, OH

MOLASSES CRINKLES

3/4 cup shortening
1 cup brown sugar
1 egg
1/4 cup molasses
2 1/4 cups flour
2 t. soda
1/2 t. cloves
1 t. cinnamon
1 t. ginger

Mix sugar, shortening, egg and molasses thoroughly. Measure flour and the rest of dry ingredients together, sift, mix with first mixture. Roll dough into balls the size of a walnut; dip top with sugar, place sugared side up and place 3 in. apart on cookie sheet.

Mrs. J. David Byler
Punxsutawney, PA

SOUR MILK COOKIES

1/2 cup lard
2 cups sugar
2 eggs
1 cup sour milk
4 cups flour
1 t. soda
2 t. baking powder
1 t. vanilla
1 t. nutmeg
1 cup chocolate chips, optional

Mix together and bak; yield about 4 dz.

Mrs. Philip Yoder
Fairbank, IA

QUAKER COOKIES

2 cups brown sugar
1 cup lard
2 eggs
2 cups flour
3 cups quick oats
1 1/2 t. soda
1 t. salt2 t. vanilla
nuts
raisins

Roll in balls and then in powdered sugar and bake.

Mrs. Raymond S. Miller
Millersburg, OH

BUTTERSCOTCH DELIGHT COOKIES

2 1/2 cups white sugar
2 1/2 cups brown sugar
2 cups shortening
2 1/2 t. soda
2 1/2 t. baking powder
5 eggs
2 T. vanilla
1/4 cup milk
5 cups flour
2 t. salt
5 cups quick oatmeal

Mix sugar and shortening. Add eggs, then dry ingredients and oatmeal and milk. Form into balls. Roll in powdered sugar and press flat onto baking sheets. Bake.

Mrs. Clarence Miller
Medford, WI

RAISIN PUFFS

1 cup dark raisins
1/2 cup light raisins

Add 1 cup water to these and boil until water is taken up - set aside while preparing.

1 cup shortening (oleo or Crisco)
1 1/2 cups white sugar
2 eggs
1 t. soda
1 t. vanilla
1/2 t. salt

Mix shortening, eggs and sugar until creamy; add rest of the ingredients. Roll in balls about the size of a walnut and roll in white sugar; bake at 375 deg. or until light brown.

Ella Hershberger
Oakland, MD

What this country needs is family trees
That produce fewer nuts and more lumber

GINGER SNAPS

3/4 cup shortening
1 cup brown sugar
1/4 cup molasses
2 1/4 cups sifted flour
1 egg
2 t. soda
1/2 t. salt
1 t. ginger
1 t. cinnamon
1/2 t. cloves

Cream together shortening, brown sugar, molasses, and egg till light and fluffy. Sift together dry ingredients; stir in molasses mixture till blended. Form in small balls; roll in granulated sugar and place 2 in. apart on greased cookie sheets.

Ella Hershberger
Oakland, MD

Home is the place where we grumble the most
And are treated the best

PEANUT BUTTER & JELLY THUMBPRINTS

1 cup butter or margarine
1 3/4 cups brown sugar (packed)
2 eggs
2 t. vanilla
3 cups unsifted all-purpose flour
1 t. baking powder
1 t. salt
2 cups (12 oz. package) Reese's peanut butter chips
1 1/2 cups quick oats
3/4 cups jelly or preserves (apple, grape, peach, etc.)

Cream butter or margarine and brown sugar in a large bowl. Add eggs and vanilla. Beat until light and fluffy. In a separate bowl combine flour, baking powder and salt. Gradually add flour mixture to creamed mixture. Reserve 1/2 cup peanut butter chips. Stir in oats and 1 1/2 cups peanut butter chips. Shape dough into 1 in. balls. lace balls on an ungreased cookie sheet. Press the center of each with your thumb to make a deep depression about 1 in. wide. Bake at 400 deg. for 7-9 min. or until lightly browned. Remove from cookie sheet. Cool on a wire rack. Fill center of each cookie with 1/2 t. jelly or preserves; top with several of the reserved peanut butter chips. Makes approximately 5 doz.

Aaron Brubacker
Liverpool, PA

RAISIN OATMEAL COOKIES

1 cup brown sugar
1 cup shortening (scant)
1 t. baking powder
1 t. soda
1 t. salt
1 cup white sugar
2 eggs
1 t. vanilla

Mix together, then add 3 cups quick rolled oats and 1 1/2 cups flour. You may add a cup of chocolate chips, nuts, coconut, or raisins. Let dough set overnight. Make little balls and flatten with a fork. Bake at 400 deg. till done.

Sue Wickey
Norfolk, NY

MOLASSES WHOOPIE PIES

2 cups brown sugar
1 cup shortening
1 cup Brer Rabbit molasses
2 cups sour milk or buttermilk
6 cups flour, sifted
3 t. soda
1 t. salt
2 t. cinnamon
1 t. vanilla
2 eggs, unbeaten

Beat together brown sugar, eggs and shortening; add molasses and buttermilk and vanilla. Add dry ingredients and drop by spoonfuls on cookie sheets. When cool put icing in between 2 cookies.

Esther Fisher
Millersburg, PA

DATE FILLED COOKIES

1 cup butter
1 cup white sugar
1 cup brown sugar
4 cups flour
1 t. soda
1 t. cinnamon
1/2 t. salt
3 eggs

Cream butter, sugar, eggs; then sift in flour, soda and cinnamon. Then roll about 1/2 in. thick and spread with the following and roll up like a jelly roll; let stand overnight.

1 lb. dates, cut fine
1/2 cup water
1/2 cup brown sugar
1 cup nuts (opt.)

Combine dates, sugar, and water, cook until thick paste and cool; then add nuts. Slice off ext morning and bake at 350 deg. or until brown.

Ella Hershberger
Oakland, MD

SOFT EGGLESS COOKIES

2 cups brown sugar
3/4 cup shortening
1 cup sweet or sour milk
1 t. baking powder
1 t. soda
1/2 t. salt
1 t. flavor, maple, black walnut, or vanilla may be used
3 1/2 cups flour, added last.

First mix sugar and shortening; then add the rest of the ingredients; mix good, then add flour. Drop by teaspoonsful on a greased cookie sheet; flatten slightly with a fork. Bake till done in 400 deg. to 450 deg. oven.

Sue Wickey
Norfolk, NY

SMALL COOKIES

2 cups white sugar
1 cup butter and lard (1/2 of each)
1 cup sweet milk (rich)
2 t. baking powder
4 cups flour
2 eggs
1 t. vanilla
1 t. soda
1/2 t. salt

Mix sugar and shortening; add eggs; mix real good. Add rest of ingredients except flour. Mix real good, stir in a little flour at a time, and keep mixing till all the flour is added. Roll and cut and bake in 400 deg. oven till slightly brown.

Sue Wickey
Norfolk, NY

CHURCH COOKIES

4 cups white sugar
4 cups brown sugar
4 cups shortening
4 cups buttermilk
8 eggs
4 t. salt
8 t. soda
4 t. baking powder
4 t. maple or vanilla flavoring

Put together in order given; mix good, then stir 18-20 cups sifted flour. Roll, cut, bake on greased cookie sheet in 400-450 deg. oven until done.

Sue Wickey
Norfolk, NY

CHOCOLATE CHIP COOKIES

Mix in order given:

6 eggs, beaten
2 cups brown sugar
1 cup white sugar
2 cups shortening
1 t. vanilla
2 t. salt
4 t. soda
4 t. cream of tartar
7 cups flour
1 cup chocolate chips

Drop by t. on greased cookie sheet and bake 10-12 min. in 375 deg. oven.

Sue Wickey
Norfolk, NY

SOFT RAISIN GINGER COOKIES

1 cup lard
1 cup sugar
1 cup molasses
1 cup lukewarm water
2 eggs
1 T. soda
1 T. ginger
1 t. salt
1 cup raisins
5 cups flour (drop by spoon)

Martha Hostetler
Fort Plain, NY

OLD-FASHIONED MOLASSES COOKIES

2 cups molasses
2 1/2 cups sugar
2 cups sour milk
2 eggs
2 t. cream of tartar
5 t. soda
cinnamon and ginger to taste

Flour to roll out, soft dough.

Martha Hostetler
Fort Plain, NY

SUGAR COOKIES

2 cups white sugar
1 cup oleo
3 eggs
1 cup sour or buttermilk
2 t. soda
2 t. baking powder
1 t. vanilla
5 cups flour

Mix together in order given and bake.

Mrs. Ammon A. Troyer
Ashland, OH

CRISP GINGER COOKIES

2 cups butter or shortening
1 cup sugar
1 cup molasses
4 eggs
2 t. soda
2 t. ginger
1 t. salt
1 t. cinnamon
1 t. nutmeg
9 cups flour

Shape into rolls and let stand a while, then slice off and bake.

Fannie Gingerich
Ethridge, TN

AMISH HATS

1 3/4 cup flour
1 t. salt
1 t. soda
1/4 cup cocoa

Sift the 4 above ingredients and add:

1 cup brown sugar
1/2 cup margarine
1/2 cup milk
1 t. vanilla
1 egg
1/2 cup chopped nuts

Drop by t. on baking dish. Bake at 350 deg. for 8 min. Take from oven and put half of marshmallow on top and bake a few min. longer. When cool, frost with the following:

5 T. cocoa
2 cups 10X sugar
Dash of salt
2 T. melted butter
1/2 t. vanilla
4 T. cream or milk

Place a walnut on top

Esther Fisher
Millersburg, PA

BIRD'S NEST COOKIES

1 cup soft butter or margarine
1/2 cup brown sugar (packed)
2 egg yolks (unbeaten)
1/2 t. vanilla
1/4 t. salt
2 cups flour (sifted)
2 egg whites (unbeaten)
1/4 cup finely chopped nuts
jam, jelly or candied cherries

Cream butter till light and fluffy; gradually add brown sugar and egg yolks. Mix well. Blend in vanilla, salt, flour. Shape dough in 1 in. balls, dip in egg white, then nuts. Place on ungreased cookie sheet 1 in. apart, make hole in center and fill with jam.

Esther Fisher
Millersburg, PA

WHITE SUGAR COOKIES

2 cups sugar
1 cup lard
1 cup cream, sweet or sour milk (sour is best)
3 eggs
1 t. soda
4 t. baking powder
Flour to roll out.

Martha Hostetler
Fort Plain, NY

BROWN SUGAR COOKIES

4 cups brown sugar
2 cups lard
4 eggs
7 cups flour
4 t. soda
4 t. cream of tartar
1/2 t. ginger
Cool before baking; roll in a roll and slice.

Mrs. Noah Wenger, Jr., Conewango Valley, NY
Martha Hostetler, Fort Plain, NY

If you listen to too much
You wind up making other people's mistakes

MOLASSES COOKIES

2 cups shortening
1 cup brown sugar
1 egg
4 T. molasses
1/2 t. salt and cloves
2 t. soda
1 t. cinnamon and ginger
2 1/4 cups flour

Cream shortening and sugar together. Add egg and molasses and beat till well blended. Sift flour. Measure and add salt, soda and spices. Add dry ingredients to creamed mixture and mix thoroughly. Chill dough in refrigerator. Shape into balls; roll in white sugar and place on greased baking sheet. Bake at 350 deg. for 12-15 min. Makes 4 doz.

Barbara Schrock
Spartansburg, PA

WHOOPIE PIES

4 cups flour
2 cups sugar
2 t. soda
1/2 t. salt
1 cup shortening
1 cup cocoa
2 eggs
2 t. vanilla
1 cup thick sour milk
1 cup cold water

Cream together sugar, salt, shortening, vanilla and eggs. Sift together flour, soda and cocoa. Add this to the first mixture alternately with water and sour milk. Add slightly more flour if milk is not thick. Drop by t. Bake at 400 deg.

Filling:

1 egg white, beaten
1 T. vanilla
2 T. flour
2 T. milk
2 cups powdered sugar or as needed
3/4 cup Crisco or oleo

Beat egg white, sugar and vanilla; then add remaining ingredients. Beat well.

Barbara Schrock
Spartansburg, PA

VALENTINE COOKIES

2 cups brown sugar
3/4 cup boiling water
3/4 cup shortening
1 t. soda
1 t. vanilla

Put in enough flour so you can roll them thin. Bake. Frost. Very good with tea.

Barbara Schrock
Spartansburg, PA

KNEE PATCHES

3 eggs
1 cup cream
4 cups flour
1/2 t. salt

Beat eggs and add cream. Sift flour and salt together and stir into mixture to make a soft dough. Take a piece of dough the size of a large marble and roll as thin as possible. (The Swiss used to cover the knee with a tea towel and then stretch dough over the knee until very thin.) Fry in deep fat, 375 deg., till a delicate brown. Drain and dist with powdered or white sugar. Makes 24-30 patches.

Barbara Schrock
Spartansburg, PA

Don't expect smooth sailing
When you're kicking up a storm

CLARK BARS

1 cup sugar
1 cup peanut butter
1 cup dates, cut up
1 cup chopped nuts
1/2 cup crushed corn flakes

Mix well. Shape in balls and let set overnite, then dip in chocolate.

Barbara Schrock
Spartansburg, PA

LITTLE DEBBIE COOKIES

1 cup oleo
3 cups brown sugar
4 eggs
2 t. cinnamon
1 1/2 t. nutmeg
1 t. soda
3 cups oatmeal
3 cups flour

Cream oleo, sugar, eggs, and spices. Add rest of ingredients. Roll into smallballs and flatten on cookie sheets. Bake at 350 deg.
Filling: Beat 2 egg whites, add 2 t. vanilla, 4 T. milk, and 2 cups powdered sugar. Beat thoroughly and add 2 more cups powdered sugar, and add 1 scant cup Crisco.

Barbara Schrock
Spartansburg, PA

MAPLE NUT DROPS

3 eggs
1 cup butter
2 cups brown sugar
3/4 cup milk
1 1/4 t. maple flavoring
1 t. soda
1/4 t. salt
3/4 cup chopped walnuts
4 cups flour

Mix in order given. Bake at 350 deg. for 10 min.

Frosting: Brown 1/4 cup butter. Add 1 beaten egg, 2 1/4 cups powdered sugar, 1 t. maple flavoring and 2 T. water.

Barbara Schrock
Spartansburg, PA

Tact is the knack of winning a point
Without making an enemy

SOUR CREAM MOLASSES COOKIES

3/4 cup lard
1 3/4 cups sugar
1/4 cup butter
3 eggs
1 cup sour cream
1 cup molasses
4 cups flour
1/2 t. each of ginger, cinnamon and nutmeg
2 t. soda, dissolved in a little hot water

Flour enough to roll and bake at 350 deg. or put in more flour around 9 cups in all and drop them on cookie sheet and bake.

Elizabeth Stutzman
Union City, PA

GRANDMA'S DROP COOKIES

3 eggs, keep 1 big spoonful out to put on top of cookies
1 cup butter or lard
1 cup hot water
3 t. baking powder
2 t. soda
6 cups flour
3 cups sugar

Mix together sugar, lard, water, and eggs; then mixture of baking powder and soda; then last the flour. Make a spoon wet with egg to mold it.

Mrs. Joe J. Yoder
Lawrenceburg, TN

GINGER SNAPS

2 cups brown sugar
1 cup Brer Rabbit molasses
1 cup shortening
1 egg
4 cups flour (sifted)
2 t. soda
2 t. ginger
1/2 t. salt
1 t. vanilla

Cream shortening, sugar and egg; add molasses and add to the creamed mixture. Chill dough 4 hrs. or overnight. Makes balls the size of a walnut and put on greased cookie sheet and bake in a slow oven 150-200 deg. Don't flatten as they will flatten themselves while baking. When done, leave them on the cookie sheet for 5 min. before removing from the sheet.

Emma Hershberger
Dover, DE

If we feel the storm
We feel the worth of the anchor

OATMEAL WHOOPIE PIES

2 cups brown sugar
1 1/2 cups margarine
4 eggs
1 t. salt
4 cups flour
4 cups oatmeal
2 t. cinnamon
2 t. baking powder
2 t. soda, dissolved in 6 T. boiling water

Cream together sugar, margarine and eggs. Add flour, oatmeal, salt, cinnamon and baking powder. Add soda water last. Beat. Drop on greased pans and bake at 350 deg.

Filling:

2 egg whites
2 t. vanilla
4 cups powdered sugar
2 T. flour
4 T. milk
1 cup Crisco

Beat egg whites until stiff. Add remaining ingredients and mix. Spread between 2 cookies.

Emma Hershberger
Dover, DE

BUTTER SCOTCH COOKIES

3 1/2 cups brown sugar
6 cups flour
2 t. cream of tartar
2 t. soda
1 cup butter and lard
5 eggs
2 t. vanilla

Mix dry ingredients, then work in shortening. Put in well-beaten eggs; mix and shape into rolls. Let set overnite.

Fannie Gingerich
Ethridge, TN

BUTTERSCOTCH CRUNCH COOKIES

2 cups lard
2 cups brown sugar
2 cups white sugar
2 t. vanilla
4 eggs

Beat and add:

3 cups flour
2 t. salt
2 t. soda
6 cups oatmeal

Roll up and chill overnite.

Mrs. Joe J. Yoder
Lawrenceburg, TN

CHEWY OATMEAL COOKIES

4 cups sifted flour
3 t. soda
2 t. salt
4 t. cinnamon
1 t. nutmeg
3 cups soft shortening
5 1/3 cups brown sugar
8 eggs
8 cups oatmeal
4 cups raisins
vanilla

Sift flour, salt, soda, and spices in a bowl. Add shortening, sugar, eggs, and vanilla. Beat until smooth. Stir in oats and raisins.

Fannie Gingerich
Ethridge, TN

A sharp tongue a dull mind
Are usually found in the same mind

CHOCOLATE OATMEAL COOKIES

2 cups sugar
1/2 cup milk
2 T. cocoa
1/2 stick butter
1 t. vanilla

Let cook for 3 min. after bubbling. Then add 1/2 cup peanut butter and 2 cups oatmeal and drop by spoonful on greased cookie sheet or wax paper.

Fannie Gingerich
Ethridge, TN

PEPPERNUTS

2 cups sugar
2 cups buttermilk
1 cup shortening
1 t. vanilla
1 cup syrup (dark)
1 cup nuts (chopped)
1 t. cinnamon
1/2 t. cloves
1 t. nutmeg
1/2 t. ginger
1 t. soda
6 or 7 cups flour, enough to make a stiff dough

Put all ingredients in a large bowl, adding just 2 cups flour the first time. Mix well, keep adding flour until it is stiff enough to roll into small rolls (1/4 x 1/2 in. in diameter); work flour in with hands near the end. Make rolls and put on cookie sheet right next to each other. Refrigerate overnite. Cut into 1/2 in. pieces. Bake at 350 deg., 8-10 min.

Treva Headings
Hutchinson, KS

If you insist on perfection
Make the first demands on yourself

MATTIE COOKIES

8 cups sugar
3 cups shortening
3 cups sour milk or buttermilk
12 eggs
8 t. soda
8 t. baking powder
flour enough to make a soft dough.

Saloma J. Byler
Dewittville, NY

POOR MAN'S COOKIES

1 cup sugar 1 cup shortening
Cream together
2 cups flour 1 t. soda
1/2 t. salt
Add:
1 egg 1 t. cinnamon
1 cup raisins cooked in 1 cup water about 5 min. 1 t. cloves
1 t. nutmeg

Spread over greased cookie sheet. Bake in 400 deg. oven 10-12 min. Ice while still warm.

Mrs. J. David Byler
Putnxsutawany, PA

BUSHEL COOKIES

5 lb. sugar 2 1/2 lb. lard
2 lb. raisins chopped 1 lb. salted peanuts chopped
2 lb. quick oats 6 lb. flour
1 qt. sweet milk 1 doz. eggs
1 c. maple syrup 2 oz. soda 2 oz. baking powder
nutmeg for flavor

Put together in eve and bake next morning if you wish. Add more flour if you want to roll them.

Saloma J. Byler
Dewittville, NY

SOFT MOLASSES DROP COOKIES

1 cup shortening 2 cups brown sugar
1 cup molasses 1 egg
1 t. salt 5 cups flour
1 t. cinnamon 1 t. soda
1/2 t. ginger 2/3 cup hot water

Cream shortening with sugar and molasses. Add egg unbeaten. Sift flour and spices. Add alternately with the hot water in which soda is dissolved. Bake on greased cookie sheet.

Naomi Peachey
Little Falls, NY

RAISIN FILLED COOKIES

9 cups sugar
3 cups lard
6 eggs
3 cups milk
14 cups flour
9 t. soda
9 t. baking powder
4 t. vanilla

Filling:
4 cups raisins or dates (grind)
2 cups sugar
4 t. salt
4 cups water
8 T. flour

Boil till thick and smooth.

Mrs. Noah Wenger, Jr.
Conewango Valley, NY

PEANUT BUTTER OATMEAL COOKIES

1 cup brown sugar
1 cup white sugar
1 cup shortening
1 1/2 cups flour
3 cups oatmeal
2 eggs
1 t. baking powder
1 t. soda
3/4 cup peanut butter

Cream together sugar and shortening. Add peanut butter and eggs. Next add all dry ingredients.

Mrs. Henry Stutzman
Conewango Valley, NY

PUMPKIN NUT COOKIES

1/2 cup shortening
1 cup sugar
2 eggs beaten
1 cup cooked mashed pumpkin
2 cups sifted flour
4 t. baking powder
1 t. salt
1/4 t. ginger
1/2 t. nutmeg
2 1/2 t. cinnamon
1 cup raisins
1 cup chopped nuts

Cream shortening and sugar till light. Add eggs and pumpkin, mix well. Sift flour, baking powder, salt and spices. Stir into pumpkin mixture. Add raisins and nuts. Bake 350 deg. 15 min.

Naomi Peachey
Little Falls, NY

DEBBIE OATMEAL COOKIES

1 1/2 cup oleo
3 cups brown sugar
4 eggs
2 t. cinnamon
1 1/2 t. soda
1/2 t. nutmeg
2 t. vanilla
2 cups flour
4 cups oatmeal
pinch salt

Mix and bake cookies. Fill with filling:

2 egg whites, beaten
1 t. vanilla
3 cups 10X sugar
1 1/2 cups Crisco
Marshmallow cream (optional)

Saloma Petersheim
Mifflintown, PA

No man can hold another in the gutter
Unless he stays there himself

FROSTED MOLASSES COOKIES

1 cup sugar
1 cup shortening
2 large eggs
1 cup molasses
1/2 cup warm water
5 cups all-purpose flour
1 T. soda
1 T. cinnamon
1 t. baking powder

Mix in order given. Roll out or drop by t. and press with glass dipped in sugar. Bake at 375 deg. till done. Frost.

Lydiann J. Bricker
Panama, NY

BUTTERSCOTCH ICEBOX COOKIES

2 cups brown sugar
3/4 cup shortening
2 eggs
4 cups all-purpose flour
1 t. baking powder
1 t. soda
1 t. vanilla
1/2 cup chopped nuts

Mix in order given. Form into rolls. Chill. Slice 1/4" thick. Bake on ungreased pans, at 350 deg. for 15 min. or till done. Don't overbake.

Lydiann J. Bricker
Panama, NY

OATMEAL COOKIES

4 1/2 cups sifted flour
1/2 t. salt
3 t. baking powder
3 t. soda
3 cups shortening
6 eggs, beaten
1 t. vanilla
6 cups brown sugar
9 cups quick oats
powdered sugar
pecan halves

Sift flour, salt, baking powder and soda. Set aside. Cream together sugar and shortening. Add beaten eggs and vanilla. Beat well. Stir in dry ingredients and oats. Chill dough. Form into balls the size of a walnut. Roll in powdered sugar until heavily coated. Place on cookie sheets and flatten with a fork. Top with a pecan half. Bake at 375 deg. for 8-10 min. or until golden brown. Makes 150 cookies.

Mrs. Daniel C. Borntreger
Riceville, IA

ICE BOX COOKIES

Cream 1 cup brown sugar, 1 cup white sugar and 1 cup shortening (or butter or lard). Add 3 eggs (well beaten), 4 cups flour and 1 t. soda dissolved in 2 t. cld water. Add vanilla and nuts.

Mrs. Daniel C. Borntreger
Riceville, IA

CHOCOLATE CHIP COOKIES

2 cups brown sugar
1 cup white sugar
2 t. salt
2 cups shortening
1 t. vanilla
4 t. soda
6 eggs
4 t. cream of tartar
7 cups flour
2-3 pkg. chocolate chips
Nuts (optional)

Mix well in order given. Drop by teaspoon onto cookie sheet. Bake at 375 deg.

Mrs. Daniel C. Borntreger
Riceville, IA

GINGER COOKIES

3 eggs
1 cup lard
2 t. ginger
pinch of salt
2 cups cane molasses
3 t. soda
flour (enough to roll)

Mrs. Daniel C. Borntreger
Riceville, IA

BUTTERMILK COOKIES

2 cups white sugar
2 cups lard
2 t. baking powder
vanilla
flour
2 cups brown sugar
2 t. soda
3-5 eggs
2 cups buttermilk

Mrs. Daniel C. Borntreger
Riceville, IA

BEST MOLASSES COOKIES

2 cups butter or lard
2 cups sugar
1 cup boiling water
2 t. ginger
a little cinnamon and vanilla
2 cups baking molasses
2 eggs
2 T. soda
2 t. salt

Mix well. Add flour to make a soft dough, approx. 9 cups. Roll out on floured board. Bake at 350 deg.

Catherine Swarey
Belleville, PA

RANGER COOKIES

1 cup white sugar
1 cup shortening
2 T. cream
1/2 t. baking powder
2 eggs
1 cup brown sugar
2 cups flour
1 t. soda
1/2 t. salt

Cream sugar and shortening until fluffy. Add beaten eggs. Mix well, add flour with baking powder and soda and salt. Then add 2 cups rolled oats, 2 cups Rice Krispies and 1 cup coconut. Mix well. Drop by t. on floured cookie sheet. Bake at 375 deg.

Louella Borntrager
Sugar Creek, OH

BANANA CHOCOLATE CHIP COOKIES

2 1/2 cups flour
2 t. baking powder
1/4 t. soda
2/3 cup shortening
1 cup sugar
2 eggs
1 t. vanilla
1 cup mashed bananas
1/2 t. salt
1 cup chocolate chips

Beat shortening until creamy, add sugar, eggs one at a time, stir in vanilla. Add flour, baking powder and soda and salt mixture alternately with bananas. Fold in chips. Drop by t. on ungreased cookie sheets. Bake at 400 deg. for 12 min.

Louella Borntrager
Sugar Creek, OH

COCONUT DROP COOKIES

1 cup brown sugar
1 cup white sugar
1 cup oleo
1 t. soda
a little salt
3 cups oatmeal
1 1/2 cups shredded coconut
1 1/2 cups flour
1/2 cup raisins or nuts

Mix, drop, and bake.

Mrs. Samuel D. Beachy
Clark, MO

DATE COOKIES

1 cup shortening
2 cups brown sugar
3 beaten eggs
4 cups flour
1/4 t. salt
1/2 t. soda

Chill for 2 hr. Roll out and cut out.

Filling:

2 1/2 cups dates
1 cup white sugar
1 cup boiling water

Boil till thick and add:

1 cup nuts

Chill, fill cookies with filling and bake at 400 deg.

Mrs. Leroy J. Byler
Fredericktown, OH

BROWN SUGAR COOKIES

4 cups brown sugar
1 t. vanilla
1 cup milk
4 t. baking powder
1/4 t. salt
7 cups flour unsifted
2 t. soda
2 cups oleo
6 eggs

Cream shortening and brown sugar together. Add eggs and mix well. Add milk and vanilla and mix. Bake at 400 deg.

Mrs. Leroy J. Byler
Fredericktown, OH

PRIZE WINNING COOKIES

4 cups brown sugar
2 cups sweet milk
4 t. soda
2 t. salt
2 cups shortening
4 eggs, well beaten
10 t. baking powder
2 t. vanilla

Flour as needed to drop. Bake at 350 deg. Frost with Crisco frosting.

Mrs. Leroy J. Byler
Fredericktown, OH

STONE CREEK COOKIES

1 cup shortening
1 t. nutmeg
1 t. salt
1 t. vanilla
1 t. soda
1 t. cream of tartar

Combine these 6 ingredients. Add:
2 cups brown sugar and cream well.
Add:

2 eggs beaten
4 1/2 cups flour (sifted)
1/4 cup milk
1 cup nutmeats

Mix well. Make into small balls the size of a walnut and flatten with potato masher or whatever you prefer. Bake

Mrs. Samuel D. Beachy
Clark, MO

Were we supposed to talk more than listen
We would have one ear and two tongues

FRUIT COOKIES

1 cup sugar
3/4 cup lard or oleo
2 eggs
1/2 t. salt
1/2 t. cinnamon
1/2 t. nutmeg or cloves
1 cup raisins cooked in 1 cup water
1 t. vanilla
1 t. soda dissolved in 2/3 cup raisin water
1 t. baking powder
2 1/2 or 3 cups flour
1/2 cup nutmeats (walnuts)

Shift from bottom of oven to grate in oven.

Mrs. Samuel D. Beachy
Clark, MO

PRIDE OF IOWA COOKIES

1 cup brown sugar
1 cup white sugar
1 cup shortening
2 cups flour
1 cup coconut
3 cups quick oats
2 eggs
1/2 t. salt
1 t. soda
1 t. baking powder
1 t. vanilla
1/2 cup nuts

Blend sugar, shortening, add beaten eggs. Sift flour, salt, soda and baking powder together. Mix all together and drop by t. on greased cookie sheet; flatten with bottom of a glass or fork. Bake at 350 deg. for 8 min.

Louella Borntrager
Sugar Creek, OH

SOFT SOUR CREAM COOKIES

1 3/4 cups white sugar
1 cup or 2 sticks oleo
1 t. salt
4 eggs

Beat real well, then add:

1 t. soda in 2 T. hot water
1 cup sour cream
4 1/2 cups all purpose flour
1 t. baking powder
flavoring of your choice

Chill overnite; then roll out on floured board. Cut any shape. Makes nice heart shape cookies. Sprinkle colored sugar on top. Bake at 350 deg. Do not overbake as cookies will not be brown when done.

Louella Borntrager
Sugar Creek, OH

DELICIOUS CARROT COOKIES

1 cup shortening
3/4 cup sugar
2 cups flour
1 t. vanilla
1 egg
1 cup cooked carrots, mashed
2 t. baking powder
1/2 t. lemon extract

Cream shortening and sugar; add eggs and mashed carrots. Sift dry ingredients; add to creamed mixture. Add flavoring and drop by t. on greased baking sheet. Bake in 350 deg. until brown. Frost cookies while still warm with icing made with juice of one orange, grated orange peel and powdered sugar added to desired thickness to spread smoothly.

Joni H. Schrock
Middlefield, OH

PEANUT BUTTER COOKIES

1 cup white sugar
1 cup brown sugar
1 cup lard
1 cup peanut butter
3 1/2 cups flour
2 eggs
2 T. milk
1/2 t. salt
2 t. soda

Put chocolate wafers on top when they come out of oven.

Mrs. Ray J. Gingerich
Fillmore, NY

MOM'S DROP COOKIES

(Frosted Creames)

2 cups molasses
2 cups sugar
2 cups lard
2 cups milk
5 eggs
5 t. soda
2 t. cinnamon
2 t. ginger
1/2 t. salt

Enough flour so you can drop on pan to bake - 7-8 cups

Cream shortening and sugar. Add eggs. Beat until light. Add molasses, then add sifted dry ingredients alternately with sour milk or buttermilk. Bake at 400 deg. for 12 min. Frost with powdered sugar icing. May be spread on cookie sheet, baked and frosted, then cut in bars.

Mrs. Vernon E. Bontrager
Iowa City, IA

APPLE COOKIES

4 cups white sugar
4 cups brown sugar
2 cups shortening
8 eggs
4 t. vanilla
4 t. baking powder
4 t. soda
12 cups flour
4 cups nuts
4 cups raisins
8 cups raw or dried apples
2 cups sour cream

Mrs. Ray J. Gingerich
Fillmore, NY

COWBOY COOKIES

2 cups white sugar
2 cups brown sugar
4 cups flour
2 cups shortening
4 cups oatmeal
2 cups chocolate chips
4 eggs
2 t. vanilla
2 t. soda
1 t. baking powder
1 t. salt.

Bake at 350 deg. for 10-15 min.

Mrs. Ray J. Gingerich
Fillmore, NY

Today is the tomorrow
You worried about yesterday

BUTTERMILK COOKIES

1 1/2 cups brown sugar
1 1/2 cups white sugar
1 1/4 cups lard
1 1/4 cups buttermilk
4 eggs
5-5 1/2 cups flour
1 t. soda
1 T. baking powder
1 t. vanilla
1/2 t. maple flavor
1/2 t. salt

Roll out to 1/3 in. thick and bake at 350 deg. for 15 min.

Mrs. Ray J. Gingerich
Fillmore, NY

SNICKERS

1/2 cup white sugar
1 cup brown sugar
1 cup shortening
2 eggs
2 cups flour
1 t. soda
2 t. cream of tartar
1/4 t. salt

Mix well; chill dough overnight, form into balls. If dough is too stiff, use 1/4 cup less flour. Mix 1/2 cup brown sugar and 1 tsp. cinnamon. Roll balls in the mixture and bake.

Mary A. Kinsinger
Meyersdale, PA

AUNT MATTIE COOKIES

4 cups sugar
1 cup lard
2 cups milk
4 eggs
3 t. soda
3 t. baking powder
flavor vanilla, lemon or nutmeg
8 cups flour

Mix and bake. Good for church cookies.

Mrs. Neal Kauffman
La Plata, MO

Your chances of loosing you shirt
Are lessened if you keep your sleeves rolled up

SPICY HONEY COOKIES

1 cup lard
2 cups white sugar
2 eggs
1/2 cup honey
4 t. soda
1 t. salt (scant)
4 T. milk
2 t. vanilla
2 t. cinnamon
5 cups bread flour
2 t. nutmeg

Cream lard and sugar; blend in eggs, honey, milk, and vanilla; beat until fluffy. Add sifted dry ingredients and mix well. Form dough into small balss. Dip one side in milk, then in sugar. Place on greased cookie sheet sugared side up. Bake at 375 deg. for 8-10 min. or until done.

Mrs. Dan J. Troyer
Mercer, PA

HEALTH COOKIES

Sift together into large bowl:

1 cup sifted flour
2 t. baking powder
1/2 t. salt

Add and mix in:

1 cup whole wheat flour
1/2 cup wheat germ
1 1/2 cups rolled oats
3/4 cup raisins

Mix in separate bowl:

2 eggs unbeaten
2 T. applesauce
1 1/2 cups brown sugar
1 cup vegetable oil
1 t. vanilla extract

Add liquid ingredients to dry ingredients and mix well. Drop by t. onto greased baking sheet. Bake in moderate oven at 350 deg. for 15 min. or till done.

Mrs. Dan J. Troyer
Mercer, PA

SUGAR FROSTED COCOA COOKIES

1 cup butter, softened
2 cups sugar
1/2 cup milk
3 cups flour
1 cup cocoa
1 egg
2 t. vanilla
1 t. soda
1 t. salt

Mix butter, sugar and eggs in large bowl until well blended. Beat in milk and vanilla. Add flour, cocoa, soda and salt and beat until ingredients are combined. Roll small amounts of dough into 1 in. balls. (Dough should be chilled to handle better.) Roll in sugar and top each with walnut half. Bake at 375 deg. for 8-10 min. or till done.

Mrs. Dan J. Troyer
Mercer, PA

OHIO FRUIT BAR COOKIES

1 lb. shortening
2 lbs. brown sugar
5 eggs
1 cup water
1 cup baking molasses
3 1/2 lb. flour
2 T. soda
1 T. vanilla
2 lb. raisins

Nuts may be added if desired.
Cook raisins - add 1 cup of water for each lb. of raisins.

Mrs. Dan J. Troyer
Mercer, PA

FILLED COOKIES

1 cup shortening
2 cups brown sugar
1 t. soda
3 eggs, beaten
2 cups flour or more
1/2 cup hot water
salt and vanilla to taste

Roll mixture out 1/8 in. thick. Cut with a cookie cutter. Put a t. or more of the filling between 2 cookies. Bake 350 deg. Takes longer to bake with filling.

Filling for the above cookies:

2 cups raisins
1 cup brown sugar
2 cups water
2 T. flour

Mix and cook till thick. Cool it a little before putting onto cookies.

Joe Borntreger
Cashton, WI

SORGHUM COOKIES

2 cups white sugar
1 t. salt
2 t. cinnamon
2 t. ginger
1 1/2 cups shortening

Mix together the above ingredients and add:

4 t. soda
5 cups flour
2 eggs beaten
1 cup molasses

Mix well. Do not overbake—are better if slightly underbaked. Drop on cookie sheets. Bake at 350 deg.

Joe Borntreger
Cashton, WI

COCOA DROP COOKIES (UNBAKED)

Boil together 5 min:

2 cups white sugar
1/2 cup cocoa
1/2 cup milk
1/2 cup butter
1 t. vanilla

Mix well with 3 cups quick oats. Drop by spoonfuls on waxed paper and cool.

Mrs. Emma Stutzman
Bronson, MO

TWINKIES

1 yellow cake mix
1 - 3 oz. instant vanilla pudding
1 cup water
4 eggs
1/2 cup oil

Mix cake mix, pudding, water, eggs and oil. Put on a greased cookie sheet. Bake at 350 deg. for 20 min.

Frosting for Twinkies:

5 T. flour
1 cup milk
1 cup sugar
1 t. vanilla
dash of salt
1/2 cup oleo
1/2 cup Crisco

Cook flour and milk until thick; cool. Mix sugar, vanilla, salt, oleo and Crisco. Beat until fluffy; mix with cooled milk and flour. Cut cake Twinkie size and slice in middle; fill with frosting. Wrap in plastic wrap.

Elizabeth Mae Raber
Montgomery, IN

CRUNCHY OATMEAL COOKIES

3/4 cup shortening
1 cup brown sugar
1 1/2 cups flour
1 1/2 cups oats
1 cup coconut
3/4 cup chopped nuts
1 egg
1 t. vanilla
2 t. baking powder
1 t. soda
1/2 t. salt

Cream shortening and sugar; add egg and vanilla, then dry ingredients. Add oats, coconut and nuts. Roll in balls and press. Bake in hot oven.

Elizabeth Mae Raber
Montgomery, IN

RAISIN DROP COOKIES

1 cup lard
2 cups brown sugar
1/2 cup hot water
4 1/2 cups flour
3 eggs beaten
2 t. baking powder
1 t. soda
1 cup raisins

Cream shortening and sugar. Add hot water then beaten eggs. Sift together dry ingredients. Add to other mixture; add raisins and drop on cookie sheet and bake.

Elizabeth Mae Raber
Montgomery, IN

VANILLA GINGER COOKIES

1 cup lard
2 cups sorghum
1/2 cup hot water
6 cups flour (more or less)
1/2 t. ginger or 1 t. cinnamon
3 t. soda
3 eggs beaten
2 t. vanilla

Heat sorghum and lard till melted; put soda in hot water and add to sorghum and lard. Add beaten eggs, vanilla, ginger or cinnamon, and flour.

Drop on cookie sheet and bake in hot oven.

Elizabeth Mae Raber
Montgomery, IN

PUMPKIN COOKIES

Cream together:
1 cup shortening
2 cups brown sugar
2 cups pumpkin or squash
Sift together:
4 1/2 cups flour
2 t. baking powder
1 t. salt
2 t. soda
2 t. cinnamon
Add to pumpkin mixture and mix well. May add 1 cup nuts if you wish. Bake.

Elizabeth Mae Raber
Montgomery, IN

CHERRY WINK COOKIES

5 cups corn flakes
2 1/4 cups sifted flour
1 t. baking powder
1/2 t. baking soda
1/2 t. salt
3/4 cup margarine
1 cup sugar
2 eggs
1 t. vanilla
1 cup chopped nuts
1 cup dates (cut fine)
1/3 cup maraschino cherries (cut in quarters)
Measure cornflakes, crush into crumbs, set aside. Sift together flour, baking powder, baking soda, and salt; set aside. Measure margarine and sugar into large mixing bowl. Beat until fluffy. Add eggs and vanilla, beat well. Add sifted dry ingredients, mix. Stir in dates, nuts and cherries. Shape level T. dough into ball. Roll in crushed cornflakes. Place on greased cookie sheet. Top with cherry quarters. Bake at 375 deg. oven about 12 min.

Aaron Brubacker
Liverpool, PA

Success in marriage
Is not only finding the right person
It is being the right person

PEANUT OATMEAL COOKIES

2 cups shortening
4 cups brown sugar
2 t. vanilla
4 eggs
3 cups all purpose flour
2 t. baking soda
6 cups oatmeal
1 lb. salted Spanish peanuts or 1 cup peanut butter

Cream shortening and sugar. Add vanilla and eggs, beat well. Stir in blour and baking soda. Add oatmeal and peanuts. Drop onto greased cookie sheet. Bake at 375 deg. for 10-12 min. If using peanut butter, add it with shortening.

Aaron Brubacker
Liverpool, PA

PEANUT BLOSSOMS

1/2 cup shortening
3/4 cup peanut butter
1/3 cup granulated sugar
1/3 cup packed brown sugar
1 egg
2 T. milk
1 - 9 oz. package (about 54) Hershey's Milk Chocolate Kisses
1 t. vanilla
1 1/2 cups unsifted flour
1 t. baking soda
1/2 t. salt
granulated sugar

Cream shortening and peanut butter in large bowl. Blend in granulated sugar and brown sugar. Add egg, milk, and vanilla. Beat well. In a separate bowl combine flour, baking soda and salt. Gradually add flour mixture to creamed mixture, blend thoroughly. Shape dough into 1 in. balls. Roll in granulated sugar. Place on an ungreased cookie sheet. Bake at 375 deg. for 10-12 min. Remove from oven. Immediately place an unwrapped kiss on top of each cookie, pressing down so that cookie cracks around the edges. Remove from cookie sheet. Cool on a wire rack. Makes approximately 4 doz.

Aaron Brubacker
Liverpool, PA

Where love is thin
Faults are thick

GOOD OATMEAL COOKIES

2 cups butter
2 cups brown sugar packed
1/2 t. salt
2 t. vanilla
2 eggs
1 t. soda
2 t. baking powder
2 2/3 cups flour
3 cups oatmeal
1 1/2 cups coconut

Joe Borntreger
Cashton, WI

Whenever the going is easy
Be sure you are not going down hill

ANDY GERTIE COOKIES

2 cups brown sugar
1 cup white sugar
1 cup lard
1 1/2 cups cream, sweet or sour
6 eggs
1/2 cup milk
4 t. baking powder
4 t. soda
pinch of salt
flour (what you need)
flavor

Mix sugar and lard, then eggs, milk, cream, and about 5 cups flour.

Joe Borntreger
Cashton, WI

COCONUT COOKIES

1 cup sugar
1/2 cup shortening
1 cup milk
1 cup coconut
2 cups flour
1 egg unbeaten
1 t. vanilla
1/4 t. salt
2 t. baking powder

Stir together shortening, sugar, eggs, flour and milk. Add coconut, gradually stir in sifted dry ingredients and drop on greased pan. Bake at 350 deg.

Joe Borntreger
Cashton, WI

BANANA OATMEAL DROP COOKIES

1 cup sugar
3/4 cup shortening
1 cup mashed bananas
1 egg
1 1/3 cups uncooked rolled oats
2 1/4 cups sifted flour
1 t. salt
1/2 t. baking powder
1/2 t. nutmeg
1/4 t. cinnamon
2/3 cup nut meats

Combine sugar, shortening, egg and banana in a bowl; beat until well-blended. Add rolled oats, sifted dry ingredients and nuts, stirring to make a soft dough. Drop by t. onto greased baking sheet about 2 1/2 in. apart.

Joe Borntreger
Cashton, WI

A man of words and not of deeds
Is like a garden full of weeds

APPLESAUCE COOKIES

3/4 cup soft shortening
1 cup brown sugar (packed)
1 egg
1/2 cup applesauce
2 1/4 cups sifted flour
1/2 cup nuts
1/2 t. soda
1/4 t. salt
3/4 t. cinnamon
1/4 t. cloves
1 cup raisins

Mix together thoroughly shortening, sugar and eggs; stir in applesauce. Sift together dry ingredients and stir in. Add raisins and nuts. Drop by t. on greased cookie sheet. Bake at 375 deg. 10-12 min.

Joe Borntreger
Cashton, WI

OLD COOKIES RECIPE

2 cups sugar
2 cups sour cream
2 t. soda with hot water
then flavor and add flour

Joe Borntreger
Cashton, WI

BUTTERSCOTCH COOKIES

4 cups brown sugar
6 cups flour
2 t. cream of tartar
2 t. soda
1 cup shortening

Mix 4 eggs and 2 t. vanilla, then mix dry ingredients; work in shortening; last add well beaten eggs and flavoring. Shape into rolls and let stand overnight and slice and bake next morning at 350 deg. Avoid hard baking.

Ella Hershberger
Oakland, MD

OLD FASHIONED COOKIES

2 eggs
2 cups brown sugar
1/2 cup hot water
1 cup oleo or lard
1 t. soda
1 t. baking powder
1 t. vanilla
1 t. maple flavor
4 cups flour

Roll out and sprinkle with white sugar on top and bake.

Ella Hershberger
Oakland, MD

PUMPKIN WHOOPIE PIES

2 heaping cups brown sugar
1 cup Crisco
2 cups pumpkin
2 eggs
3 1/2 cups flour
1 t. cinnamon
1 t. salt
1 t. baking powder and soda
1 t. vanilla
1/2 t. cloves
1/2 t. ginger

Cream together sugar, Crisco and eggs. Add pumpkin and vanilla; sift together flour, baking powder, soda, and spices. Add to above mixture. Drop by t. on cookie sheet. Bake 10 min. in 400 deg. oven.

Filling:

1 egg white
2 T. flour
2 T. milk
1 t. vanilla
1 cup powdered sugar

Beat together and add: 1/4 cup Crisco, 1 cup powdered sugar. Beat until fluffy and put between two cookies.

Esther Marie Fisher
Conneautville, PA

DOUBLE CRUNCHERS

1 cup shortening
1 cup white sugar
1 cup brown sugar
2 eggs
1/2 t. salt
1 t. soda
2 cups crushed corn flakes
1 cup coconut
2 cups quick oats
2 cups flour
12 oz. semi sweet chocolate chips
1 cup granulated sugar
2 T. water
6 oz. cream cheese

Melt above in double boiler and spread between two cookies immediately.

Esther Marie Fisher
Conneautville, PA

CHOCOLATE SANDWICH COOKIES

2 cups brown sugar
1/4 cup cocoa
4 cups flour
1 t. vanilla
1/2 cup shortening
2-3 eggs
1 t. soda

Roll thin and bake. Spread icing between 2 cookies.

Esther Marie Fisher
Conneautville, PA

A good disposition is worth more than gold

RANGER JOE COOKIES

1 cup shortening
1 cup white sugar
1 cup brown sugar
2 eggs
1 t. vanilla
1/2 cup chocolate chips
1 t. soda
1/2 t. baking powder
2 cups flour
2 cups rice krispies
2 cups oatmeal
1 cup coconut
1/2 t. salt
1/2 cup walnuts

Bake at 375 deg.

Esther Marie Fisher
Conneautville, PA

SAND TARTS

1 lb. granulated sugar except 1/3 cup brown
10 oz. butter and lard (scant)
1/4 t. cinnamon
1 lb. flour
1/2 t. soda
2 egg yolks

Roll out and cut. Spread with slightly beaten egg whites. Sprinkle with nuts, white sugar and cinnamon.

Esther Marie Fisher
Conneautville, PA

PUMPKIN COOKIES

1 cup lard
2 t. baking powder
2 cups pumpkin
2 t. soda
2 cups sugar
2 t. cinnamon
4 cups flour sifted

Cream cooked pumpkin, sugar and lard. Add dry ingredients. Stir 1 cup chopped dates, raisins or nuts; drop on cookie sheet. Bake at 375 deg. Ice while still warm with confectioner's sugar, milk and butter; flavor with maple flavor.

Enos Yoders
Park City, KY

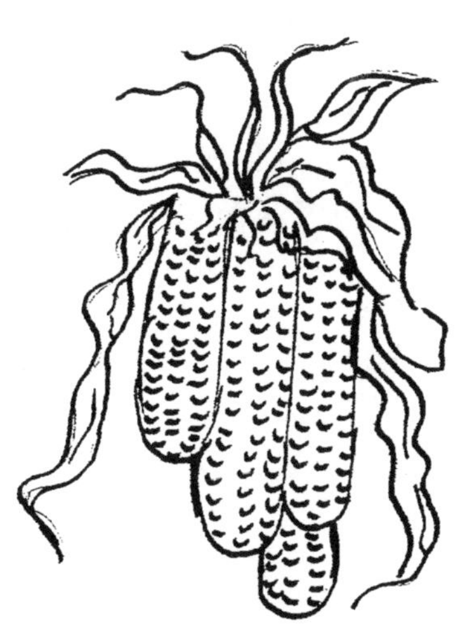

CHOCOLATE MARSHMALLOW COOKIES

1/2 cup cocoa
1 cup sugar
1/2 cup milk
1 3/4 cups flour
1/2 t. soda
36 marshmallows
1/2 cup shortening
1 egg
1 t. vanilla
1/2 t. salt
1/2 cup chopped nuts

Sift flour with soda, salt and cocoa. Cream shortening. Add sugar gradually. Add egg and beat well. Add flour mixture and milk alternately beating after each addition. Add nuts. Drop mixture by t. Bake in 350 deg. oven. Top with 1/2 marshmallow. Return and bake 2 min.

Frosting:
2 cups powdered sugar
5 T. cocoa
4 T. cream
3 T. butter

Esther Marie Fisher
Conneautville, PA

PINEAPPLE COOKIES

1 cup shortening
1 t. soda
1 cup brown sugar
4 cups flour (more might be needed)
1 cup pineapple (crushed)
1 t. vanilla
1 cup white sugar
2 eggs
1/2 cup nuts if desired

Mix and drop by spoonfuls on cookie sheets. Bake in moderate oven.

Clara Hochstetter
Canton, MO

APPLE RAISIN COOKIES

Cream:
1/2 cup oleo
1 cup brown sugar
Mix:
2 cups sifted flour
1 t. baking powder
1/2 t. salt
1 t. cinnamon
1/2 t. cloves
1/2 t. nutmeg
Stir into creamed mixture. Add:
3/4 cup chopped apples
1 cup raisins
1/2 cup nuts (opt.)
Drop by T. on well greased cookie sheet. Bake at 350 deg. 14-16 min.

Martha Mast
Revere, MO

SNICKERDOODLES

Mix:
1 cup oleo
1 1/2 cups sugar
2 eggs
Add:
2 3/4 cups sifted flour
2 t. cream of tartar
1 t. soda
1/4 t. salt
Roll into balls size of small walnuts. Roll into mixture of 2 T. sugar and 2 t. cinnamon. Place 2" apart on ungreased cookie sheet. bake until lightly brown, but still soft.

Martha Mast
Revere, MO

NO BAKE COOKIES

Mix the following:
2 cups sugar
2 T. cocoa (heaping)
1/2 cup milk
1/2 t. salt
1/2 t. vanilla
1/2 cup butter
Bring to a rolling boil; remove from heat and add 3 cups instant oatmeal and 1 cup coconut, 1/2 cup nuts. Mix and drop by t. on wax paper. Let cool.

Clara Hochstetter
Canton, MO

OATMEAL WHOOPIE PIES

2 cups brown sugar
3/4 cups butter or margarine
2 eggs
1/2 t. salt
1 t. cinnamon
1 t. baking powder
3 T. boiling water
1 t. soda
2 1/2 cups flour
2 cups quick oats

Mix sugar, shortening, eggs, salt and cinnamon, baking powder. Mix soda with hot water, add flour and oats. Bake at 350 deg. for 10 min.

Filling:

2 beaten egg whites
1 T. vanilla
2 cups 10X sugar
3/4 cup Crisco

Mix together and put between 2 cookies.

Lydia Stoltzfus
Bloomsburg, PA

You cannot purchase happiness
It's something you must earn
Give happiness to other folks
And get joy in return

MONSTER COOKIES

3 eggs
1 cup brown sugar
1 cup white sugar
1 t. vanilla
2 t. soda
1/2 cup margarine
1 cup peanut butter
4 1/2 cups oatmeal
1 cup M & M's

Mix in order given. Drop on greased cookie sheet. Bake at 350 deg. for 12 min.

Cathryn Schmucker
Litchfield, MI

SOFT SPICE COOKIES

2 cups brown sugar
1 cup shortening
1 cup milk
3 eggs
2 t. baking powder
2 t. soda
1 t. cinnamon
1 t. vanilla
4 cups flour

Mix in order given. Drop by t. on greased cookie sheet. Bake at 375 deg. for 10 min. Ice while warm.

Icing:
1/2 cup butter
1 cup brown sugar
1/4 cup milk

Boil together 2 min. Add powdered sugar until thick enough to spread.

Cathryn Schmucker
Litchfield, MI

Advice is a poor substitute
For a good example

CHOCOLATE MOUNTAIN DROP COOKIES

1 3/4 cups flour
1 cup sugar
1/2 cup cocoa
1/2 t. soda
3/4 t. salt
1/2 cup butter
1/2 cup milk
2 T. water
1 egg
27 large marshmallows

Mix in order given. Bake at 350 deg. When baked, add marshmallow, cut in half, on top of cookie, while hot. Frost with chocolate frosting.

Chocolate Frosting:
3 cups powdered sugar
1 T. cocoa
1 T. butter
3 T. milk

Put on cookies while warm.

Cathryn Schmucker
Litchfield, MI

CHOCOLATE CRISPY COOKIES

5 cups flour
2 t. soda
1 t. salt
2 cups oleo, softened
4 cups sugar
4 eggs
4 t. vanilla
8 cups rice krispies
2 - 12 oz. pkg. chocolate chips or M & M's.

Beat oleo and sugar until smooth. Beat eggs and vanilla. Mix in flour, soda and salt. Stir in cereal and chips. Drop on greased baking sheet. Bake at 350 deg. about 10 min. or until lightly browned.

Joni H. Shrock
Middlefield, OH

PARKER COOKIES

2 cups brown sugar
1 cup shortening
3 eggs
1/2 cup milk
2 t. soda
2 t. baking powder
3 1/2 cups flour
1/2 t. nutmeg
1/2 t. salt
1 t. vanilla

Drop on cookie sheet and bake.

Elizabeth Stutzman
Union City, PA

CRUNCHY COOKIES

2 cups brown sugar
1/2 cup shortening
2 eggs
1 t. vanilla
3 cups flour
1 t. soda
3/4 t. baking powder

Make in balls and press down with fork. Bake.

Elizabeth Stutzman
Union City, PA

Kindness is the sunshine
In which virtue grows

DATE PINWHEEL COOKIES

1 cup butter
1 cup white sugar
1 cup brown sugar
4 cups flour
3 eggs
1 t. cinnamon
1 t. soda
1/2 t. salt

Cream butter and sugar; add eggs, then add dry ingredients. If dough is too soft, chill a while. Roll on floured board 1/2 in. thick. Spread with filling and roll in jelly roll fashion. Cool until firm. Slice and bake in hot oven.

Filling:

1/2 cup dates
1/2 cup sugar
1/2 cup water
1/2 cup nuts

Combine dats, sugar and water. Cook until thick, then add nuts. This may be enough for 2 batches cookies.

Elizabeth Stutzman
Union City, PA

Those that most need advice
Usually like it the least

IVA'S SUGAR COOKIES

1 cup sugar
1 cup powdered sugar
1 cup butter
1 cup vegetable oil
2 eggs
1 t. vanilla
4 1/2 cups flour
1 t. baking soda
1 t. cream of tartar
1 t. salt

Cream together sugars and butter. Add vegetable oil and eggs and beat well. Beat in vanilla. Sift together flour, soda, cream of tartar, and salt and add, mixing thoroughly. Shape into balls and flatten with a glass dipped in sugar or refrigerate and roll out for cut cookies. Bake at 350 deg. for 8-10 min. Frost or decorate, if desired. These cookies do not brown a lot.

Ida Miller
Medford, WI

PINEAPPLE CREAM CHEESE TWIST

1/2 lb. oleo
4 cups flour
3/4 t. salt
2 pkgs. dry yeast
3/4 cup water
2 eggs, beaten

Combine flour, salt and oleo. Dissolve yeast in warm water and add eggs. Add to flour mixture and blend well. Knead and let double in size. Divide into 4 balls. Rout out dough.

Cheese filling:
1/3 cup sugar
1 t. vanilla
2 - 8 oz. pkg. cream cheese
1 1/2 T. lemon juice

Combine all ingredients and beat well.

Pineapple filling:
1# can crushed pineapple
3 T. cornstarch
1/2 cup sugar

Cook together until thick. Cool. Spread cheese filling in center of dough. Spread pineapple filling on top of cheese filling. Cut slits on each side of filling and overlap. Put on greased cookie sheet. Let rise 25 min. Bake at 350 deg. Cool and frost. Sprinkle with chopped nuts.

Frosting:
powdered sugar
vanilla
milk
butter flavor

Joni H. Shrock
Middlefield, OH

SOFT GINGER MOUNDS

4 1/4 cups flour
2 t. soda
1 t. ginger
3/4 t. cinnamon
1/2 t. nutmeg
1 cup raisins
3/4 cup sugar
3/4 cup shortening
1 1/4 cups molasses
1 egg
1 cup hot tap water

Cream sugar, shortening, molasses and egg thoroughly. Add blended dry ingredients alternately with hot tap water. Mix well; stir in raisins. Drop by heaping t. onto greased baking sheet. Bake at 375 deg. for 8-10 min.

Joni H. Shrock
Middlefield, OH

OATMEAL CRISPIE COOKIES

1 cup lard
1 cup white sugar
1 cup brown sugar
3 cups oatmeal
2 cups flour
2 eggs
1 t. soda
1/2 t. salt
1/2 t. baking powder
1/2 t. vanilla

Cream shortening, sugar, eggs. Sift flour, soda, salt and baking powder. Add oatmeal and vanilla. Shape into balls and press down. Bake 350 deg. for 10 min.

GRANDMA'S MOLASSES COOKIES

2 cups sugar
1 cup molasses
1 cup butter or oleo

Boil these together and cool; then add:

3/4 cup boiling water with 1 t. soda; also add 1 t. cinnamon
5 eggs
1 t. salt
2 cups flour to make a thin cake dough

Pour in greased cookie sheets and bake at 300 to 350 deg. oven for 20 min. or until done. Cut in squares and cool. Can be put together with fluffy frosting.

Sue Wickey
Norfolk, NY

ANYTHING COOKIES

3/4 cup margarine
1 cup white sugar
1 cup brown sugar
1 egg
1 t. cream of tartar
1 cup salad oil
3 t. vanilla
1 t. salt
1 t. soda
1 cup oatmeal
2 3/4 cups all-purpose flour
1 cup rice krispies
12 oz. chocolate chips

Mix until well blended. Drop by spoonful onto cookie sheet. Bake at 325 deg. till lightly brown.

Catherine Swarey
Belleville, PA

If you have nothing to say
Don't publish it by talking

Cheeses & Dips

CHEDDAR CHOWDER

2 cups boiling water
2 cups diced potatoes
1 1/2 t. salt
1/2 cup chopped celery
1/2 cup chopped onion
1/4 t. pepper
Boil about 8-10 min.
Mix together:
1/4 cup melted butter
1/4 cup flour
Add:
2 cups milk
2 cups grated cheddar cheese
1 1/2 cups diced ham
Mix everything together and heat. Do not boil.

Mrs. Wilma Mast
South Hutchinson, KS

KRAFT CHEESE

5 gal. skimmed milk
Let set till thick, then scald ontop of stove until hot enough that it is uncomfortable for the hand. Then drain through a cloth and squeeze real dry. Put through a food grinder to make real fine. Cook the following in double boiler till smooth—approximately 1 hour or more:
5 cups dry cheese
1 t. soda
2 t. salt
1/2 cup butter
1 - 1 1/2 cups cream or milk
Stir occasinally while cooling to make a softer cheese. Add more milk. Cheddar cheese powder put in last. Will make it more like velvetta cheese.

Mrs. Henry Stutzman
Conewango Valley, NY

HOMEMADE CHEESE

Slowly heat milk to 92 deg. stirring now and then. Then add the rennet which has been dissolved in 1/2 cup cold water. Stir for a few minutes. Then let set quiet for 30 min. It should thicken like jello within 30 min. Then cut the curds lengthwise and crosswise. Then start heating till temp. around 110-115 deg. Never heat it higher than 117 deg. It is usually ready at 110-115 deg. Stir the curds all the time you are heating it. Then let it set, stirring every now and then till when you take a handful of curds and press them together real hard, and it breaks apart nice and crisp, it is ready to put in press, but if it is still rubber-like it is not ready. Press it 12 hr. then take it out of press and put in salt brine for about 3 days, turning it every day. After taking it out of salt brine, wash it off with clear water everyday for 4 weeks and turn it over every day. Keep it at a temp. of 72-75 deg., then you may put it in a cooler place. Should be ready toeat at 4-6 wks. old. For 10 gal. milk, use 1 rennet tablet. For hostein milk, it might take a little more. It is good to have morning and evening milk to get right acid.

Fannie Gingerich
Ethridge, TN

CHEESE

100 lb. sweet whole milk
1 rennet tablet dissolved in3 oz. cold water
Heat milk to 80 deg. Remove from heat, add rennet tablet, stir one minute. Let stand till thick (about 1 hr.) Cut in small pieces, then heat to 114 deg., stirring constantly. Remove from heat; stir 1/2 hr.; take off whey and put curds in a large cloth and press 24 hr. While cheese is in press put salt in curds.

Clara Hockstetter
Canton, MO

No one has a right to do as he pleases
Unless he pleases to do right

CREAM CHEESE OR SCHMRIE'R KASE

Mix 3 t. soda in 6 cups cheese crumbs; let stand overnight (or until crumbs are all melted).
Add 3 cups milk, 3 cups cream, 3 t. salt, 1# cheespread. Heat in double boiler till smooth and all melted. Stir every now and then while cooling.

Martha Mast
Revere, MO

CHEESE LOGS

1 - 8 oz. cream cheese
4 oz. blue cheese
2 t. Worcestershire sauce
1 t. mustard
1/2 lb. sharp cheddar cheese
2 t. grated onion
1 t. lemon juice
1/2 t. paprika
1/2 t. salt

Form rolls. Roll in ground nuts. Serve on crackers.

Fannie S. Miller
Bird-in-Hand, PA

CHEESE BALLS OR LOGS

8 oz. cream cheese
1/2 can Spam (shredded)
1 sm. onion, chopped
1/8 t. Worcestershire sauce
salt and pepper to taste (if desired)

Mix together and form into rolls, then roll in ground nuts. Variation: nuts and ground parsley may also be mixed to roll them in. Then wrap them in Saran Wrap and refrigerate.

Fannie S. Miller
Bird-in-Hand, PA

CHEESE SPREAD

2 lb. cheese
1 can Carnation milk
2 cups milk
1 stick butter

This is a substitute for cup cheese. Any kind of cheese can be used. Heat the milk and add the rest of ingredients. When it has become a smooth sauce, it is finished.

Fannie S. Miller
Bird-in-Hand, PA

VEGETABLE DIP

8 oz. sour cream
1 cup real mayonaisse
1 T. dill seed
1 T. minced onion
1 T. parsley flakes
1 T. Beau Monde spice

Mix until smooth and creamy. Serve with crackers, cauliflower, celery, chips, etc.

Mrs. Emma Stutzman
Bronson, MI

DIP FOR CRACKERS, VEG. ETC.

Beat:

2 eggs
2 T. sugar
1 T. vinegar

Cook till thickened. Then beat in:

8 oz. cream cheese

A small onion if preferred or a pk. of onion soup mix.

Fannie S. Miller
Bird-in-Hand, PA

CHEESE WHIZ

1 - 2 lb. box Velveeta Cheese
1 can milnot
1 cup milk
1/2 cup oleo

Melt slowly in saucepan or double boiler. Beat with beater until smooth. Put in jars while ht and seal. Will keep. Very good.

Mary Ann Hilty
Monroe, IN

QUICK CHEESE

1 t. salt
1 qt. cottage cheese
1 1/2 T. soda
1 cup cream

Mix salt, soda and cheese together. Let stand for 2 hrs. Add cream and a little butter and melt over hot fire till smooth.

Ida Miller
Medford, WI

SWISS CHEESE

Heat milk to 90 deg. stirring all the time. Turn off heat. Put in one cheese rennet tablet (dissolved) or 2 oz. liquid rennet to 100 lb. milk, stir well, cover and let stand till it is set like jello, about 30 min. Now cut real fine both ways with long sharp knife. Heat again slowly to 114 deg. stirring all the time. Press together a handful of curds and when it breaks fairly straight it is ready to take off. Do not heat over 118 deg. Now put it in a cheese cloth and in a press and weight it down real well with bricks. Take out after 12 or 15 hr. Now put it in salt brine for 36 hrs. Then wash off in clean water and keep at about 72 deg. for several weeks, turning the cheese about every day.

Elizabeth Stutzman
Union City, PA

CHEESE WHIZ

3 boxes (2 lb.) cheese
2 cans milnot or 3 1/4 cup cream
1/2 qt. milk
1 stick oleo

Melt and mix in double boiler.

Mrs. Philip Yoder
Fairbank, IA

CHEESE BALLS

2 - 8 oz. cream cheese
8 oz. shredded med. cheddar or sharp cheese
1 T. pimentos
1 T. onion chopped fine
1 t. Worcestershire sauce
1 t. lemon juice

Roll in finely chopped nuts; cherry on top.

Harry Martins
New Holland, PA

Brownies & Bars

ZUCCHINI BROWNIES

Beat together:

4 eggs
1 1/4 cups oil
2 cups sugar

Sift together:

2 cups flour
2 t. soda
2 t. cinnamon
1 t. salt
4 T. cocoa

Add:

1 t. vanilla
1 cup nuts
3 cups shredded zucchini

Mix all together and spread on a 15" x 10" jelly roll pan. Bake at 350 deg. for 30 min. You can frost them if you desire, but we like them as they are.

Mary A. Kinsinger
Meyersdale, PA

COCONUT BARS

1 cup flour
2 t. baking powder
1 t. salt or less
1/2 cup shortening
2 cups brown sugar, firmly packed
2 eggs
2 t. vanilla
1 1/2 cups coconut
1/2 cup nuts

Mix dry ingredients together in a bowl. Melt shortening in saucepan over low heat. Remove from heat and add sugar, eggs and vanilla. Mix well and add dry ingredients, coconut and nuts. Spread in well-greased pan. Bake at 350 deg. for 25 to 30 min. Cool and cut into bars.

Joe Borntreger
Cashton, WI

The interest is too high on borrowed trouble

ZUCCHINI BARS

1/2 cup butter or oleo
1/2 cup brown sugar
1/2 cup white sugar
2 cups shredded zucchini
1 cup coconut
3/4 cup chopped nuts
2 eggs
1 t. vanilla
1 1/2 t. baking powder
1 3/4 t. flour

Cream butter and sugar until light. Add eggs. Beat in vanilla and flour sifted with baking powder. Stir in zucchini, coconut, and nuts. Spread batter in greased jelly roll pan. Bake 30-35 min. While bar are baking, make cinnamon frosting. Spread frosting over warm baked cake. Cut into bars.

Cinnamon Frosting:
1 cup powdered sugar
1 T. milk
1 1/2 T. melted butter or oleo
1 t. vanilla
1 t. cinnamon

Beat all ingredients in small bowl until smooth.

Mrs. Wilma Mast
S. Hutchinson, KS

One way to keep your friends
Is not to give them away

TRIPLE TREAT BARS

Cream together:
3/4 cup shortening
3/4 cup brown sugar
1/2 cup peanut butter
2 eggs
1 t. vanilla
1/4 cup milk

Add rest of ingredients and mix well:
1 1/2 cups flour
2 cups rolled oats
1 t. soda
1 cup chocolate chips
1/2 t. salt
1 cup chopped nuts

Bake in 10x15 in. pan at 350 deg. for 20-25 min.

Ida Miller
Medford, WI

CALIFORNIA DREAM BARS

1/4 cup brown sugar
1/2 cup melted butter
1 cup flour

Mix as for pie crust and line bottom of 8x10 in. pan, pressing flat. Bake at 350 deg. for 15 min. Take out and while still hot cover with chocolate chips.

Beat 2 eggs until light then add:

1/4 cup brown sugar
2 T. flour
1 t. salt
1/2 t. baking powder

Mix and spread over baked crust. Sprinkle peanuts and return to oven and bake 15 min.

Ida Miller
Medford, WI

It is better to fill a little place right
Than a big place wrong

ICE CREAM BARS

1/2 cup cocoa
1/2 cup sugar
1 t. vanilla
1 1/2 cups milk
6 egg yolks
1/3 cup sugar

Crumb mixture:

2 cups graham crumbs
1/4 cup sugar
1/2 cup oleo
1/4 t. salt
6 egg whites (beaten)
3/4 cup sugar
2 cups cream (whipped)

Mix cocoa, 1/2 cup sugar and milk. Bring to a boil. Add beaten egg yolks to which the 1/3 cup sugar has been added; cook until slightly thick. Cool.

Mix crumbs. Put half in bottom of cake pan. Beat 6 egg whites. Add salt and 3/4 cup sugar. Beat until stiff and glossy. Add to cocoa mixture. Also add whipped cream. Pour on top of crumbs. Sprinkle remaining crumbs on top. Freeze until firm.

Mrs. Wilma Mast
S. Hutchinson, KS

CHEWY CHOCOLATE CHIP BARS

1 cup butter or oleo (soft) — 1/2 cup sugar
1 cup brown sugar (divided) — 2 cups flour
3/4 cup chocolate chips — 3/4 cup finely chopped walnuts
1 T. water — 1 t. vanilla
2 eggs, separated — 1/2 t. salt
1 t. baking powder — 1/2 t. baking soda

Cream together butter, sugar, and 1/2 cup brown sugar until light and fluffy. Add water, vanilla and egg yolks (reserve whites in seaparate bowl). Beat for 2-3 min. Beat in flour, salt, baking powder and soda. Spread batter onto lightly greased 13x9x2" baking pan. Sprinkle on chocolate chips.

Beat egg whites until they form soft peaks; then add reserved brown sugar, blending well. Carefully spread over chips. Sprinkle with chopped nuts. Bake at 350 deg. for 35 min. or until meringue is golden brown. Cut with sharp knife while still hot. Yield 3 doz. bars.

Lucinda Hilty
Monroe, IN

MAPLE BARS

8 oz. cream cheese — 8 oz. oleo or butter
3 lbs. powdered sugar — 1 T. maple flavoring

Form in patties. Chill. Then dip in melted chocolate. Mix peanuts in rest of chocolate and put dabs on top.

Irene Wengard
Shipshewana, IN

Fools can make money
But it takes wise men to know
How to spend it

PINEAPPLE BARS

2 cups flour
1 cup sugar
1/2 cup lard
1/2 cup butter
pinch of salt
1/2 t. vanilla

Work together and line 1/2 of the mixture in a cake pan.

Topping:

1 large can pineapple, cherries, or blueberries
1 egg yolk
1 T. flour
1/2 cup sugar

Boil till thick; pour into crust and cover with remainder of crumbs. Bake at 350 deg. for 1/2 hr.

Mrs. Clarence Miller
Medford, WI

MARSHMALLOW BROWNIES

3/4 cup oleo
1 1/3 cups sugar
1 1/3 cups flour
1/2 cup chopped nuts (optinal)
2 T. cocoa
3 eggs
1/2 t. baking powder
1/3 t. balt
1 1/2 t. vanilla

Mix and bake at 350 deg. for 30 min. Take out of oven and cover with marshmallows. Put back in oven for 3 min.

Icing:

3/4 cup sugar
1/3 cup milk
1 1/2 t. vanilla
2 T. cocoa
4 T. oleo

Boil for 3 min. Let cool. Add 2 cups powdered sugar.

Cathryn Schmucker
Litchfield, MI

Getting old may be feeling your corn
More than your oats

DOUBLE CHOCOLAGE CRUNCH BARS

1/2 cup oleo
3/4 cup flour
1/4 t. salt
3/4 cup sugar
1/2 cup nuts
2 eggs
1/2 t. baking powder
1 heaping T. cocoa
1 t. vanilla

Cream oleo and sugar. Add eggs. Stir flour, nuts, cocoa, baking powder and salt. Stir into egg mixture. Spread in bottom of greased 13x9 in. pan. Bake at 350 deg. for 15 min. Sprinkle 2 cups marshmallow on top. Bake 3 min.

2 cups semi-sweet chocolate chips
1 heaping T. peanut butter
1 1/2 cup Rice Krispies

Combine chips and peanut butter; cook and stir over low heat till chocolate is melted. Stir in cereal. Spread mixture on top of cooled bars.

Chill and but in bars.

Mary Swartzentruber
Apple Creek, OH

Everybody knows that Pa is boss around here
But what Ma says goes

PEANUT BUTTER CEREAL BARS

2/3 cup sugar
1 1/2 cups chunky peanut butter
4 squares Baker's semi-sweet chocolate
2/3 cup light corn syrup
3 cups corn flakes

Combine sugar and corn syrup in saucepan; bring to a boil. Remove from heat, stir in peanut butter. Pour over cereal in bowl and mix well. Melt chocolate in saucepan over very low heat, stirring constantly. Spread over cereal mixture in pan. Let stand till chocolate is firm. Cut into 2x1 in. bars. Makes about 32 candies.

Mary Swatzentruber
Apple Creek, OH

ICE CREAM BARS

1/2 cup melted butter
2 cups graham cracker crumbs
1/2 cup sugar

Mix and press into bottom of pan.

1/4 cup cocoa
1 1/4 cup sugar
1 1/2 cups milk
1/4 t. salt
2 cups whipped cream
6 egg yolks
6 egg whites

Bring 1 cup sugar, milk and cocoa to a boil. Add beaten egg yolks with remaining 1/4 cup sugar. Boil until thickened. Cool. Beat egg whites and cream separately. Combine with cooked mixture. Pour over graham cracker layer. Freeze. You can freeze these outside. It freezes best if temperature is below zero. Variations: Instead of using a graham cracker crumb crust, use a layer of whole graham crackers on bottom and another layer on top. Also instead of cocoa, you may use 1/4 c. flour and add vanilla flavoring.

Mrs. Daniel C. Borntreger
Riceville, IA

MAPLE FROSTED SPICE BARS

2 cups flour
1 t. salt
1 cup sugar
1 t. cinnamon
1/2 cup applesauce
2 t. baking powder
1/4 t. nutmeg
1/4 t. allspice
1/4 t. soda
3/4 cup milk
2 eggs
1/2 cup nuts or raisins

Combine first nine ingredients; stir and blend well, add remaining ingredients. Spread in greased jelly roll pan. Bake at 350 deg. for 25-30 min. Cool on rack; frost. (Can cut cake through and put frosting in between.)

Maple Frosting

1 pkg. 8 oz. cream cheese
1 t. vegetable shortening
1/2 t. maple flavoring
1/2 t. vanilla
1 1/2 cups powdered sugar

Clara Hochstetter
Canton, MO

YUM YUMS BARS

2 cups flour
2 cups butter
1/2 cup brown sugar

Top part:

2 cups brown sugar
1 T. flour
1/2 t. baking powder
1 cup coconut
1/2 cup nut meat
1 t. vanilla
3 eggs, beaten
1 t. salt

Mix first 3 ingredients and press in bottom of 10x14 in. pan. Mix other ingredients and spread over bottom part. Bake at 300 deg. for 20 min. or until brown. When cool, cut in squares.

Clara Hochstetter
Canton, MO

BROWNIES

1 1/4 cups margarine
3/4 cup brown sugar
3/4 cup white sugar
5 eggs, separated
1 1/2 t. vanilla
3 cups flour
1 1/2 t. baking powder
1/2 t. soda and 1/2 t. salt
1 cup milk

Spread thin on shallow pan. Beat egg whites until fluffy and add 1 1/2 cups brown sugar. Spread on batter. 5 or 10 min. before finished baking, sprinkle with toll house bits or coconut.

Fannie Miller
Bird-in-Hand, PA

CARMEL BROWNIES

2 cups brown sugar
1 cup flour
3/8 cups shortening
1 cup chopped nuts
2 t. baking powder
1 t. salt or less
2 t. vanilla
2 eggs

Sift flour, baking powder and salt together. Melt shortening; add sugar, eggs,vanilla and dry ingredients. Mix with the nuts. Spread thinly in a well-oiled and floured pan. Bake in 350 deg oven 30 min. Cool and cut into bars.

Joe Borntreger
Cashton, WI

MUD HEN BARS

1 1/2 cups flour
1/2 cup lard
1 cup sugar
1 whole egg
2 egg yolks
1 t. baking powder
pinch of salt
Press in butter pan.
Topping:
1 cup chopped nuts
1 cup small marshmallows
1 cup chocolate chips
2 egg whites, beaten stiff
1 cup brown sugar, packed
Beat in brown sugar after egg whites are stiff. Bake 30-40 min.

Ida Miller
Medford, WI

A smooth sea never makes a skillful mariner

CHURCH WINDOWS

1 stick oleo
10 1/2 oz. pkg. chocolate chips
10 1/2 oz. pkg. miniature marshmallows
1 cup chopped nuts
coconut

Melt oleo and chocolate chips in double boiler. Cool. Add nuts and marshmallows. Put some shredded coconut on wax paper, pour mixture on coconut. Form into two rolls and cover with coconut. Chill. Slice when ready to serve.

Saloma J. Byler
Dewittville, NY

FRESH APPLE BARS

3 eggs
1 cup cooking oil
1 3/4 cups white sugar
Beat above ingredients well; then add the rest.
2 cups all-purpose flour
1/2 t. salt
1/2 t. cinnamon
1 t. soda
2 cups chopped fine fresh apples
1 cup chopped nuts
This is enough for a large cookie sheet.

Joni H. Shrock
Middlefield, OH

CRUNCHY BARS

1 cup sugar
1 cup cream
2 cups Rice Krispies
1 cup corn syrup
5 cups cornflakes
2 cups salted peanuts

Cook sugar, cream, and syrup to soft ballstage. Remove from heat and pour at once over cereal and peanuts. Mix well and pack into pan. When cook, cut into bars.

Fannie Gingerich
Ethridge, TN

EXTRA EASY FRUIT CAKE SQUARES

6 T. butter or margarine
1 1/2 cups graham cracker crumbs
1 cup shredded coconut
2 cups mixed candied fruit
1 - 14 oz. can sweetened condensed milk
1 cup chopped pitted dates
1 cup coarsely chopped walnuts

Melt butte in 15 1/2x10 1/2x1 jelly roll pan. Sprinkle graham cracker crumbs into bottom of pan, shaking pan to distribute crumbs evenly. Layer in coconut, candied fruit, dates and nuts. Press mixture down lightly with hands to level it. Pour sweetened condensed milk evenly on top. Bake in 350 deg. for 25-30 min. or until set. Cool in pan on rack. Cut into 1 1/2" squares. Makes 60.

Joni H. Shrock
Middlefield, OH

MAGIC COOKIE BARS

1/2 cup margarine
1 1/2 cups graham cracker crumbs
1 can sweetened condensed milk
1 - 6 oz. pkg. chocolate chips
1 1/3 cups coconut (if you prefer)
1 cup chopped nuts

Preheat oven to 350 deg. In 13x9 in. pan melt margarine. Mix and press into pan. Pour milk evenly over crumbs. Top evenly chocolate chips, coconut, and nuts. Bake 25-30 min. cool and cut.

Anna Mary Lapp
Quarryville, PA

CHOCOLATE ZUCCHINI BROWNIES

2 cups sugar
1 1/2 cups vegetable oil
4 eggs
4 T. cocoa
3 cups grated zucchini
1 cup nuts
2 cups flour
2 t. soda
1 t. salt
2 t. cinnamon
1 t. vanilla

Bake in sheet cake pan; frost if desired.

Mrs. Ray J. Gingerich
Fillmore, NY

CHOCOLATE REVEL BARS

1 cup butter
2 cups brown sugar
2 eggs
2 t. vanilla
2 1/2 cups flour
1 t. soda
1 t. salt
3 cups oatmeal

Spread 2/3 in pan; then filling; dot with the rest.
Filling: Melt in double boiler
12 oz. chocolate chips
1 can Eagle Brand milk
2 T. butter
1/2 t. salt
2 t. vanilla
1 cup nuts

Bake at 350 deg. for 25-30 min.

Mrs. Ray J. Gingerich
Fillmore, NY

TURTLE BARS

No. 1:
1 box Swiss or German Chocolate cake mix
1 stick melted butter or oleo
1/3 cup evaporated milk or cream

Mix and pat 1/2 of dough in 13x9 in. greased pan and bake at 350 deg. for 10 min. and cool to room temp. and add 2nd layer of:

No. 2:
14 oz. melted caramels
1/3 cup evaporated milk or cream

Then spread on top of caramel layer:
1 cup nuts
12 oz. chocolate chips

No. 3:
Take remaining dough and press flat with hands and lay on top. Bake approx. 15-20 min. longer or until dough loses its gloss. May sprinkle it with powdered sugar and cut into bars.

Mrs. Ray J. Gingerich
Fillmore, NY

EASY TIME HOLIDAY SQUARES

Cream:
1 1/2 cups sugar
4 beaten eggs
1 cup margarine
Add:
1/2 t. lemon extract or 1 t. vanilla
2 cups flour

Pour batter into greased loaf cake pan. With a spoon or such, make little wells every inch or 1 1/2 inch, fill with a dab of cherry pie filling. Bake 40 min. or less. When cool, ice with white frosting carefully so as not to deck the filling.

Mose E. Helmuth
Edgewood, IA

CHOCOLATE CHIP OATMEAL BROWNIES

2 eggs
2/3 cup white sugar
2/3 cup brown sugar
1 t. baking powder
1 t. cinnamon
1/4 t. nutmeg
2 t. vanilla
1 cup flour
2 cups quick oats
2 cups chocolate chips
pinch of salt
1 cup shortening

Combine all except for half of chocolate chips, Spread in 15x9 in. buttererd pan. Sprinkle with 1 cup chips. Bake 20 min. at 350 deg.

Mose E. Helmuth
Edgewood, IA

If you don't at first succeed
Try, try a grin!

DOUBLE CHOCOLATE CRUMBLE BARS

1 cup sugar
1/3 cup shortening
1 egg
1/2 cup sour milk
1 1/4 cups flour
1/4 cup cocoa
1 t. soda in 1/2 cup boiling water (add last)

Bake at 350 deg. until done. Melt 2 cups marshmallows on top of hot cake. Cool. Melt 1 1/2 cups choco. chips and 1/3 cup peanut butter in double boiler. Stir in 1 1/2 cups rice krispies. Spread on top of cake. Before completely chilled, cut into bars.

Mose E. Helmuth
Edgewood, IA

ICE CREAM BARS

1/2 cup melted butter
2 cups graham cracker crumbs or whole graham crackers laid on bottom and again on top
1/2 cup sugar
1/4 cup cocoa or 1/4 cup flour and vanilla
1 1/4 cups sugar
1 1/2 cups milk
1/4 t. salt
2 cups whipped cream
6 egg yolks
6 egg whites

Bring milk, flour or cocoa, and 1 cup sugar to a boil. Add beaten egg yolks with 1/4 cup sugar. Boil till thick. Cool. Beat egg whites and cream separately. Combine with cooked mixture. Put in pan with graham crackers.

Mose E. Helmuth
Edgewood, IA

GOLDEN GRAHAM'S S'MORES

3/4 cup light corn syrup
3 T. margarine or butter
1 pkg. (11.5 oz.) Nestle milk chocolate morsels
3 cups Kraft miniature marshmallows
1 t. vanilla
1 pkg. (12 oz.) golden grahams
9 cups cereal

1. Grease rectangular pan 13x9x2 in.
2. Heat syrup, margarine and morsels to boiling, stirring constantly. Remove from heat; stir in vanilla.
3. Pour over cereal in bowl; toss until coated. Fold in marshmallows, 1 cup at a time. Press in pan with buttered back of spoon. Let stand 1 hr.
4. Cut into 2" squares. Store loosely covered at room temperature up to 2 days. 24 squares.

Mrs. J. David Byler
Punxsutawney, PA

Throw mama from the train a kiss

MARSHMALLOW BARS

1/2 cup oleo
1 cup brown sugar
1 egg
1 t. vanilla
1/4 cup cocoa
1/2 cup flour
1/2 t. soda
1/2 t. salt
1/2 cup milk

Combine sugar, oleo, egg and vanilla. Add dry ingredients. Spread on greased cookie sheet. Bake at 375 deg. for 8 min. Remove from oven. Sprinkle a few miniature marshmallows over top and return to oven 1 min.

Icing:

1/3 cup butter
1 cup brown sugar
2 T. cocoa
1/4 cup milk

Combine. Boil till it forms large bubbles. Cool and add powdered sugar to thicken. Spread thinly over bars.

Mrs. J. David Byler
Punxsutawney, PA

TOFFEE BARS

1 cup brown sugar
1 stick oleo
1 cup flour
1 egg yolk
1 t. vanilla

Whip butter and add in this order—sugar, egg yolk, vanilla and flour. Bake at 350 deg. Remove from stove and put chocolate on top.

Mrs. Ray J. Gingerich
Fillmore, NY

MARSHMALLOW BARS

1/2 cup butter
1 cup brown sugar
1 egg
1 t. vanilla
1/4 cup cocoa
1/2 t. soda
1/2 t. salt
1/2 cup milk
2 cups flour
1 bag miniature marshmallows

Bake about 15 min. Then put marshmallows on till melted.

Icing:

1/3 cup butter
1 cup brown sugar
1/4 cup milk
2 T. cocoa

Cook until it forms large bubbles. Cool and add 1 cup powdered sugar.

Mrs. Ray J. Gingerich
Fillmore, NY

CHOCOLATE & BUTTERSCOTCH BROWNIES

Blend:

1/2 cup brown sugar
1/2 cup white sugar
3/4 cup margarine
3 egg yolks
1 t. vanilla

Add:

2 cups flour
1 t. baking powder
1/4 t. soda

Press in a large greased baking pan; sprinkle with: 6 oz. chocolate chips and 6 oz. butterscotch chips and 1 cup coconut on top. Beat: 3 egg whites with 1 cup brown sugar till stiff. Spread on top and bake at 300 deg. for 40 min-1 hr.

Mrs. Ray J. Gingerich
Fillmore, NY

BABE RUTH BARS

Melt:
1 cup white syrup
1 cup white sugar
Add:
1 cup peanut butter
2 heaping T. marshmallow cream
5 cups Rice Krispies

Press in 13x9 in. pan; cut in bars and dip in chocolate.

Elizabeth Mae Raber
Montgomery, IN

YUMMY CHOCOLATE SQUARES

1 lb. marshmallows
1 t. vanilla
1 pkg. semi-sweet chocolate bits
1 cup chopped nuts
3 T. oleo
1 cup Rice Krispies

Melt marshmallows, chocolate and oleo over low heat stirring constantly. Mix in rest of ingredients. Spread in well-buttered 8" pan. Cut in squares after itsets.

Elizabeth Mae Raber
Montgomery, IN

MARSHMALLOW BARS

1/2 cup shortening
1 cup sugar
1 egg
1 t. vanilla
1 1/3 cups mashed bananas
1 t. baking soda dissolved in 1 T. water
1 1/2 cups flour
1 t. baking powder

Mix in order given. Spread in greased 15x10 jelly roll pan. Bake at 350 deg. for 25-30 min. Remove from oven. Drop spoonfuls of 7 oz. jar of marshmallow creme on bars. Let stand 2 min. Spread and cool. Frost with:

2 cups powdered sugar
1 T. butter
2 T. milk
1 t. vanilla
few drops yellow food color

Mrs. Joe J. Miller
Apple Creek, OH

LISA'S CHERRY SQUARES

1/2 lb. butter or margarine
1 cup sugar
2 eggs
1 cup chopped walnuts
1 t. vanilla
2 cups flour
1 can cherry pie filling

Cream butter and sugar. Add vanilla and stir in eggs one at a time. Add nuts and mix well. Stir in flour. Spread 3/4 of the thick batter in 9x13 in. ungreased pan. Cover with pie filling. Drop remaining batter by spoonfuls on top of cherries. Spread around a little with wet knife. Bake at 350 deg. for 45 min. Let cool; cut and may be sprinkled with confectioner's sugar.

Mrs. Joe J. Miller
Apple Creek, OH

GRAHAM CRACKER BARS

Put graham crackers broken in halves in a 8x8" pan.
Cook:
2 cups sugar, brown and white
1/2 cup cream
Cook till blended; pour over crackers
Put slivered almonds on top. Bake at 350 deg. for 12 min. When completely cold, break in graham cracker halves sizes.

Ida Schrock
Haven, KS

OATMEAL BARS

1 cup butter
1 cup brown sugar
1 cup sugar, optional
1 1/2 cups flour
3 cups oatmeal
2 eggs
1 t. vanilla
1 t. soda
3/4 cup raisins, chocolate chips or nuts

Cream butter, sugar and eggs. Add remaining ingredients. Put into a large pan 12x18x1 in. or 9x13 in. and 8x8 in. Bake 20 min. at 350 deg. Combine frosting ingredients and beat to spreading consistency. Frost bars while still warm.

Frosting:
6 T. butter
1 1/2 cups powdered sugar
1 t. vanilla
a little milk

Ida Schrock
Haven, KS

To make both ends meet
Take some out of the middle

GRANDMA'S OATMEAL BARS

1 cup shortening
1 cup white sugar
1 cup brown sugar
2 eggs
1 1/2 cups flour
1 t. soda
1 t. vanilla
1/2 t. salt
3 cups quick oatmeal
cinnamon to taste

Cream shortening and sugar; add eggs and vanilla. Sift flour, soda and salt together and add with oatmeal. Bake about 30 min. in a large greased pan. Frost while warm.

Mrs. Joseph Schrock
Agusta, WI

PUMPKIN BARS

4 eggs
1 2/3 cups sugar
1 cup oil
1 6 oz. can pumpkin
2 cups flour
2 t. baking powder
2 t. cinnamon
1 t. salt
1 t. soda

Beat eggs, sugar, oil and pumpkin. Blend in dry ingredients. Spread in ungreased 15x10 pan. Bake at 350 deg. for 25-30 min. Cool before frosting.

Frosting:
3 oz. cream cheese
2 cups powdered sugar
1/2 cup oleo
1 t. vanilla

Beat together. Spread on cooled bars. Sprinkle with chopped nuts.

Mrs. Jacob Stutzman
Jeromesville, OH

Desserts

HOMEMADE DREAM WHIP

1/2 cup hot water, blended with 1 T. gelatin
Add:
2 egg yolks
1/2 cup Wesson oil

Set in refrigerator to set. This can be made in advance. When ready to use, beat 2 egg whites very stiff and add 1 t. vanilla and 1/2 cup raw sugar or honey. If you use honey, use only 1/3 cup. Beat gelatin until stiff and smooth. Add to egg whites and fold by hand. Will last for hours at room temperature. May also be frozen for ice cream.

Ida Miller
Medford, WI

CHERRY DESSERT

18 graham crackers
3 T. sugar
1/4 cup melted butter

Mix together, put in pan and press. Bake 10 min.

1 - 8 oz. cream cheese
1 cup powdered sugar

1 pkg. Dream Whip as directions on box (or about 1 cup whipping cream). Whip, then mix with cream cheese and put on top of graham cracker crust and let set. Then put one can cherry pie filling on top. Ready to eat.

Joe Borntreger
Cashton, WI

RHUBARB DUMPLINGS

2 cups flour
3/4 cup milk
3 T. lard
2 t. baking powder
dash of salt

Sift together flour, salt and baking powder and then work the shortening into this. Add milk and mix well. Roll dough into 3/4 in. rectangle and spread this with enough diced rhubarb to cover well. Sprinkle with sugar and nutmet (or cinnamon). Roll into long rectangle (as for rolls) and cut into 1 1/2-2" slices. Place in baking dish and pour Sweet Sauce over this. Bake in moderate oven until done.

Sweet Sauce
1 cup white sugar
1 heaping T. flour
1/4 t. salt

Mix well together. A 1 cup hot water, a small lump oleo, and a dash of nutmeg. Pour over dumplings. Serve with milk while warm.

Mary Ann Hilty
Monroe, IN

Happy people usually want very little
And enjoy that very much

PINEAPPLE PUDDING

1 cup pineapple juice
4 T. sugar
2 T. flour
1/2 t. salt
1 egg beaten
1 can pineapples
10 cents worth of cheese
1 cup nuts

Drain juice from pineapples, then put on stove till boiling. Mix the sugar, flour, salt and egg together. Then stir into boiling juice and cook till done. Put in pineapple and set away to cool. When ready to use, put in cheese, nuts and whipped cream.

Joe Borntreger
Cashton, WI

AUNT CLARA'S DESSERT

1 pkg. raspberry jello
1 cup boiling water
1 cup pineapple juice
1/4 cup butter
1 1/2 cups powdered sugar
2 eggs, separated
1/2 cup melted butter
1/4 cup brown sugar
16 graham crackers, crushed
1 cup drained crushed pineapple

Dissolve gelatin in boiling water. Add pineapple juice. Chill until mixture is slightly thickened. Cream 1/4 cup butter and the powdered sugar. Blend in well beaten egg yolks. Beat egg whites until stiff but not dry. Fold into creamed mixture. Combine melted butter and brown sugar with cracker crumbs. Put half of crumbs mixture in bottom of buttered 9x12" pan. Spread evenly with egg mixture. Spread pineapple over filling. Pour gelatin on top. Chill until set. Cut in squares. Top with whipped cream.

Mary A. Kinsinger
Meyersdale, PA

You must forgive someone their little faults
Or you will never get close enough
To admire their goodness

MYSTERY PUDDING

1 cup flour
1 cup sugar
1 t. soda
1/4 t. salt
1 egg
1/2 cup brown sugar
1/2 cup nuts
1 t. vanilla
1 - 16 oz. can fruit cocktail

Sift dry ingredients. Mix in bowl with egg, vanilla and undrained fruit. Pour in ungreased pan and sprinkle with nuts and brown sugar. Bake at 325 deg. for 40 min.

Joe Borntreger
Cashton, WI

SPECIAL

2 beaten egg yolks
1 cup white sugar
1/2 cup milk
Boil 1 min.
Dissolve 1 pkg. plain gelatin in 1/3 cup cold water; pour this in hot mixture. let stand till cool and kind of thick.
Add:
2 beaten egg whites
1 cup cream (whipped)
flavor
Whip all together with cooked mixture. Have ready 16 finely rolled graham crackers with 1/3 cup browned butter and some brown sugar. Mix and arrange in layers and chill.

Joe Borntreger
Cashton, WI

DONE

1 cup white flour
1 cup whole wheat flour
a little lard
1 t. soda
1 t. baking powder
3/4 cup sugar
pinch of salt
milk till a good batter
This is good for supper with milk and canned blackberries.

Enos Yoders
Park City, KY

DELICIOUS APPLE ROLLS

Beat:
2 egg
3/4 cup milk
Add:
3 T. sugar
4 1/2 T. shortening
3 t. baking powder
3 cups flour
6 apples, cut fine or amount desired.
Take 1 1/2 cup brown sugar; add water for syrup to suit your taste. Roll dough about 1/2 in., then spread with butter, sugar, cinnamon and apples. Roll and slice off and put in pans. Then pour syrup over and bake. Serve warm with milk.

Mary Swartzentruber
Apple Creek, OH

MOCHA FUDGE PUDDING

1 cup Robin Hood all-purpose flour
3/4 cup sugar
2 T. cocoa (scant)
2 t. baking powder
1/2 t. salt
1/2 cup milk
2 T. melted butter
1 t. vanilla
1/2 cup brown sugar, firmly packed
1 1/2 T. cocoa
1 cup hot strong coffee

Add flour, sugar, 2 T. cocoa, baking powder and salt. Stir well to blend. Add milk, butter and vanilla. Mix well, spread in cake pan. Combine brown sugar and 1 1/2 T. cocoa. Sprinkle evenly over batter. Pour hot coffee over batter in pan—more coffee if preferred. Bake at 350 deg. for 25-30 min.

Mary Swartzentruber
Apple Creek, OH

BROWN STONE FRONT

Mix dry:
2 cups sugar
2 cups flour
pinch of salt
2 t. soda
6 t. cocoa
Beat well:
4 eggs
2 cups cream

Add to dry mixture and beat well. Bake in a moderate oven.

Alma Yoder
Lovington, IL

BAKED CHOCOLAGE FUDGE PUDDING

Cream together:
3 T. lard
3/4 cup white sugar
Sift together:
1 cup flour
1 1/2 t. baking powder
1/2 t. salt
1/2 cup milk

Put in ungreased pan. Put nuts or raisins in. To spread on top of batter:
1 cup brown sugar
1/4 cup cocoa
1/4 cup salt

Mix together and sprinkle on top of batter. DO NOT STIR. Pour 1 1/4 cup boiling water over top of batter and all. Bake at 350 deg. for 40-45 min. cut in blocks and fix like date pudding.

Mrs. Joe J. Yoder, Lawrenceburg, TN
Mrs. Ammon A. Troyer, Ashland, OH

BROWN SUGAR DUMPLINGS

1 cup brown sugar 2 cups flour
1 1/2 t. baking powder 2 T. butter
3/4 cup milk 1 cup raisins, dates, or nuts (optional)

Drop by spoonfuls in boiling syrup made of 3/4 cup brown sugar, 3/4 cup syrup, 2 cups water, 2 T. butter. Bake. Serve with whipped cream.

Fannie Gingerich
Ethridge, TN

Of course life does not begin at 40
For the fellow who went like 60
When he was 20

APPLE SALAD DRESSING

1 egg (beaten) 1/2 cup sugar
1 T. flour or clear jell 1/2 cup water
dash of salt butter size of walnut

Heat just till it cooks before adding butter. Cool; mix 1 cup whipped cream before serving. Put diced apples and bananas (if desired) in bowl and pour dressing over top. Mix and serve.

Bertha Beiler
Loganton, PA

JELLO TAPIOCA

1 cup baby pearl tapioca 10 cups water
soak 4-6 hrs.
Cook, then add:
2 cups sugar pinch salt

Cook 10 min. or till pearls are clear. Add 3/4 cup orange jello and let cool. Before serving you may add 2 pkg. dream whip. Also orange slices may be added.

Bertha Beiler
Loganton, PA

SWEETHEART PUDDING

1/2 cup flour — 3/4 cup sugar
4 egg yolks — 1 cup milk
1 qt. milk — 2 t. vanilla
4 egg whites — 1/2 cup sugar
26 graham crackers — 2/3 cup sugar
1/4 cup butter

Combine flour, sugar (3/4 cup) and the egg yolks; gradually add 1 cup milk; beat until smooth. Add 1 qt. milk and boil. Add vanilla. Melt butter; add to crushed graham crackers mixture. Line large shallow baking pan, pressing firmly. Beat egg whites till it holds soft peaks. Add the 1/2 cup sugar. Pour cooked mixture in baking pan, cover with meringue. Top with remaining crumbs. Bake in mod. oven at 325-350 deg. for 30 min.

Mrs. Noah Wengerd, Jr.
Conewango Valley, NY

CHERRY PUDDING

2 cups flour — 3/4 cup sugar
2 eggs — 2 t. soda
2 cups cherries

Enough juice to make the dough right. A good supper cake!

Mrs. Noah Wengerd,Jr.
Conewango Valley, NY

CRAZY PUDDING

Syrup:
1 cup brown sugar — 2 cups hot water
2 T. butter

Dough:
1/2 cup white sugar — 1 cup flour
2 t. baking powder — 1/2 cup milk
1/2 cup raisins

Bring syrup to a boil. Pour syrup into a cake pan. Drop dough mixture into the syrup. Bake. Serve hot with milk.

Naomi Peachy
Little Falls, NY

DELICIOUS UNCOOKED ORANGE ICE CREAM

Beat together:
2 cups sugar
5 eggs
2 cups heavy cream
2 pkg. (4 serving size) orange jello dissolved in one cup boiling water. Add enough milk to above mixture to fill a one gallon freezer. Any other flavor jello can be used with vanilla added.

Naomi Peachy
Little Falls, NY

VANILLA ICE CREAM

8 eggs, well beaten
2 boxes instant pudding
1 cup brown sugar
1 cup white sugar
1 cup powdered sugar
Milk and cream as you wish.
Mix together cold. Fill the freezer a little more than 1/2 full. This recipe is for a 1 1/2 gal. freezer.

Mrs. Joe J. Yoder
Lawrenceburg, TN

CHOCOLATE ICE BOX PUDDING

1/2 lb. sweet chocolate (Hershey bar)
3 t. sugar
4 eggs, separated
1 t. vanilla
1/2 cup chopped nuts
1 cup whipped cream
1 pkg. vanilla wafers
Melt chocolate in double boiler, add sugar and egg yolks, cool at once. Add nuts and vanilla, fold in whipped cream and beaten egg white. Combine choc. mixture. Line bottom of dish with vanilla wafers, then choc. etc. Last top with whipped cream and nuts.

Mrs. J. David Byler
Punxsutawney, PA

They say talk is cheap
But you pay dearly for it

YUM YUM

Bottom Part: 2 cups flour
1/2 cup brown sugar 1/2 cup butter or oleo
Mix together and press firmly into a 10x14" pan.
Top Part:
3 eggs beaten 2 cups brown sugar
1/4 t. baking powder 1/2 t. salt
1 T. vanilla 1 cup chopped nuts
Bake until nice and brown on top.

Mrs. J. David Byler
Punxsutawney, PA

PINE SCOTCH PUDDING

Sift together:
3/4 cup flour 1 t. baking powder
1 t. salt 1 t. soda
Beat 2 eggs till fluffy.
Add:
1 cup sugar 1 t. vanilla
1 cup nuts 1 cup crushed pineapple
Mix all together. Bake at 350 deg. for 35 min.
Sauce:
Melt 1/4 cup butter
Add 1 T. flour, 1 cup brown sugar, 1/4 cup water, 1/4 cup pineapple juice. Boil 3 min. Add vanilla. Serve with whipped cream if desired.

Mrs. J. David Byler
Punxsutawney, PA

BASIC VANILLA ICE CREAM

4 T. unflavored gelatin 6 cups milk
3 cups sugar 1/4 t. salt
10 eggs 3 qt. light cream and milk
2 (3 3/4 oz.) pkg. instant pudding mix 2 T. vanilla
Soften gelatin in 1 cup cold milk; scald 3 cups milk and stir into gelatin until it dissolves. Add sugar and salt, stirring till dissolved. Add remaining 2 cups milk. Beat eggs at high speed; add light cream, pudding mix, vanilla, then gelatin mixture. Mix well.

Mrs. Philip Yoder
Fairbank, IA

FUDGE PUDDING

1 1/4 cup sugar — 2 T. cocoa
2 cups flour — 1/2 t. salt
4 t. baking powder — 1 cup milk
4 T. shortening — 1 cup chopped nuts, if desired

Mix all together; put in pan 9x12 inches.

Mix:

1 1/2 cups sugar — 4 T. cocoa

Sprinkle on top of dough; pour 2 3/4 cups boiling water over it. Bake 45-50 min.

Mrs. Clarence Miller
Medford, WI

RHUBARB DESSERT

First layer: Crumble together

1/2 cup butter — 1 cup flour
2 T. sugar

Press in cake pan 9x13 in. Bake 10 min. at 350 deg.

Second layer:

5 cups rhubarb, cut fine — 6 egg yolks
4 T. flour — 1 cup cream
2 cups sugar — 1/4 t. salt

Put sugar and cream together, then eggs. Mix and pour on top of baked crust. Bake again at 350 deg. 40-45 min. or until firm.

Third layer:

Beat 6 egg whites; add 12 T. sugar, 2 at a time. Beat well. Add 2 t. vanilla and a little salt. Put this on top of baked custard filling and sprinkle with coconut. Bake again until brown.

Mrs. Clarence Miller
Medford, WI

BAKED APPLE AND GRAHAM CRACKER PUDDING

12 graham crackers — 8 apples, sliced
1/2 cup raisins — 1 1/2 cups sugar
2 cups thin cream

Put layers of apples, sugar, raisins and cracker crumbs in baking dish and pour cream over it. Bake in oven.

Mrs. Clarence Miller
Medford, WI

COTTAGE PUDDING

1 cup sugar
1 egg
3 T. butter
1 t. vanilla
2/3 cup milk
2 1/2 t. baking powder
1 1/2 cups flour

Mix in order given. Beat well. Bake at 350 deg. till done.
Serve with Hote Sauce:

1/2 cup butter
3 T. flour browned in heavy pan.

Add water to desired thickness, stirring to dissolve lumps. Remove from heat and add:

1 cup sugar
1 t. vanilla

Lydiann J. Bricker
Panama, NY

PISTACHIO FRUIT SALAD

1 box pistachio pudding
1 - 6 oz. can crushed pineapple
1 - 6 oz. can fruit cocktail - drained
1 bowl Cool Whip
2 cups marshmallows

Mix pudding according to directions. Fold in the remaining ingredients. Chill before serving.

Lydiann J. Bricker
Panama, NY

BROWN SUGAR DUMPLING

3/4 cup milk
1 cup sugar
1 t. butter
1 1/2 t. baking powder
2 cups flour
1 cup raisins
1 cup nuts
1 cup dates

Syrup:

2 cups brown sugar
2 cups hot water
1 T. butter

Mix above ingredients and drop into boiling syrup. Bake 20 min. Serve with whipped cream.

Saloma J. Byler
Dewittville, NY

CHERRY DANISH

1 1/2 cups sugar
1 cup oleo
4 eggs
1 t. vanilla
3 cups flour
1 t. almond extract
1 1/2 t. baking powder
1 can cherry pie filling

Mix all ingredients except pie filling. Spread 3/4 of batter on cookie sheet. Spread pie filling on top. Drop remaining batter by teaspoon on cherry pie filling. Bake at 350 deg. for 30 min. Drizzle glaze on cherry danish.

Glaze:
1 cup 10X sugar
1 to 2 T. milk

Saloma Petersheim
Mifflintown, PA

You can increase face value with a smile

TAPIOCA PUDDING

4 egg whites
1 cup sugar
1 t. vanilla
1/2 t. salt
4 egg yolks
8 cups milk
3/4 cup tapioca

Boil milk. Add the rest of ingredients except egg whites. Boil 3 min. Then add egg whites.

Alma Yoder
Lovington, IL

RICE KRISPIE ICE CREAM TOPPING

3 1/3 cups Rice Krispies
1 cup coconut
1 stick margarine
1 cup chopped nuts
1 cup brown sugar

Melt margarine in a bowl; mix in remaining ingredients. Spread in a pan; brown in oven. Serve sprinkled over ice cream.

Lydiann J. Bricker
Panama, NY

FLUFFY MINUTE TAPIOCA PUDDING

Cook together until thickened:

1/3 cup sugar
1/8 t. salt
3 T. tapioca
1 egg yolk
2 cups milk

Beat 1 egg white. Slowly add 2 T. sugar while beating egg white rapidly. Add to tapioca mixture. (Crushed pineapples, nuts, and bananas may also be added, or put in layers with graham crackers.)

Mrs. Daniel C. Borntreger
Riceville, IA

CHOCOLATE CHIP PUDDING

24 large marshmallows or 240 small
1/2 cup milk
1/2 pkg. chocolate chips, ground in nut chopper
1 cup cream, whipped
1/2 t. vanilla

Heat marshmallows with milk in top of double boiler until melted. Fold in whipped cream, vanilla and ground chocolate chips. Pour into graham cracker crust and freeze. Also good chilled inteasd of frozen.

Mrs. Daniel C. Borntreger
Riceville, IA

DAIRY QUEEN ICE CREAM

Soak 2 T. or 2 envelopes unflavored gelatin in 1/2 cup cold water. Heat 4 cups whole milk until hot, but not boiling. Remove from heat. Add gelatin mixture, 2 cups sugar, 2 t. vanilla and 1 t. salt. Cool. Add 3 cups cream or 1 can evaporated milk. Put in cold place to chill 5-6 hours before freezing. Fruit may be added if desired. Makes 1 gallon.

Catherine Swarey, Belleville, PA
Mrs. Ammon A. Troyer, Ashland, OH

A cheerful heart and a smiling face
Put sunshine in the darkest place

CHERRY DELIGHT

2 cups graham cracker crumbs
1/2 cup melted oleo or butter
1 T. powdered sugar

Mix all in a flat 9x13 in. casserole dish; set in a cool place for 15 min.

Filling:

1 box Dream Whip Caream (1 1/4 cup cream can be used)
1 - 8 oz. pkg. cream cheese
1/2 cup powdered sugar
1 t. vanilla

Mix together and spread on graham crust; next add cherry filling and chill. Put whipped cream on top. Can also use other fruit filling to suit taste.

Clara Hochstetter
Canton, MO

If more husbands were self-starters
Less wives would be cranks

DELICIOUS EASY ICE CREAM BARA

2 cups cream
6 eggs (separated)
1 cup sugar

Beat cream, egg yolks, and egg whites separately. Then mix together with 1 cup sugar. Drop mixture onto graham crackers. Top with another layer of graham crackers. Freeze in freezer or set out in very cold weather. Instant pudding may also be used. Makes a large amount.

Mrs. Daniel Borntreger, Riceville, IA
Catherine Swarey, Belleville, PA

STEAMED GRAHAM PUDDING

4 cups whole wheat flour
1 cup raisins
1 cup sugar
2 cups sweet milk
2 t. soda
4 t. molasses
1 t. salt

Steam 1 hr. Don't lift lid. Good hot with milk.

Martha Hostetler
Fort Plain, NY

STRAWBERRY JELLO MOLD

1 large pkg. strawberry jello
2 cups boiling water
2 cans frozen strawberries thawed with juice
1 - 4 oz. can crushed pineapple (drained)
1/2 cup chopped nuts
1 pt. sour cream

Dissolve jello in boiling water; add strawberries, pineapple and nuts. Pour 1/2 of mixture into 9x9 in. pan or mold. Let set until firm, about 1 1/2 hrs. Spread sour cream over jello mixture; pour rest of jello over sour cream. Let set.

Joni H. Schrock
Middlefield, OH

CREAMY LIME PINEAPPLE SALAD MOLD

1 - 3 oz. pkg. lime jello
1 cup boiling wate
1/2 pt. sour cream
1 cup crushed pineapples with syrup
1/2 cup chopped nuts
12 maraschino cherries (halved)

Dissolve jello in boiling water; refrigerate until partially set. Fold in sour cream, fruits and nuts. Chill until firm.

Joni H. Schrock
Middlefield, OH

Some people create a vacuum in their heads
By overworking the built -in blower attachment

PINEAPPLE ANGEL DELIGHT

1 envelope plain gelatin
1/2 cup cold water
1/2 cup boiling water
3/4 cup sugar
1 cup crushed pineapple
1 pt. whipping cream
chopped pecans
angel food cake (broken in pieces)

Dissolve gelatin in cold water. Stir in boiling water, sugar and pineapple. Chill until jelled. Whip cream. Fold in pineapple mixture. Pour over layers of cake. Sprinkle with nuts. Chill overnight.

Mrs. Wilma Mast
S. Hutchinson, KS

ORANGE PUDDING

3 cups orange juice
1/3-1/2 cups heaping cornstarch (mix with water)
Heat orange juice. Add 1/2 cup sugar and cornstarch and cook. Beat 2 egg yolks. Add a bit of hot pudding to yolks, then add to rest of pudding. Boil. Add a dab of butter. Cool.
Add 8 oz. whipped topping, orange chunks, bananas, coconut and nuts.

Mrs. Wilma Mast
S. Hutchinson, KS

SUNBURST ORANGE JELLO

1 - 6 oz. pkg. orange jello
1 pt. small curd cottage cheese
1 #2 can crushed pineapple (drained)
1 large carton Cool Whip

Prepare jello according to package directions. Pineapple juice can be substituted for cold water. Cool. Add cottage cheese; mix well; add pineapple and fold in Cool Whip. Chill until firm.

Joni H. Schrock
Middlefield, OH

COTTAGE CHEESE DESSERT

1 - 1 lb. box cottage cheese
1 can crushed pineapple, drained
1 - 3 oz. box orange jello
1 small whipped cream

Mrs. Emma Stutzman
Bronson, MI

APPLE CRUSPET

1 qt. apples, sliced
3/4 cup sugar
1 cup flour
1/2 cup ater
3/4 cup brown sugar
5 T. butter

Peel and slice the apples, and pour the water over them. Mix the other ingredients as for pie crust and pour over apples and water. Do not stir together. Bake in a shallow pan 45 min. When cool, cut in squares and serve with ice cream or whipped cream.

Mrs. Emma Stutzman
Bronson, MI

RHUBARB CRUNCH

Syrup:
1 cup white sugar
1 cup water
2 T. cornstarch

Crunch:
1 cup flour
3/4 cup oatmeal
1 cup brown sugar
1 1/2 cups butter
1 t. cinnamon

Add 3 cups rhubarb. Put half of crunch in bottom of 9x9 in. pan. Then put rhubarb in. Pour syrup over this. Add rest of crumbs on top. Bake at 350 deg. for 1 hr. This is also good with apples.

Alma Yoder
Lovington, IL

BROWNIE PUDDING

2 cups sifted flour
4 t. baking powder
1 t. salt
1 cup white sugar
1 cup chopped nuts
2 T. cocoa
1 cup milk
4 T. melted shortening
2 t. vanilla

Sift flour, baking powder, salt, sugar and cocoa. Add milk, shortening and vanilla. Mix until smooth. Add nuts and pour in a greased casserole.

Syrup:
1 cup brown sugar
1 1/2 cups boiling water
1 T. cocoa

Sprinkle over batter. Pour boiling water over and bake. Serve with milk or whipped cream.

Mrs. Jacob Stutzman
Jeromesville, OH

FRUIT PUDDING

1 cup fruit - fill with juice or water
1 cup flour
3/4 cup sugar
2 eggs
1 t. soda
2 t. vinegar

Mix all together. Put in 8x8 in. pan. Bake at 350 deg. for 45 min.-1 hr. or till done.

Ida Schrock
Haven, KS

COCONUT PUDDING

4 cups milk, heated, not boiling. Add beaten yolks of 3 eggs, 2/3 cup sugar; bring to a boil. Remove from heat and add 2 cups coarsely crushed soda crackers, 1 cup coconut. Beat whites of eggs stiff, add sugar and vanilla to taste; spread on top while other mixture is hot, then brown in oven. Best when eaten same day pudding is made, when cool.

Martha Hostetler
Fort Plain, NY

FLUFFY PUDDING

Separate one egg; beat white till foamy. Measure 1/3 cup sugar, gradually add 2 T. to whites, beat to soft peaks. Mix rest of sugar, egg yolk, 3 T. tapioca, 1/8 t. salt and 2 cups milk. Bring to full boil in double boiler. Very slowly add to the beaten white, stirring rapidly to blend. Add 3/4 t. vanilla. Cool 20 min., then beat it well.

Sadie Miller
Fort Plain, NY

ICE CREAM

3 pt. whole milk
2/3 cup flour
1 cup sugar

Heat milk, Stir up flour and sugar with a little milk. Add to hot milk and stir till itgets a little thick; do not boil.

Beat hard 6 eggs, 1 cup sugar. Add 1 more cup sugar, beat again. Add 3 cups cream, vanilla and enough milk for a 6 qt. freezer. A little karo instead of all sugar makes it good if cream isn't plenty.

Fannie Gingerich
Ethridge, TN

YOU'RE LUCKY IF THERE'S ANY LEFT PUDDING

2 cups flour
2 sticks oleo
1 cup finely chopped nuts

Mix together and press into ungreased loaf pan like graham crackers. Bake at 350 deg. until light brown. Cool completely.

Mix:
1 - 8 oz. pdg. cream cheese (room temp.)
1 cup confectioner's sugar
1 bowl whipped cream (Cool Whip)

Spread on crust. Mix 3 pkg. instant pudding, any flavor, with 4 1/2 cups milk. Spread on top. Top with large carton whipped cream and sprinkle with chopped nuts. Chill. Lemon pudding is best.

Mrs. Ammon A. Troyer
Ashland, OH

PINK FLUFF

1 - 20 oz. can crushed pineapple
1 - 13 oz. can evaporated milk
1/2 cup sugar
3 oz. pkg. strawberry jello
8 oz. cream cheese

Boil crushed pineapple and sugar slowly for 5 min. Add jello (dry) mix until dissolved. Cool till it starts to set. Beat cream cheese and milk until fluffy. Fold in pineapple and jello mixture. Chill until firm. Fills a 9x13 in. pan. Can be served as a salad with lettuce leaf or a dessert. Good on crushed brown crackers.

Mrs. Ammon A. Troyer
Ashland, OH

CHOCOLATE PUDDING

1 cup flour
1 cup dark corn syrup
1/4 t. salt
2 T. melted butter
2 t. baking powder
1/2 cup chopped nuts
1/4 cup milk
1 1/2 T. cocoa
1/2 t. vanilla

Mix together and put in greased baking pan. Combine 3/4 cup brown sugar and 4 T. cocoa. Put on top of first mixture. Then pour 1 cup hot water over both mixtures in pan. Bake.

Mrs. Daniel C. Borntreger
Riceville, IA

FRUIT DIP

1 can Eagle Brand milk
8 oz. Cool Whip
6 oz. pink lemonade
Eagle Brand Milk:
1 cup, plus 2 T. dry milk
1/2 cup warm water
3/4 cup sugar

Mix milk and water. Stir sugar to dissolve. This recipe equals 1 can Eagle Brand Milk.

Mrs. Wilma Mast
South Hutchinson, KS

WHITE HOUSE PUDDING

2 pkg. plain gelatin
2 cups milk
1 1/2 cups sugar
4 eggs, separated
2 cups whipping cream
1 lb. vanilla wafers or graham crackers, crushed
1/4 cup margarine or butter

Dissolve gelatin in 1/2 cup cold milk. Scald remaining milk. Combine sugar and beaten egg yolks. Add to scalded milk, stirring constantly until slightly thickened. Add gelatin mixture. Cool. Fold whipped cream and stiffly beaten egg whites into cold gelatin mixture. Mix margarine with crumbs. Cover bottom of pan with half of crumbs. Top with gelatin mixture and then the remaining crumbs. Chill. Cut into squares and top each with whipped cream and a maraschino cherry.

Mrs. Daniel C. Borntreger
Riceville, IA

HEAVENLY CREME

Crush: 4 cups corn flakes
1 T. sugar
1/4 cup soft butter
Combine first 3 things and save 1/4 for on top.
1 pkg. Cool Whip
1/2 cup sugar
2 eggs

Mrs. Ray J. Gingerich
Fillmore, NY

PARADISE PUDDING

Mix 1 box powdered sugar with pineapple juice or butter and spread over finely ground graham crackers.
Mix 2 boxes lucky whip till stiff.
Add miniature marshmallows and a can of drained crushed pineapples and vanilla. Spread on top of powdered sugar. If desired, sprinkle nuts over top.

Mrs. Ray J. Gingerich
Fillmore, NY

GLORIFIED RICE

2 cups boiled rice, chilled
1 - 8 oz. can crushed pineapple (drained)
3/4 cup sugar
1 - 3 oz. pkg. strawberry jello
1 cup cream, whipped

Dissolve jello in hot drained pineapple juice and add water to make 1 pt. Add sugar when mixture begins to thicken. Whip until pale pine. Fold in pineapple rice and whipped cream. Mold in cups. Serve with whipped cream topped with cherry.

Mrs. Dan J. Troyer
Mercer, PA

UPSIDE DOWN DATE PUDDING

1 cup pitted dates, cut up
1 cup boiling water
1 1/2 cups flour
1/2 t. salt
1 egg
2 T. butter
1/2 cup each of white and brown sugar
1 t. soda
1/2 t. baking powder
1 cup chopped walnuts
1 recipe brown sugar sauce

Combine dates and water. Blend sugars, egg and butter. Sift together dry ingredients. Add to sugar mixture. Pour into baking dish.
Top with Brown Sugar Sauce:
Combine:
1 1/2 cups brown sugar
1 T. butter
1 1/2 cups boiling water

Bake in 375 deg. oven for 40 min. Cut in squares; invert on plates. Serve warm with whipped cream. Can be made day before.

Barbara Schrock
Spartansburg, PA

CORNFLAKE PUDDING

Beat 2 eggs
Add:
1 t. vanilla — 1 1/2 cups sugar
8 oz. cream cheese softened
Cream real well and fold in 8 oz. Cool Whip.
Crush 1 1/2 cups cornflakes; add 1/4 cup butter and 1/2 cup sugar. Layer bottom of serving bowl with crumbs; then layer of pudding mixture; layer of crumbs; etc., ending with layer of crumbs on top.

Barbara Schrock
Spartansburg, PA

FRUIT PIZZA

Layer 1: Crust:
1/2 cup butter (softened) — 1/4 cup brown sugar
1/4 cup chopped nuts — 1 cup flour
1/4 cup quick oats
Bake at 375 deg. for 10-15 min.
Layer 2: Combine:
8 oz. cream cheese — 5 oz. Cool Whip
Put on top of crust.
Layer 3: Arrange fruits in an interesting pattern...Kiwi, mandarin oranges, grapes, pineapples, peaches (your choice).
Layer 4: Sauce: Stir together:
1/2 cup sugar — dash of salt
1 T. clear jell or cornstarch — 1/2 cup orange juice
2 T. lemon juice — 1/4 cup water
Boil till thickened; remove from heat and add 1/2 t. orange peel (do not omit). Cool before spooning over fruit.

Fannie S. Miller
Bird-in-Hand, PA

PEACH CRUNCH

1 qt. peaches
1 T. sugar
1 T. flour
1/2 cup peach juice
1 cup sugar
1 cup flour
2 t. baking powder
1/2 t. salt
2 T. oleo
1 egg, beaten

Place peaches in baking dish. Mix 1 T. sugar, 1 T. flour and 1/2 cup peach juice and pour over peaches. Combine the rest of ingredients and sprinkle over the peach mixture. Bake at 400 deg. till browned. Serve with milk.

Miss Sara Shetler
Glasgow, KY

APPLE CRISP

8 cups apples (sliced)
1 1/2 cups brown sugar
1 1/2 cups flour
1 cup oleo
2 cups oatmeal
1 t. salt
cinnamon

Line an oblong cake pan with apple slices. Sprinkle with cinnamon. Mix all the ingredients together and pour over apples. Bake 40 min. at 350 deg. or until done.

Miss Sara Shetler
Glasgow, KY

PINEAPPLE CHEESE PUDDING

1 cup pineapple juice
1/4 cup sugar
2 T. flour
1 egg

Beat egg, add pineapple juice. Mix sugar and flour and blend with juice; heat to boiling. Cool.

Add:

1/2 cup cheese
1/2 cup nut meats
pineapple chunks from which you have drained the juice
1 cup cream, whipped

Miss Sara Shetler
Glasgow, KY

Middle age is youth gone to waist

KOOL-AID DESSERT

1 large pkg. or 4 scoops Kool Aid 1 cup sugar
2 qts. water 4 heaping T. clear jell
Cook till clear and add:
1 small pkg. or 1/2 cup jello same flavor as Kool Aid. When cool, add fruit. If fruit has juice, use it to mix clear jell. Can be used for Danish Dessert.

Esther Fisher
Millersburg, PA

A cheerful heart and a smiling face
Put sunshine in the darkest place

ORANGE SHERBERT

1 large pkg. orange jell 3 3/4 cups hot water
Mix and cool till warm and add:
1 pt. orange sherbert 1 med. box Cool Whip
1/2 pkg. small marshmallows
Mix all together; pour in mold and chill till firm.

Esther Fisher
Millersburg, PA

LEMON LUSH

1 cup flour 1/2 cup margarine (melted and cooled)
1/2 cup chopped nuts
Mix and pat in baking pan. Bake at 350 deg. for 20 min.
Mix together:
9 oz. cream cheese 1/2 cup 10X sugar
1 1/2 cups Cool Whip
Mix and spread over cooled crust.
Mix:
2 pkg. lemon instant pudding 3 cups milk
Spread over creamed cheese mixture. If preferred, top with Cool Whip. Hint: When using instant pudding, heat the molk and cool it before mixing with pudding. It does not have that aftertaste.

Fannie S. Miller
Bird-in-Hand, PA

FLUFFY TAPIOCA PUDDING

Heat 4 cups milk and 1 cup sugar
Mix:
6 T. minute tapioca
2 egg yolks
1 cup milk

Add to hot milk; bring to a good boil. Add a pinch of salt, beat the 2 egg whites; slowly fold tapioca into egg whites. Stir a few times while cooling. May add sliced bananas or crushed, drained pineapples or chopped nuts or chocolate chips, or plain whipped cream.

Martha Mast
Revere, MO

APRICOT DELIGHT

1/2 lb. apricots
1 qt. water
pinch of salt
1 cup sugar
4 rounded T. tapioca
1 pkg. 6 oz. orange jello

Cook apricots until tender to mash. Take 1 qt. water, bring to a boil, add sugar and tapioca. Boil till clear. Put in jello; add apricots and mix. Cool; top with whipped cream.

Mrs. Joe . Miller
Apple Creek, OH

HOR XEMWL SUMPLINFA

Make a sauce of:
1 T. butter
1 1/2 cups boiling water
1/8 t. salt
1 cup brown sugar

Put all in a kettle and let come to a boil while preparing dough.
Dumplings:
1 1/4 cups flour
1 1/2 t. baking powder
1/4 cup sugar
1/8 t. salt
1 T. butter
1/2 cup milk
1/2 t. vanilla

Sift dry ingredients together; cut in butter; add milk, vanilla and mix. Drop by round spoonfuls in boiling sauce. Boil lightly over low heat for 10 min. without removing cover.

Mrs. Joseph Schrock
Agusta, WI

VERY GOOD FRUIT ICE CREAM

5 large ripe bananas (mashed)
4 oranges (cut in small chunks and add a little sugar and let set till the rest is mixed)
1 - 20 oz. can crushed pineapples
Approximately 6 cups cream and 6 cups milk
2 cups sugar 1/2 t. salt
3 T. vanilla
Use 1 1/2 gal. freezer.

Mrs. Ray J. Gingerich
Fillmore, NY

ANGEL FOOD CAKE DESSERT

1 pkg. raspberry jello 2 cups water
1 cup sugar 2 pt. cream or millnot
2 cups crushed pineapples 12 marshmallows
1 angel food cake
Chill mixture till it starts to thicken; melt marshmallows in jello. Slice cake in a big bowl and arrange in layers. Pour jello mixture over top. Strawberries can be used instead of pineapples. Chill in refrigerator.

Alma Yoder
Lovington, IL

There is no food value in wild oats

FRUIT COBBLER

1 T. shortening 1 cup sugar
1 egg beaten 1 cup flour
1 t. baking powder pinch of salt
4 cups undrained fruit, sweetened to taste
Put fruit on bottom of pan. Blend other ingredients and put crumbs on top of fruit. Bake at 400 deg. for 20-25 min. in an 8x8 in. pan. Good with ice cream or with milk and sugar.

Mrs. Amos W. Yoder
Jamesport, MO

LEMON DESSERT

Beat 8 egg whites till frothy; add 1 t. cream of tartar. Beat stiff. Gradually add 1 1/2 cups sugar. Spread in 9x13" pan. Bake at 250 deg. for 20 min., then 300 deg. for 40 min. Cool.
Filling:
Beat 8 yolks till thick; gradually add 1 cup sugar, juice of 1 lemon, grated rind of 1 lemon. Cook over hot water till thick. Cool. Whip 2 cups of cream. Spread 1/2 over meringue. Spread lemon mixture over cream, then top with remaining cream. Refrigerate 24 hrs.

Lydiann J. Bricker
Panama, NY

RHUBARB PIZZA

2 cups flour
1 t. baking powder
1/2 t. salt
1/2 cup sugar
5 T. milk
2 eggs

Mix all together. Spread over bottom and sides of pan. Spread 3 cups chopped rhubarb over top. Sprinkle with 1 1/2 T. strawberry jello. Melt 1/2 cup butter and 1 cup sugar. Pour over the top. Bake 40 min. at 350 deg. Serve warm with milk.

Catherine Swarey
Belleville, PA

BAKED APPLE DUMPLINGS

1 cup flour
1 t. baking powder
pinch of salt
butter size of an egg
milk to make soft dough

Sift flour, baking powder and salt. Add butter and milk to make dough. This is enough for 3 apples. Roll out dough. Cut in circles. Place apples inside to make dumplings. Set in pan. Pour over dumplings:
Sauce: 1/2 cup sugar, 1 T. butter, 1 cup boiling water.
Bake at 350 deg. for 1 hr. Serve warm with milk.

Catherine Swarey
Belleville, PA

RASPBERRIES WITH KNEPP

Bring to a boil:
2 cups whole raspberries or juice
3/4 cup sugar
2 cups water
Mix:
1 cup flour
5 t. baking powder
3 t. sugar
1/4 t. salt
1 cup milk

Mix 3 level T. cornstarch with enough water to make a smooth sauce. Stir into the hot raspberry mixture and bring to a boil. Drop the dough part by spoonful into the boiling rasp. mixture. Cover with a tight lid and let boil slowly for 20 min. Do not uncover during the boiling period. Serve with milk. Other fruit may be used.

Mrs. Noah Wengerd, Jr.
Conewango Valley, NY

RHUBARB BUTTER CRUNCH

3 cups diced rhubarb
1 cup white sugar
3 T. blour
1 cup brown sugar
1 cup rolled oats
1 1/2 cups flour
3/4 cup butter

Combine white sugar, rhubarb and 3 T. flour and place in a baking dish. Combine brown sugar, rolled oats and 1 1/2 cups flour. Mix in butter and sprinkle over rhubarb mixture.

Mrs. Henry Stutzman
Conewango Valley, NY

BAKED APPLES

12 apples
3 T. cornstarch
1 1/2 cups sugar
1 t. cinnamon
1/2 t. salt
2 cups boiling water

Peel and slice apples and place in a large greased baking dish. Combine remaining ingredients and cook until clear. Pour over apples and bake in a moderate oven. Serve either hot or cold with whipped cream.

Mrs. Daniel C. Borntreger
Riceville, IA

RHUBARB CRUNCH

Mix until crumbly:

1 cup flour
3/4 cup uncooked oatmeal
1/2 cup melted margarine
1 cup brown sugar
1 t. cinnamon

Press half of crumbs in a greased 9 in. baking pan. Cover with 4 cups diced rhubarb.

Combine the following and cook until thick and clear:

1 cup sugar
2 T. cornstarch
1 cup water
1 t. vanilla

Pour over rhubarb and top with remaining crumbs. Bake at 350 deg. for 1 hr.

Louella Borntrager
Sugar Creek, OH

STRAWBERRY ANGEL FOOD CAKE DESSERT

1 angel food cake
3 qts. fresh strawberries
whipped cream

Mix together:

2 cups water
2 cups sugar
4 T. corn syrup
dash of salt

Bring to boil and thicken with 6 T. clear jel mixed with water. Remove from heat; add 1 pkg. strawberry Kool Aid. Cool. Alternate cake, strawberries and sauce in a large bowl. Cover with whipped cream. chill and serve.

Cathryn Schmucker
Litchfield, MI

To get his wealth
He spends his health
And then with might and main
he turns around and spends his wealth
To get his health

STRAWBERRY TAPIOCA

6 cups boiling water
2/3 cup tapioca
pinch of salt

Heat water to boiling; add tapioca and salt. Boil about 2 min. Remove from heat; cover and let stand until tapioca looks clear. Add:

1 cup sugar
1 small box strawberry jello (or 1/2 cup)
1 pkg. strawberry Kool-aid

Before serving, add fresh or canned strawberries and whipped cream.

Cathryn Schmucker
Litchfield, MI

ICE CREAM SANDWICHES

3 eggs
1 cup cream
1/2 cup sugar

Separate eggs; beat egg whites until stiff; add vanilla; fold in beaten up cream and add yolk mixture.

Mrs. Noah Wengerd, Jr.
Conewango Valley, NY

DANISH DESSERT

1 1/2 T. cornstarch
1 1/2 cups juice or water
1/4 t. salt
1/4 cup jello (any flavor)
1/3 cup white sugar

Heat to boiling - 1 cup liquid. Combine jello, sugar and cornstarch. Make a paste with 1/2 cup liquid. Stir into boiling juice until thick and clear. Cook a few minutes and pour over mixture of fruit and chill well. Fresh or frozen strawberries are especially good.

Lydia Stoltzfus
Bloomsburg, PA

PEACH MARMALADE

5 cups peaches, sliced and chopped
1 can crushed pineapples
6 cups sugar

Cook together 15 minutes and add 3/4 cup or 1 large box orange or other flavor jello. Pour in jars and seal.

Lydia Stoltzfus
Bloomsburg, PA

BROKEN GLASS

1 pkg. lime jello
1 pkg. cherry jello
1 pkg. orange jello

Dissolve each kind separately in 1 cup hot water. Add 1/2 cup cold water; chill till firm. Cut into 1/2 in. cubes.

Now soften 2 T. plain gelatin in 1/2 cup cold water. Add 1 cup hot water to dissolve. Put aside till it starts to thicken. Cook 1 cup pineapple juice with 3 T. sugar. Cool. Beat 1 pint whipping cream. Mix plain gelatin, pineapple juice, whipped cream and 3 jello flavors together.

Crush 24 graham crackers; mix with 1/4 cup butter. Add 3 T. sugar. Put in pan, toast 15 min. at 250 deg. Cool. Take out 1/2 cup to put on top.

Martha Mast
Revere, MO

BAKED GRAHAM PUDDING

Mix together:

2 eggs
1 1/2 cups sugar
2 cups sour milk
2 t. soda
1/2 t. salt
2 cups raisins or dates
2 cups whole wheat flour
2 cups white flour

Bake at 350 deg.

Martha Mast
Revere, MO

GRAHAM PUDDING

1 cup graham flour
1 cup white flour
1 cup raisins
1 cup milk
1/4 cup molasses
1/4 cup sugar
1/2 t. cinnamon
1 t. soda
1 egg
salt

Steam 1 hr. Serve with milk.

Fannie Gingerich
Ethridge, TN

DAIRY QUEEN ICE CREAM

Soak 2 pkgs. Knox gelatin in 1/2 cup cold water. Heat 4 cups milk to hot (not boiling). Remove and add gelatin and 2 cups white sugar, 2 t. vanilla and 1 t. salt.

Set aside and cool. When cooled, add 3 cups cream or some evaporated milk instead of all cream. Put in ice box to chill 5 or 6 hrs. Before freezing, add 2 eggs beaten. If you wish, add jello. Makes 1 gal. This ice cream is easy to freeze in a bowl if no freezer.

Mrs. Joe J. Yoder
Lawrenceburg, TN

APPLE GOODIES

3/4 cup sugar
1/2 t. cinnamon
1/8 t. salt
4 T. flour
4 cups sliced apples or more

Topping for above:

1/2 cup oatmeal
1/2 cup brown sugar
1/2 cup flour
1/8 t. soda
1/8 t. salt
1/4 cup butter

Bake.

Mrs. Samuel D. Beachy
Clark, MO

APPLE ROLLS

2 cups flour
4 t. baking powder
2 T. sugar
3/4 cup milk
2 T. lard
1/2 t. salt

Mix and roll out. Cut 4 or more apples fine and sprinkle over dough; add cinnamon if desired. Roll together and cut in pieces and put in pans.

Cook the following syrup 5 min. and pour over rolls:

1 cup brown sugar
1/2 cup white sugar
2 cups water

Bake. Eat with milk.

Mrs. Samuel D. Beachy
Clark, MO

CHOCOLATE DUMPLINGS

1 1/2 cups water | 1 T. butter
salt | 1 cup sugar
3 T. flour | vanilla

Heat water to boiling. Mix other ingredients and add to boiling water. Cook till thick. Set off flames until ready for dumplings to go in.

Dumplings:

1/2 cup flour | 1/2 t. baking powder
1 T. butter | 2 T. milk
2 T. sugar | 1/2 t. salt
1 egg | vanilla

Put flour, baking powder, salt and sugar in a bowl and work butter in it. Add egg, vanilla and milk. Have the syrup boil and drop in the dumplings by spoonfuls. Cover and cook for 20 minutes. Do not stir. Serve while still hot with milk or cream or chill and top with whipped cream.

Mrs. Samuel D. Beachy
Clark, MO

BROWN BETTY

2 1/2 cups oats | 2 1/2 cups flour
1 1/2 cups sugar | 1 cup lard (scant)
2 t. soda | 2 t. salt

Mix this altogether. Put 1/2 of it in; then put 3 cups diced apples on; then put the rest of crumbs on top. sprinkle with butter and molasses or karo and bake. Serve with milk.

Fannie Gingerich
Ethridge, TN

PERFECT DAIRY WHIP

1 qt. powdered milk or non-dairy creamer can also be used
1 canevaporated milk
2 cups white sugar or less
2 t. vanilla

This is for a 4 qt. freezer. 1 pkg. of instant pudding mix can be added. This will not come out right if cow's milk or cream is used.

Mary A. Kinsinger
Myersdale, PA

PRISM DESSERT

1 (3 oz.) pkg. orange jello
1 (3 oz.) pkg. cherry jello
1 (3 oz.) pkg. lime jello

Disslve each pkg. of jello in 1 cup hot water in separate pans. Add 1/2 cup cold water to each. Chill until set.

1 (3 oz.) pkg. lemon jello
1/4 cup sugar
1 cup hot pineapple juice

Dissolve the jello and sugar in pineapple juice. When this is chilled (until it is just like a syrup), fold it into 2 cups heavy cream, whipped. Cut the orange, cherry, and lime jello into cubes and fold this into the cream mixture.

1 cup graham cracker crumbs
1/4 cup melted butter

Mix together and line pan with the above mixture. Pour the cream and jello mixture into it. Garnish the top with chopped nuts and put into refrigerator. Chill 12 hrs. Serves 18.

Mrs. Amos W. Yoder
Jamesport, MO

LIME BAVARIAN CREAM

(Drain reserving juice) 1 - 20 oz. can crushed pineapples
Combine, stirring to dissolve:
1 -3 oz. pkg. lime gelatin
1 cup hot water
Add 1 cup pineapple juice; add water if necessary to equal 1 cup.
Let set until quivery
Blend in:
1 cup whipping cream (whipped)
1/2 cup halved maraschino cherries
1 cup miniature marshmallows

Pour into 12x8 in. pan or 7-cup mold or glass dish. If using an oblong pan, garnish each square with nut meat. Chill until set. Variation: whip gelatin before blending in remaining ingredients.

Mrs. Joe J. Miller
Apple Creek, OH

BAKED APPLES

9 apples, cut in halves
1 cup hot water
Butter and cinnamon
1 cup sugar
1 T. flour

Put apples in pan. Mix up rest of ingredients and pour over apples. Bake. Is good to serve with whipped cream.

Fannie Gingerich
Ethridge, TN

PEACH OR APPLE COBBLER

4 cups sliced fresh peaches or apples
1 cup sugar
1 cup water
3 T. tapioca
cinnamon
2 T. oleo

In a baking pan combine the fruit, tapioca, sugar, cinnamon and water; dot with oleo.

Crust:

1 1/2 cups flour
1/2 t. salt
1 1/2 t. baking powder
6 T. shortening

Add milk to make a soft dough; roll or press to fit top of pan; make slits to permit escape of steam. Bake in hot oven until crust is done.

Elizabeth Mae Raber
Montgomery, IN

FRUIT DESSERT

1 large Cool Whip
1 can fruit cocktail
1 instant vanilla pudding
1 can pineapples

Optional: mini marshmallows and nuts; also bananas, if desired.

Mrs. Ray J. Gingerich
Fillmore, NY

What you don't know won't hurt you
But it often amuses others

JELLY ROLL

2 egg yolks (beaten)
3/4 cup granulated sugar (add slowly)
4 T. cold water
1 cup flour (sifted)
1 1/2 t. baking powder
1/2 t. salt
2 egg whites (beaten)

Spread thinly on large greased pan. Bake 15 min.

Filling:

1 1/2 t. cocoa
1/4 cup flour
1/4 cup cold milk
1 T. butter
1 cup sugar
1 egg
1/4 t. salt
1 T. vanilla

Cook until thick.

Bertha Beiler
Loganton, PA

APPLE DUMPLINGS

Dough:

2 cups flour
2 1/2 t. baking powder
1/2 t. salt
2/3 cup shortening
1/2 cup milk

Sauce:

2 cups brown sugar
2 cups water
1/4 cup butter
1/2 t. cinnamon
6 apples, cut in halves

Roll out dough, cut in squares. Place one apple half on each square. Set dumplings in the pan; pour sauce over and bake.

Bertha Beiler
Loganton, PA

FRENCH VANILLA ICE CREAM

2 cups sugar
1/4 t. salt
4 cups milk
12 egg yolks (beaten)
1 T. vanilla
4 cups whipping cream

Mix together sugar, milk and egg yolks and bring to a boil, but don't let it boil hard, just so it starts to bubble. Cool, add vanilla, whipping cream without whipping. Freeze according to directions on freezer. Enough for 1 gal. freezer.

Mrs. Ammon A. Troyer
Ashland, OH

APPLE BLOSSOM DESSERT

Mix:

2 beaten eggs
1 1/4 cups cooking oil
2 cups sugar
1 t. vanilla
3 cups grated raw apples
2 t. soda
1 t. cinnamon
1 t. nutmeg, optional
3 cups flour
dash of salt

Topping:

1/3 cup sugar
1 t. cinnamon
1 cup chopped nuts, optional

Sprinkle on batter and bake 25-30 min. at 325 deg. Spread into 12x18 in. jelly roll pan. This dessert may be cut up into squares and topped with whipped cream or eaten with ice cream. When served plain as for cake is a good choice also.

Mose E. Helmuth
Edgewood, IA

ICE CREAM SANDWICHES

3 eggs
1 cup cream, whipped
1/2 cup sugar

Separate eggs; beat egg yolks until light. Add sugar; beat well. Beat egg whites until stiff; add vanilla. Fold beaten egg whites and whipped cream in egg mixture. Put graham crackers on bottom of pan and on top. Set out to freeze a couple hrs. or overnight. Must have zero weather to freeze. Must set pan outside or in freeer to make them firm.

Clara Hochstetler
Canton, MO

PINEAPPLE PUDDING

1 can eagle brand milk
1 can crushed pineapples
1 large Cool Whip
cherry pie filling
chopped nuts

Mix and chill.

Mrs. Ray J. Gingerich
Fillmore, NY

RASPBERRY VANILLA CLOUD

1 2/3 cups graham cracker crumbs
1/4 cups white sugar
1 t. cinnamon
1/3 cup butter, melted
1/4 cup sugar
1/4 cup flour
1 pkg. unflavored gelatin
1/2 t. salt
1 3/4 cups milk
3 egg whites
1/4 t. cream of tartar
1/2 cup sugar
1 t. vanilla
1/2 cup heavy cream, whipped
Raspberry Sauce (recipe follows)

Mix together crumbs, sugar, cinnamon and butter. Press into a 9 in. square pan. Bake at 375 deg. for 4 min; cool. Combine 1/4 cup sugar, flour, gelatin and salt in 2 qt. saucepan. Slowly stir in milk. Bring to a boil, stirring constantly. Boil 1 min. Cool thoroughly. Beat egg whites with cream of tartar until stiff. Gradually beat in 1/2 cup sugar. Add vanilla. Fold egg whites and whipped cream into cooled mixture. Turn into crust. Chill well. Cut into squares and serve topped with raspberry sauce. makes 9 servings.

Raspberry Sauce:

Drain 2 - 10 oz. pkg. frozen raspberries, thawed. Add water to juice to make a 1/2 cups.

Combine with:

1/4 cup sugar
2 T. cornstarch
1 T. lemon juice

Cook, stirring until mixture boils 1 min. Add raspberries. Cool.

Mose E. Helmuth
Edgewood, IA

CRUNCHY CRUMBS

1 cup flour
2/3 cup brown sugar
1/4 cup oleo

Mix till crumbly and bake in slow oven. To use as crust under puddings or in layers between puddings.

Mrs. Neal Kauffman
La Plata, MO

GRAPENUT PUDDING

3 cups milk
1 cup grapenuts
3 rounded T. flour
1 t. maple flavor
1 cup raisins
1 cup brown sugar
2 egg yolks

Cook raisins first. Cook rest of ingredients in double boiler or or saucepan. When taken off stove, add 2 stiffly beaten egg whites. When cold, top with whipped cream, if desired.

Ella Hershberger
Oakland, MD

APPLE GOODIE

1/2 cup flour
3/4 cup sugar
1 t. cinnamon
1 qt. sliced apples
1/4 t. salt

Sift dry ingredients and combine with apples. Mix and place in a greased casserole.

Topping:
1 cup oatmeal
1 cup flour
1/4 t. soda
3/4 cup brown sugar
1 cup butter
1/4 t. brown powder

Combine dry ingredients and rub in butter to make crumbs. Put on top of apple mixture. Bake at 375 deg. for 35 to 40 min.

Esther Marie Fisher
Conneautville, PA

TAPIOCA

4 cups water
1/2 cup jello
6 T. tapioca - medium or pearl

Cook on low heat until tapioca is almost clear; add jello and chill.
Then add:
pinch of salt
sugar to taste

Fold in any fruit desired: strawberries, etc. Fold in whipped cream.

Esther Marie Fisher
Conneautville, PA

BUTTERSCOTCH ICE CREAM TOPPING

2 cup packed light brown sugar
1 1/2 cup light cream
4 Tblsp cornsyrup
4 Tblsp butter
1/2 tsp butterscotch, vanilla, or maple flavor

Place all ingredients, except flavor, in a heavy saucepan. Bring to a boil. Stir constantly. Boil 3 or 4 min. Let stand until nearly cool; add flavor. Beat for a few min. Pour into jars.

Mary Swartzentruber
Apple Creek, OH

It isn't so much what a man has
That makes him happy
As it is what he doesn't want

FLUFFY MINUTE TAPIOCA PUDDING

Cook together:
1/3 cup sugar
1 egg yolk
1/8 t. salt
2 cups milk
3 T. tapioca

Beat one egg white; add 2 T. sugar very slowly (and beat rapidly). Add tapioca mixture into whites. Can also add crushed pineapple, nuts and bananas, or fix in layers with graham crackers.

Enos Yoders
Park City, KY

GINGERICH BOYS' RECIPE

Mix 2 1/2 cups crushed graham crackers with oleo and put in a greased cake pan.

Spread on a layer of chocolate chips, a layer of coconut, then nuts if desired. Drizzle a can of Eagle Brand milk over all and bake at 350 deg. for approx. 30 min. (Not too thick layers of the things)

Mrs. Ray J. Gingerich
Fillmore, NY

CHOCOLATE CREAM CHEESE PUDDING

1 cup chocolate chips or sweet chocolate
1 - 8 oz. cream cheese
3/4 cup brown sugar — 1/8 t. salt
1 t. vanilla — 2 eggs, separated
1 cup cream (whipped) — 9" graham cracker crust

Melt chocolate in double boiler; cool 10 min. Blend cheese, sugar, salt and vanilla; beat in egg yolks; add cooled chocolate. blend well. Beat egg whites till stiff and blend in. Add whipped cream and pour over graham crackers.

Mrs. Ray J. Gingerich
Fillmore, NY

RAISIN PUDDING

1 cup flour — 1 cup sugar
1 cup raisins — 1/2 cup milk
2 t. baking powder

Place in dish and cover with a sauce made from:

2 cups boiling water — 1 cup sugar
1 T. butter

Stir till well blended; pour over batter. Bake at 350 deg.

Joe Borntreger
Cashton, WI

APPLE CRISP

Slice apples or fruit in a cake pan.
Mix together with a fork until crumbs:

1 cup flour — 1/2 cup sugar
1 t. baking powder — 1/4 t. salt
1 unbeaten egg

Sprinkle over apples, or fruit. Sprinkle over top cinnamon, cream of melted butter. Bake at 350 deg. for 30-40 min.

Joe Borntreger
Cashton, WI

BROWN SUGAR DUMPLINGS

Syrup:
1 cup brown sugar
2 cups hot water
2 T. butter
Bring to a boil.
Mix:
1/2 cup sugar
1 cup flour
2 t. baking powder
1/2 cup milk
1/2 cup nuts or raisins
Pour syrup into a cake pan. Drop the dough mixture into the syrup. Bake in moderate oven. Before serving, break into small pieces and top with whipped cream.

Mary Ann Hilty
Monroe, IN

PINEAPPLE CHERRY CRISP

1 cup canned crushed pineapples
2 1/2 cups (pitted) cherries
3 T. minute tapioca
1 T. lemon juice
1 cup sugar
Combine and cook till clear, stirring constantly.
Mix crumbs together:
1 cup flour
1 cup oatmeal
1/2 cup melted butter
2/3 cup brown sugar
1/4 t. soda
Put 1/2 of crumbs mixture on the bottom of a baking pan. Add cherry and pineapple mixture, cover with the remaining of the crumbs. Bake at 400 deg. for 25 min.

Joe Borntreger
Cashton, WI

FRUIT SLUSH

1 can crushed pineapples
1 can crushed peaches
1 can crushed pears
8-10 oranges
grapes or any other fruit
1 - 6 oz. box orange jello. Mix with only 1 cup hot water. Use tang to your taste.
Freeze and serve partially thawed.

Lucinda Hilty
Monroe, IN

KANSAS DIRT PUDDING

1 1/2 lb. oreo cookies (crushed)
2 - 3 1/2 oz. pkg. vanilla instant pudding, mixed according to directions on box.
8 oz. cream cheese, creamed until smooth
12 oz. Cool Whip
Mix pudding, cream cheese, and Cool Whip together. Layer in flour pot, starting with cookies and ending with cookies on top. This will fill 2 - 7 in. flour pots. Garnish with silk flowers and gummy worms on top.

Mrs. wilma Mast
S. Hutchinson, KS

PINEAPPLE TAPIOCA

1 1/2 cups raw tapioca
Pour into approx. 2 qt. boiling water. Boil 10 min. Cover and set aside till clear.
Add:
1 - 3 oz. box orange jello
1 small can crushed pineapples
Add around 1 cup sugar while hot.
Add whipped cream before serving.

Mrs. Neal Kauffman
La Plata, MO

CHERRY TOPPED GRAHAM DESSERT

1 - 6 oz. pkg. instant vanilla pudding
2 cups cold milk
1 cup whipped topping
1 can cherry pie filling
14 graham crackers (crushed)
Line a 9" square dish with graham crackers, filling in to cover bottom. Mix pudding mix and milk. Beat well and allow to stand 5 min. Fold in whipped topping. Pour half of pudding on crackers. Add another layer of graham crackers. Top with remaining pudding and another layer of crackers. Spoon cherry pie filling on top. Refrigerate at least 3 hrs.

Frances Helm
Shippensburg, PA

BLUEBERRY COBBLER

1 stick oleo
2 cups sugar
2 eggs
3 cups flour
1/2 t. salt
2 t. soda
4 T. vinegar
1 t. cinnamon
1 t. cloves
1/2 cup blueberry juice
1 1/2 cups blueberries

Cream butter and sugar together; add eggs and beat well till fluffy. Sift flour and measure. Sift dry ingredients and add juice and vinegar. Beat thoroughly after each addition. Add berries and stir just enough to blend into dough. Bake at 350 deg. for approximately 40 min.

Martha I. Shetler
Glasgow, KY

APPLE CRUNCH

1 cup flour
3/4 cup oatmeal, uncooked
1 cup brown sugar
1 t. cinnamon

Filling:
1 cup sugar
2 T. cornstarch
1 cup water
1 t. vanilla

Mix until crumbly.

Press half of crumbs into a 9 in. baking dish. Cover with 4 cups diced apples. Cookling filling until clear and thick. Pour over apples. Top with remaining crumbs. Bake in a moderate hot oven, about 350 deg., for 1 hr.

Mrs. Amos W. Yoder
Jamesport, MO

YOGURT

8 cups milk - heat to 180 deg.
1 T. unsweetened and unflavored gelatin - dissolve in water

Remove milk from stove and stir in the gelatin; then cool to 108 deg. Add yogurt (several tblsp. or 1/2 cup). Put in incubator until jelled (2 1/2-3 hr.); then remove from incubator, beat a little, and put in refrigerator.

Mrs. Amos W. Yoder
Jamesport, MO

Jams & Jellies

RHUBARB JAM

4 cups raw rhubarb (cut up small)
1 T. water
1 cup crushed pineapple
4 cups white sugar

Cook all together for 10 min. Stir often until sugar dissolves over low heat (before counting cooking time). Remove from heat and add 1 - 3 oz. box strawberry jello. Mix well and pour in jars and seal.

Clara Hochstetter
Canton, MO

PINEAPPLE-PEACH JELLY

5 cups crushed peaches
7 cups sugar
1 - 10 oz. can crushed pineapples

Cook 10-15 min., then add 2 - 3 oz. pkg. orange jello. Stir well and pour in jars and seal. This jelly is superior in flavor and color.

Clara Hochstetter
Canton, MO

DANDELION JELLY

In early morning pick 1 qt. dandelion flowers (no stems). Wash them and boil with 1 qt. water for 3 minutes. Drain off 3 cups liquid; add 1 pdg. pectin, or sure jell, 1 t. lemon or orange extract (use real lemon) and 4 1/2 cups sugar. Boil about 5 minutes. It tastes somewhat like honey.

Lydia Stoltzfus
Bloomsburg, PA

PEAR JELLY

4 lbs. sugar
4 lbs. grated pears
1 can crushed pineapples
Boil 20 to 30 minutes (not longer)

Lydia Stoltzfus
Bloomsburg, PA

Some of the busiest people
Are only picking up the beans they spilled

RHUBARB PRESERVE

4 cups finely cut rhubarb4 cups sugar

Let stand 2-3 hrs., stirring occasionally. Then bring to boil and boil 10 min. Add 1 lb. crushed pineapple. Boil again 7 min. Remove from heat and add 1 3 oz. box strawberry jello. Seal in jars.

Saloma J. Byler
Dewittville, NY

RED BEET JELLY

3 cups red beet juice
6 oz. raspberry jello
4 cups sugar
1 box Sure-Jell

Bring beet juice and sure-jell to a boil; then add the sugar. Boil 5-7 min. Add jello, jar and seal. Don't boil too fast or it will be too stiff.

Fannie S. Miller
Bird-in-Hand, PA

PINEAPPLE JELLY

6 cups sugar
1 cup water

Boil 10 min.
Add 3 cups crushed pineapples; boil 5 min.
Add 1 t. alum. Put in jars

Fannie S. Miller
Bird-in-Hand, PA

HOME MADE HONEY

5 lb. white sugar
1 1/2-2 cups water

Boil till clear.

Add alum size of a big cherry. Boil 2 min. Set back on stove, then put in:

8 good smelling pink roses
10 red clover blossoms
20 white clover blossoms

Press down in syrup with spoon. Let stand 10 min. Strain, then cool. This is very good.

Elizabeth Stutzman
Union City, PA

ZUCCHINI JELLY

Cook 6 cups peeled and grated zucchini in its own juice 6 min. over medium heat.

Add:

6 cups sugar
2 T. lemon juice
1 - 8 oz. can crushed pineapple including the juice

Cook 6 min. Remove from heat. Add 2 - 3 oz. boxes apricot jello. Put in jars and seal. If peach jello is used, add 1/4 t. almond flavoring.

Mary A. Kinsinger
Meyersdale, PA

PEAR HONEY

5 lbs. mashed pears, pealed and cored
10 lbs. sugar
1 qt. crushed pineapple

Boil all together to a full rolling boil for 20 min. Seal in sterile jars.

Lydiann J. Bricker
Panama, NY

DANDELION JELLY

In early morning before dew dries, pick 1 qt. blossoms. Look over for bugs. Boil in 1 qt. water for 3 min. Drain.

Add:

1 pkg. sure jell
1 t. lemon or orange extract
4 1/2 cups sugar

Boil 3 min. Pour and seal in sterile jars.

Lydiann J. Bricker
Panama, NY

RHUBARB JAM

5 cups rhubarb, cut up fine
4 cups sugar

Put on low heat to start and cook until done. Add 1 box of your favorite jello. Seal immediately.

Mrs. Samuel D. Beachy
Clark, MO

PINEAPPLE JAM

1 qt. crushed pineapple
1/2 gal. white karo
6 lb. white sugar

Mix all together and just bring to a boil. At times it gets too thick, just add a little water till it's right. Makes 1 gal.

Mrs. Samuel D. Beachy
Clark, MO

People who plant onions
Should not expect violets to bloom

STRAWBERRY HONEY

1 cup water
4 cups sugar

Boil 10 min.

Add:

2 cups mashed berries
1 t. powdered alum

Boil 1 min.

Seal in sterile jars. Will be thin until cold.

Lydiann J. Bricker
Panama, NY

APPLE JAM

2 qt. diced apples
1 cup raisins
1 cup brown sugar
2 T. clear jel
1/4 t. cinnamon
1/8 t. salt

Cook apples and raisins. Add brown sugar and salt. Thicken with clear jel. Take off heat and add cinnamon.

Aaron Brubacker
Liverpool, PA

PINEAPPLE PEACH JELLY

5 cups crushed peaches
7 cups sugar
1 - 10 oz. can crushed pineapple

Cook 10-15 min. Then add 1-3 oz. pkg. orange jello. Stir well and pour into jars and seal.

PINEAPPLE PRESERVES

2 qt. crushed pineapples
1 qt. karo
5 lb. sugar
Boil 20 min. Put in jars.

Sallie Flaud
Newburg, PA

RHUBARB JAM

Wash and prepare 4 cups rhubarb. Add 4 cups sugar. Let stand 2 1/2 hrs., mixing occasionally. Bring to a boil and boil for 10 min. Add small can crushed pineapple. Boil for 7 min. more. Remove from heat and add 1 - 3 oz. box strawberry jello. Can and seal.

Emma Hershberger
Dover, DE

RHUBARB JAM

5 cups rhubarb
4 cups sugar
Let stand overnight. Cook 5 min., add 2 boxes (3 oz.) strawberry or cherry jello; add 1 cup water.

Mrs. Leroy J. Byler
Fredericktown, OH

Meat & Vegetable Casseroles

POTATOES & DUMPLINGS

5 large potatoes
1 large onion
1 pt. chicken or however much you want to put in.
Put together and cook until potatoes are almost soft.
Dumplings:
4 large eggs
1/2 t. salt
1 t. baking powder
1/2 cup water
Flour till stiff and drop in boiling potatoes and broth. Cook about 10 min. Keep covered.

Mrs. . David Byler
Punxsutawaney, PA

NOODLE BAKE

1 lb. hamburger with onion, browned
Cook 1 pkg. noodles
Grease casserold; add noodles, hamburger and onion together.
Add:
1 can mushroom soup
1 can tomato soup
Put in casserole and bake at 350 deg. for 20 min.

Ida Schrock
Haven, KS

A man may make mistakes but he isn't a failure
Till he starts blaming someone else

BRUNCH CASSEROLE

3 cups bread crumbs
3 cups cheddar cheese, shredded
3 cups cubed ham, hamburger or sausage
6 eggs, beaten
1 t. mustard
3/4 t. salt
3 cups milk
3 T. butter
Put bread cubes, cheese and meat in a 9x13x2 in. pan. Mix the rest of ingredients and pour over the top of bread, cheese, and meat. Refrigerate overnight. Bake at 350 deg. for 1 hr.

Ida Schrock
Haven, KS

HEARTY CASSEROLE

2 cups diced carrots
6 med. potatoes
celery to taste
1 small onion
1 cup meat stock
1 cup peas
1 cup milk
3 T. butter
2 T. oatmeal or flour
bread crumbs soaked in butter

Cook first four items till tender. Add remaining ingredients. Pour into buttered casserole. Sprinkle with bread crumbs. Bake at 400 deg. for 40 min.

Fannie S. Miller
Bird-in-Hand, PA

MACARONI CASSEROLE

1 cup macaroni
1/2 cup onions
1/2 cup cheese
1 lb. chipped ham
2 T. oleo
2 cans soup: mushroom, celery

Cook macaroni till about half done. Add all other ingredients and put in baking dish. Bake till done.

Mrs. Dan J. Troyer
Mercer, PA

Smiles go a long way
Evan at home

CHICKEN CASSEROLE

12 slices bread crumbs, toasted in butter
4 cups cooked chicken
1 can cream of mushroom soup
1 cup chicken broth
1/2 cup Miracle Whip
4 eggs, well beaten
2 cups milk
1 t. salt

Mix, cover and store in refrigerator overnight. Put velveeta cheese on top. Bake at 350 deg. for an hr. Stir now and then while baking.

Mrs. Dan J. Troyer
Mercer, PA

TATER TOT CASSEROLE

2 bags tater tots
hamburger
mixed vegetables
1 can cream of mushroom soup
1 can cream of chicken soup

Brown hamburger, then mix soups, vegetables and meat together. Put a bag of tater tots in bottom of pan or roaster; spread mixture over tater tots, then put other bag on top. Put cheese on top. Bake till very bubbly.

Mrs. Dan J. Troyer
Mercer, PA

When looking for faults
Use a mirror
Not a telescope

FAST VEGETABLE SCALLOPED DISH

1 - 16 oz. jar lima beans, drained
1 - 16 oz. jar whole kernel corn, drained
1 - 16 oz. jar whole tomatoes, drained
5 T. butter
1/2 t. celery salt
1/2 t. onion salt

In a 1 1/2 quart casserole combine all ingredients except butter. Dot surface with butter. Bake in moderate oven for 1/2 hr. or until done.

Mrs. Dan J. Troyer
Mercer, PA

ONION PATTIES

Mix together:
3/4 cup flour
1/2 t. salt
2 t. baking powder
1 T. corn meal
1 T. sugar
1 T. wheat germ
Enough milk and cream for a thick batter
2 1/2 cups finely chopped onion. Fry till golden brown.

Joe Borntreger
Cashton, WI

ZUCCHINI PIZZA

4 cups shredded zucchini
1 cup Bisquick
1/2 cup oil
1/2 cup chopped onions
3 eggs
2 t. parsley
1 t. oregano

Bake at 350 deg. for 20-25 min. Then cover with pizza sauce and sprinkle cheese on top. Bake 10 more min.

Fannie S. Miller
Bird-in-Hand, PA

PIZZA CASSEROLE

1 lb. hamburger
Chopped onion and seasoning and cook
2 16 oz. cans pizza sauce
1 10 oz. pkg. mozarella cheese
7 oz. macaroni
4 oz. pepperoni
1 can mushrooms

Bake at 350 deg. for 45 min.

Esther Marie Fisher
Conneautville, PA

ZUCCHINI CASSEROLE

3 cups peeled chopped zucchini
1 cup Bisquick
1/2 cup oil
1/2 cup cheese (velveeta)
1/2 t. garlic powder
1 t. salt
4 eggs
chopped onion

Mix together in casserole. Bake at 350 deg. for 30-40 min.

Esther Fisher
Millersburg, PA

BROCCOLI CASSEROLE

Cook fresh or frozen cut broccoli, and drain. Stir in velveeta cheese whiz or cheddar cheese and a little milk. Put in a casserole and put crushed ritz crackers on top. Bake.

Esther Fisher
Millersburg, PA

A brook would lose its song
If it had no rocks

STROMBOLIES

1 T. yeast | 1 cup warm water
1 t. sugar | 1 t. salt
2 T. oil | 2 1/2 cups bread flour

Mix like bread dough and leave set for 5 min. Roll out into 6 parts and fill with meat, cheese, and onions. Fold together and seal edges. Bake 20 min. at 400 deg.

Bertha Beiler
Loganton, PA

PIZZA CASSEROLE

Melt in a med. saucepan 1/2 cup oleo. Blend until smooth 2 T. flour. Add, then cook until thickened, 2 cups milk. Remove from heat; then blend in and stir until smooth 1/4 lb. velveeta cheese. Fold together:

1 lb. noodles, cooked and drained
2 lbs. ground beef, browned and drained
4 cups spaghetti sauce | 1 can mushroom soup

Put mixture in baking dish; then top with pepperoni slices. Bake at 350 deg. for 30-45 min. Remove from oven and top with cheese. Return to oven until cheese is melted.

Mary Swartzentruber
Apple Creek, OH

MACARONI AND HAMBURGER CASSEROLE

1 lb. hamburger | 2 med.-sized onions, minced
1/4 lb. macaroni | 1 1/2 qt. boiling water
2 t. salt | 1/4 t. pepper
1 cup corn | 2 cups tomato juice

Mix chopped onion, 1/2 t. salt and pepper with hamburger. Cook macaroni in salt water until tender. Add corn, tomato juice and hamburger to the macaroni. Bake at 350 deg. for 1 hr.

Aaron Brubacker
Liverpool, PA

One way to save face
Is to keep the lower end of it closed

COPPER PENNY CARROTS

2 lbs. carrots
1 small green pepper, thinly sliced
1 med. onion
1 10 oz. can condensed tomatoe soup
1/2 cup oil
1 cup sugar
3/4 cup vinegar
1 t. prepared mustard
1 t. worcestershire sauce
salt and pepper to taste

Cook carrots 5 min., then drain. Combine with other vegetables, set aside. Combine all other ingredients, bring to a boil and pour over vegetables; mix well. Marinate at least 10-12 hrs.

Fannie S. Miller
Bird-in-Hand, PA

If your life is a grind
Use it to sharpen your wits

BAKED BEANS

(for a lot of people)

3 gal. baked beans
2 qt. king syrup
4 big onions
salt and pepper
1 large bottle ketchup
about 2 lb. bacon, fried bacon or ham chopped up.

Mix all together and bake at 300 deg. for 3 hrs.

Katie Smoker
Ronks, PA

VEGETABLE PIZZA

2 cans crescent rolls
3/4 cup mayonnaise
2 - 8 oz. cream cheese (softened)
1 pkg. Hidden Valley Ranch mix

Spread rolls on greased cookie sheet. Bake until golden. Mix cream cheese, mayonnaise, and ranch dressing. Spread on cooled crust. Top with chopped broccoli, carrots, celery, cucumbers, mushrooms, radishes, tomatoes, or any other favorite vegetables. Top with grated cheese.

Mrs. Wilma Mast
S. Hutchinson, KS

COPPER PENNIES

2 lb. carrots, diced and cooked
1 green pepper, sliced
3/4 cup vinegar
1/2 c. vegetable oil
1 can tomato soup
1 onion, sliced in rings
3/4 cup sugar
1 t. Worcestershire sauce
1 t. dry mustard

Mix all together. Marinate in refrigerator overnight. Serve cold.

Saloma Petersheim
Mifflintown, PA

GEAUGA COUNTY EGGS

(For a quick breakfast)

Make a hole in the center of a slice of bread. Put in a frying pan of hot butter. Crack an egg into the hole in the bread slice. Turn once. A slice of cheese may be added to each side.

Naomi Peachy
Little Falls, NY

Some minds are like concrete
All mixed up and permanently set

HIDDEN EGGS

Place a layer of fine bread crumbs in a buttered cake pan. Crack eggs on top of the bread crumbs until they're covered. Season with salt and pepper or your favorite seasonings. Cover the eggs with another layer of bread crumbs. Top with shredded cheese and bake until the eggs are done.

Naomi Peachy
Little Falls, NY

GOOD CREAM OF MUSHROOM PATTIES

1 can cream of mushroom soup
3 eggs
1 small onion or powder sage
2 cups quick oatmeal
2 t. beef broth flavor

Naomi Peachy
Little Falls, NY

GREEN BEAN CASSEROLE

1 1/2 lb. hamburger
1 med. onion
1 qt. breen beans
salt & pepper to taste
1 can cream of mushroom soup
Processed American or Velveeta cheese

Fry hamburger and onion until hamburger is brown and onion tender. Add salt, pepper, and soup. Mix and heat until hot. Layer green beans, hamburger mixture and put cheese on top. Bake at 350 deg. for 1 hr. This casserole can also be frozen.

Catherine Swarey
Belleville, PA

SCALLOPED CORN

2 cups canned or frozen corn
1 cup milk
2/3 cup cracker or bread crumbs
3 T. melted butter
1/2 t. salt
1/8 t. pepper
1 t. sugar
2 eggs
1 t. minced onion

Butter casserole. Bake 350 for 30 min.

Bertha Beiler
Loganton, PA

EASY BAKED SPAGHETTI

2 slices bacon (diced)
1 clove garlic (minced)
1 t. salt
1 t. chili powder
2 1/2 cups water
1 cup grated cheddar cheese
2 med. onions (chopped)
1/2 lb. ground beef
pepper to taste
2 - 8 oz. cans tomato sauce
1/2 lb. spaghetti

In heavy skillet fry bacon bronw and remove bacon. Add onions and garlic; cook until soft; add meat. Cook and stir until meat loses red color; stir in seasoning salt, pepper and chili powder, and tomato sauce and water. Cover and simmer for 25 min. Put cooked spaghetti and sauce and cheese in layers; cover with lid or foil; bake 30 min.; uncover and bake for 15 min. more in 350 deg. oven.

Sue Wickey
Norfolk, NY

MACARONI-CHEESE-BEEF BAKE

1 1/2 cups macaroni, partly cooked and drained
1 lb. ground beef, browned
1/2 cup chopped onions
1/2 cup chopped parsley
salt and pepper
1 can mushroom soup
3/4 cup milk
1 cup grated cheese

Combine all ingredients; place in greased baking dish. Bake in 350 deg. oven for 20 min.

Elizabeth Mae Raber
Montgomery, IN

SPAGHETTI AND MEAT BALLS

1/2 lb. ground beef
salt and pepper
finely chopped onion
1 1/2 cups tomato juice
1/2 cup cheese
1 cup spaghetti or macaroni

Season beef with salt and pepper. Make into tiny balls; brown in skillet. Remove and brown onions lightly; add tomatoes and cheese. Cook spaghetti in boiling water, but don't cook until completely done. Drain. Grease a 1 1/2 qt. casserole. Fill with alternate layers of spaghetti, meatballs and sauce. Bake 1/2 hr., or until done.

Elizabeth Mae Raber
Montgomery, IN

UNDERGROUND HAM CASSEROLE

4 cups chunked ham
4 T. oleo
1/2 cup chopped onion
1 T. Worcestershire sauce
2 cans cream of mushroom soup
1 cup milk
2 cups cheese, cubed
4 qts. mashed potatoes
1 pt. sour cream
browned, crumbled bason

Combine ham, oleo, onion and worcestershire sauce and cook till onions are tender. Place in bottom of a med. sized roasting pan. In a saucepan heat together soup, milk, and cheese, until cheese melts. Place over top of onions. Mash potatoes using no salt or milk, and mix with sour cream. Spread over top of mixture and sprinkle with bacon. Bake at 350 deg. for 20 min. "The soup and cheese mix comes to the top when done; that's why it's called underground ham."

Mrs. Joe J. Miller
Apple Creek, OH

SPARERIBS, SAUERKRAUT AND POTATOES

	4 qt. cooker	6-8 qt.
spareribs	2 1/2 lb. ribs	5 lbs. ribs
fat	1 T.	2 T.
salt	1 t.	2 t.
pepper	dash	1/8 t.
sauerkraut	20 oz. can or 2 1/2 cups	5 cups
brown sugar	1 T.	2 T.
potatoes, med. whole	4	8
water	2/3 cup	1 1/3 cups

Brown spareribs in hot fat in cooker. Add salt & pepper. Put sauerkraut in bottom of cooker and sprinkle with brown sugar. Place ribs and potatoes over kraut. At 10 lb. and cook 20 min. after jiggler is controlled. Reduce pressure normally 5 min.; then place cooker under faucet. Use a Mirro pressure cooker, or may be cooked 1 hr. or baked in roaster in the ordinary way.

Mrs. Joe J. Miller
Apple Creek, OH

VEGETABLE SOUP

1/2 bu. ripe tomatoes, juiced
10 onions
10 medium sized carrots
10 plants celery
2 green peppers
18 ears corn
1/2 - 1 gal. cooked soup beans

Fannie Gingerich
Ethridge, TN

A chronic kicker is never out of a job

CHEESE DISH

1 cup grated cheese
1 cup bread crumbs
2 beaten eggs
1 cup milk
1 T. butter
salt and pepper

Mix all together and bake until nicely browned. Sprinkle with pepper if desired.

Mrs. Jacob Stutzman
Jeromesville, OH

NO PEAK STEW

2 1/2 lbs stewing beef, cut fine
1 onion
6 carrots
2 potatoes
1 stalk celery
2 cups tomato juice
2 t. salt
1 t. sugar
2 1/2 t. minute tapioca

Cook 4 hrs. in a tightly covered casserole at 250 deg.

Mrs. Jacob Stutzman
Jeromesville, OH

SAUSAGE GRAVY AND BISCUITS

1 pound sausage
1 stick oleo
1/2 t. pepper
1/2 t. salt
1 t. sage
1 1/4 cups flour
1 1/2 qts. milk

Brown sausage. Add butter, pepper, salt and sage. When butter bubbles, stir in flour; mix well. Add milk. Stir rapidly till thick. Serve hot over biscuits.

Barbara Schrock
Spartansburg, PA

PENNSY SUPPER

6 weiners, sliced thin
4 medium potatoes, diced and cooked
2 T. minced onion
1/4 cup soft butter
1 cup cooked peas
1 T. prepared mustard
1 cup mushroom soup
salt and pepper

Combine weiners with potatoes, onions and butter in casserole. Combine remaining ingredients and toss with weiner mixture. Dot with reserved weiners. Cover and bake at 350 deg. for 30 min. Serves 6.

Barbara Schrock
Spartansburg, PA

I had rather be bent by hard work
Than be crooked by dodging it

CRUSTY BAKED POTATOES

6 medium potatoes
4 T. melted butter
1/2 cup cracker crumbs
1 t. salt

Pare potatoes and wipe dry. Cut in halves and roll in melted butter, then in crumbs in which salt was added. Place in greased pan and bake 1 hr.

Sadie Miller
Fort Plain, NY

BEEF AND VEGETABLE CASSEROLE

1 - 8 oz. pkg. noodles
1 can cream of mushroom soup
2 cups peas or vegetables, if desired
1 cup milk
1/2 lb. beef

Fry beef in butter until slightly browned. Add mushroom soup and milk. Cook noodles until tender; drain. Put noodles, peas, and meat in layers. Cover with buttered bread crumbs. Bake in oven till brown.

Sadie Miller
Fort Plain, NY

BEEF AND CHEESE

1 lb. ground beef
1 small onion
1 1/2 cups uncooked spagetti
1 cup tomatoes
2 T. butter
3 T. flour
2 cups milk
3/4 cup cheese
catsup as desired

Cook spagetti until tender; drain. In a skillet brown beef and onion in butter. Add flour, seasoning, and milk. Cook till thick. Mix 1/2 cup cheese with spaghetti. Sprinkle with remaining cheese. Bake at 350 deg. 25-30 min.

Sadie Miller
Fort Plain, NY

POTATOES IN CHEESE

Dice a dish of potatoes and cook until soft in salt water.
Make a cheese sauce: Soften butter in skillet, put onion in if you like; add flour as for white sauce; add milk and cheese to make it thick. Pour over hot potatoes and serve, or set in warm oven till ready to serve.

Mrs. Raymond S. Miller
Millersburg, OH

NOODLE CASSEROLE

6 oz. noodles
1 cup chicken
1 cup bread crumbs, browned in butter
1 can mushroom soup
1 cup milk

Cook noodles in salt water until tender. Combine cooked noodles with chicken and mushroom soup and milk. Put in casserole, cofer with bread crumbs and bake for 25 min.

Mrs. Raymond S. Miller
Millersburg, OH

HAMBURGER AND BEAN CASSEROLE

Brown 1 lb. hamburger
1/4 cup catsup
1 t. vinegar
4 T. brown sugar
3/4 cup water
1 t. worcestershire sauce
1/2 can pork and beans (202)

Season with salt, pepper, onion salt, and celery salt. Simmer and pour into casserole and bake at 350 deg. for 25 min.

Mrs. Raymond S. Miller
Millersburg, OH

A man who will trim himself to suit everybody
Will soon whittle himself away

BAKED HAM AND NOODLE CASSEROLE

In a 1 1/2 qt. casserole, mix:
1 can cream of chicken soup
1/2 cup milk
2 cups drained cooked noodles
2 cups diced cooked ham

Bake at 375 deg. for25 min.

Mrs. Raymond S. Miller
Millersburg, OH

CARROT PATTIES

grated carrots
1 small onion
3 eggs
pinch of salt and pepper
cracker crumbs

Drop in hot butter or lard by tablespoons and fry on both sides.

Esther Fisher
Millersburg, PA

STOVETOP BEANS

3 cups cooked navy beans
Add:
1 cup cream
3 T. butter
1/2 cup brown sugar
1/2 cup ketchup
2 t. mustard
1 small chopped onion
5 slices velveeta cheese (or more)

Cook slowly on top of stove till well heated and cheese is melted; add cut up hot dogs.

Esther Fisher
Millersburg, PA

CHICKEN 'N FILLING CASSEROLE

1 average size chicken, cut up (fryer)
1 cup diced carrots (cooked)
1 med. onion (chopped)
1 loaf bread (cubed)
2 cups milk
1 egg
salt and pepper to taste

Beat together egg and milk. Roll raw chicken pieces in flour and fry lightly in butter. Arrange chicken in bottom of roasting pan. Bake uncovered for 1 hr. at 450 deg. (For older chickens, add some water and bake longer.) Mix the vegetables, bread cubes, and milk and egg together. Spread on top of chicken. Top with dots of butter. Bake 1/2 hr. longer.

Saloma Petersheim
Mifflintown, PA

WIGGLERS

9 slices bacon
3 lb. hamburger
3 onions, chopped
3 cups carrots, cut & cooked
2 cans peas
1 cup celery, cut & cooked
2 lb. spaghetti, cooked
3 cups diced potatoes, cooked
2 cans mushroom soup
1 lb. velveeta cheese
1 1/2-2 qts. tomato soup

Fry bacon; take out. Heat hamburger and onions in bacon grease. Put in roaster. Add potatoes, carrots, celery, peas, spaghetti and mushroom soup. Then arrange cheese slices and bacon on top. Pour tomato soup over all. Bake in moderate oven, 350-375 deg. for 1 1/2-2 hrs.

Joe Borntreger
Cashton, WI

CHEESY SALMON CASSEROLE

1/4 cup chopped onions
2 T. margarine
1 can cream of mushroom soup
1/2 cup milk
1 cup shredded cheese
4 cups cooked macaroni
1 - 8 oz. can salmon
Buttered bread crumbs

In medium saucepan cook onion in margarine until tender. Stir in soup, milk, 3/4 cup of cheese, macaroni and salmon. Pour in baking dish. Bake at 250 deg. for 25 min. Top with bread crumbs and remaining cheese. Bake 5 more min.

Cathryn Schmucker
Litchfield, MI

NOODLES MEXICANO

1 lb. browned ground beef
1/2 green pepper, chopped (optional)
1 onion, chopped
2 cloves of garlic
1 t. salt
1 can corn liquid
1 can black olives and liquid (sliced)
large can tomatoes
1 t. chili powder
8 oz. noodles

Cover and cook 1/2 hr. on top of stove. Add 1/2 lb. shredded cheddar cheese. Cover and cook till cheese melts.

Joni H. Shrock
Middlefield, OH

SPAGHETTI PIZZA DELUXE

1 - 7 oz. package creamette spaghetti, uncooked
1/2 cup skim milk
1 egg beaten
]vegetable cooking spray
1/2 lb. lean ground beef
1 medium onion, chopped
1 medium green pepper, chopped
1 clove garlic, minced
2 cups shredded part skim mozzarella cheese
pepperoni
1 - 15 oz. can tomato sauce
1 t. Italian seasoning
1 t. any salt free herb seasoning
1/4 t. pepper
2 cups fresh sliced mushrooms

Prepare creamette spaghetti as package directs; drain. In medium bowl, blend milk and egg; add spaghetti and toss to coat. Spray 15x10 in. jelly roll pan with vegetable cooking spray. Spread spaghetti mixture evenly in prepared pan; top with pepperoni. In large skillet cook beef, onion, green pepper and garlic until beef is no longer pink; drain. Add tomato sauce and seasonings; simmer 5 min. Spoon meat mixture evenly over spaghetti. Top with mushrooms and cheese. Bake in 350 deg. oven for 20 min. Let stand 5 min. before cutting. Refrigerate leftovers. Makes 8 servings.

Joni H. Shrock
Middlefield, OH

When you get to the end of your rope
Tie a not and hang on to it

SCALLOPED SPINACH

2 lbs. spinach
2 eggs (beaten)
2 cups milk
2 cups bread (cubed)
4 T. butter (melted)
3/4 t. salt
1/8 t. pepper
1/2 cup bacon (cooked)

Cook and drain spinach. Add rest of ingredients except bacon. Place in greased casserole and put bacon on top. Bake at 350 deg. for 40 min. Serves 6.

Mrs. Wilma Mast
S. Hutchinson, KS

QUICK BAKED BEANS

2 cans - 16 oz. baked beans
1/4 cup brown sugar
1/2 t. mustard
1/2 cup ketchup
2 small onions
1 t. worcestershire sauce
bacon slices

Stir all together, except bacon. Put in baking dish; top with bacon slices. Bake at 350 deg. for 1 hr.

Esther Fisher
Millersburg, PA

WARM DANDELION

1 cup cut up ham, hotdogs, or bacon
Fry and add 1 cup milk.
Make thick sauce with 3 T. flour, 2 T. brown sugar, a little vinegar. Put washed, cut up dandelion greens in a bowl. When ready to eat, pour the hot sauce over it. Do not cookdandelions. Add 2 hard boiled eggs, cut up. Spinach may also be used.

Esther Fisher
Millersburg, PA

EL PASO CASSEROLE

1 3/4 lb. velveeta cheese
1 1/2 lb. noodles
2 lb. chipped ham

Sauce:
1/2 lb. butter
1/2 gal. milk
1 cup flour
1 can celery soup

Cook noodles in salt water. Blend cheese and ham in white sauce; pour over noodles in oiled pan sprinkled with toasted bread crumbs. Bake at 350 deg. for 25 min.

Mrs. Leroy J. Byler
Fredericktown, OH

ONE STEP MACARONI 'N CHEESE CASSEROLE

4 cups uncooked macaroni
2 t. worcestershire sauce
2 cups velveeta cheese
6 cups milk
1 t. salt
paprika

Put in oven. Bake at 350 deg. for 50 min.

Mrs. Leroy J. Byler
Fredericktown, OH

SCRAMBLED EGGS

In a bowl break 4 eggs; whip lightly with a fork and add 1/4 cup milk or cream, salt and pepper to taste.

Heat skillet, but not real hot. Add 1 T. oleo. Add egg mixture and mix with fork in a skillet until mixture starts to set. Cover and let heat for a minute or 2 until well set. Cut in pieces and turn with spatula to brown both sides. Makes delicious sandwiches when lettuce and mayonnaise is added or chili sauce.

Miss Sara Shetler
Glasgow, KY

ONION PATTIES (DEEP FAT FRIED)

3/4 cup flour
2 t. baking pwoder
1 T. sugar
1 t. salt
1 T. corn meal
2 1/2 cups fine chopped onions

Enough milk to make a thick batter (or use 1/2 cup powdered milk and enough cold water to make a thick batter).

Mix first 5 ingredients. Stir in enough milk (or water if powdered milk is used) to make a thick batter. Mix in onions, chopped fine, and drop by spoonfuls into deep fat. Flatten patties slightly as you turn them. Fry to a golden brown. Deep fat should be heated to 350 deg. before adding batter.

Miss Sara Shetler
Glasgow, KY

LEFTOVER MASHED POTATOES

To about 2 cups leftover mashed potatoes add:
3 eggs
2 T. flour
1/4 cup sweet milk
1/2 t. salt

Mix all together and fry as for pancakes till light brown. Eat with a meat gravy or plain.

Miss Sara Shetler
Glasgow, KY

SWEET POTATOES

6 med. size sweet potatoes
1/4 cup butter
1 cup brown sugar
1 t. salt
3/4 cup water

Melt and brown butter; add sugar, water and salt. Pour over cooked sweet potatoes. Bake at 375 deg. for 30 min.

Rebecca King
Gordonville, PA

ONE DISH MEAL

1 cup cooked diced potatoes
1/2 cup cooked diced celery
1/2 cup cooked diced carrots
or whatever vegetable you like. Put all in dish or casserole with beef or chicken with broth.

Biscuit topping:
2 cups flour
4 t. baking powder
1/2 t. salt
2 T. shortening
3/4 cup water or milk

Mix and drop by tablespoons on top of other things. Bake 20-30 min. till done. Serve with gravy.

Cora Stutzman
Union City, PA

CHICKEN AND BISCUIT CASSEROLE

1 pkg. mixed vegetables, frozen
3-4 cups cooked chicken, cut up off the bones
Gravy made with the broth of chicken

Cook vegetables until soft. Mix and pour together in a casserole dish. Top with large biscuits like Hungry Jack or Pillsbury's. Bake at 350 deg. for 30 min.

Mrs. Joe J. Miller
Apple Creek, OH

Always be ready for the unexpected

Muffins Buns Rolls

BRAN MUFFINS

1 cup white flour
1 cup graham flour
1/2 cup brown sugar
1/2 cup shortening
1 egg
1 t. baking powder
1/2 t. soda
1/2 t. salt

Mix dry ingredients, then add milk, beaten eggs, melted shortening and the rest of ingredients. Mix quickly, pour in greased muffin tins and bake 20 min. in 400 deg. oven or until done. Eat with fruit and milk, like shortcake.

Sue Wickey
Norfolk, NY

MUFFINS

1/4 cup brown sugar
1/4 cup honey
2 packages sweetner
2 eggs
1/2 cup oleo

Mix and beat well and add:

1 cup plain yogurt
1 cup bran
1 cup oatmeal
1/2 cup flour
1 t. baking soda
3/4 cup raisins
1 t. cinnamon

Bake in greased muffin tins 15-20 min. at 400 deg. or until done.

Sue Wickey
Norfolk, NY

BUNS

2 cups milk
2 cups water
1 1/2 cups shortening
1 T. salt
1 scant cup sugar
3 eggs
3 T. dry yeast (dissolved in water with 1 T. sugar)
5 lb. or less bread flour

Knead 2 or 3 times 1/2 hr. apart. Make into rolls. Bake 15-20 minutes at 350 deg. Makes 100 small rolls. Nice for large gatherins or picnics.

Catherine Swarey
Belleville, PA

CORN MEAL ROLLS

1/3 cup corn meal
1/2 cup sugar
2 t. salt
1/2 cup shortening
2 cups milk
1 T. dry yeast
1/4 cup warm water
2 eggs, beaten
4 cups flour, more as needed

Cook corn meal, sugar, salt, shortening and milk in medium-sized saucepan until thick (like cooked cereal). Cool to lukewarm. Add yeast which has been dissolved in lukewarm water, then eggs. Beat good. Add flour to form a soft dough. Knead. Place in bowl - cover - let rise. Punch down. Roll to 1 in. thickness and cut with round cookie cutter. Brush with butter, dust with corn meal. Let rise on cookie sheet. Bake for 15 min. at 375 deg., or till golden brown. Dough will keep in refrigerator several days.

Barbara Shrock
Spartansburg, PA

BISCUITS SUPREME

2 cups flour
1/2 t. salt
4 t. baking powder
1/2 t. cream of tartar
2 t. sugar
1/2 cup shortening
2/3 cup milk

Sift dry ingredients together. Cut in shortening until mixture resembles course crumbs. Add milk all at once and stir just until dough follows fork around bowl. Drop by T. on ungreased cookie sheet. Bake in hot oven, 450 deg., for 10-12 min.

Barbara Schrock
Spartansburg, PA

The easiest way to finish is a hard job
Is to get to work
After the start is made the finish is near at hand

CINNAMON ROLLS

2 1/2 cups scalded milk
3 pkg. yeast
1 cup shortening
3 eggs (beaten)
3/4 cup sugar
2 1/2 qt. flour
1 1/4 t. salt

Add shortening, sugar and salt to hot (scalded) milk and stir to dissolve. Cook to lukewarm; add yeast mixture and stir until softened. Add eggs, and add flour mix; then knead. Place in a greased bowl. Cover and let rise till double in size. Divide into two portions; roll out and brush with soft butter, sprinkle with brown sugar and cinnamon, then roll in a long roll, cut and place in greased cake pans. Let rise 20 to 30 min. Bake 25-30 min. in 350 deg. oven. This dough can be rolled out, cut with doughnut cutter, and fried in hot shortening or veg. oil; then glazed for doughnuts.

Sue Wickey
Norfolk, NY

BUNS

1 cup hot water
1 T. salt
1/2 cup sugar
3 T. butter

Mix together, let cool to lukewarm then add to yeast.

3/4 cup warm water
1 t. sugar
2 T. bulk yeast
1 egg, well beaten
5 3/4 cups Robin Hood flour

Mix all together, work down good and grease dough, cover with wax paper. When doubled in bulk, work down again; let rise again; work out in 12 buns. Bake in 2 layer cake pans. Bake at 350 deg. for 30 min.

Louella Borntrager
Sugar Creek, OH

CINNAMON YEAST ROLLS

1 1/2 cups milk
1/2 cup sugar
2 pkgs. yeast
3 eggs
2 t. salt
1 stick butter or oleo
1/2 cup warm water
6 cups flour

Scald the milk; add the salt, sugar and oleo or butter. Mix well and cool slightly. Dissolve yeast in the warm water and let stand 5 min.; then add to the above mixture. Add the egg and 3 cups of the flour and beat well. Add remaining flour and mix well and put in large bowl to rise until doubled in bulk. Roll out into 2 large rectangles - spread with soft oleo and sprinkle with brown sugar and cinnamon. Roll up as a yello roll. Cut into 3/4-1 in. slices and put in butter baking pans. Let rise until doubled in size, then bake in hot oven, 375-400 deg., for about 10-15 min. or until lightly browned. When cool, frost them with desired frosting.

Lucinda Hilty
Monroe, IN

OAT BRAN RAISIN MUFFINS

No Cholesterol

2 1/2 cups oat bran cereal
1/2 cup raisins
1/2 t. salt
4 oz. egg whites or egg substitute
2 t. brown sugar substitute
1 T. baking powder
1 cup skim milk
1 T. vegetable oil

Combine dry ingredients. Add milk, egg whites and oil. Mix just until dry ingredients are moistened. Fill muffin cups 3/4 full. Bake at 425 deg. about 18 min. or until brown.

Mrs. Dan J. Troyer
Mercer, PA

Vacation is a time when
You exchange good dollars
For bad quarters

AUDREY'S ROLLS

2 envelopes yeast (6 t.) dissolved in 1/2 cup warm water.
Pour 1 cup hot water over:

1 t. salt
3/4 cup sugar
1 cup oleo

Cool to lukewarm and add yeast and 2 eggs; then add 5 cups flour. Roll out and spread with melted butter, brown sugar and cinnamon. Roll up and slice in 1 in. slices. Lay in pans and let rise till double. Bake in hot oven till done.

Mrs. Neal Kauffman
La Plata, MO

DELICIOUS APPLE ROLLS

Dough:

2 T. sugar
3 T. lard
1/2 cup milk
2 cups flour
2 t. baking powder
1 egg

Syrup:

2 cups brown sugar
1 1/2 cups water

Enos Yoders
Park City, KY

SWEET BUNS

3 cups milk
5 t. salt
2 cups sugar
1 lb. shortening

Heat and cool to lukewarm. Add 8 beaten eggs. Dissolve about 6 T. yeast in 2 cups warm water. Add to milk solution; stir and add around 12 cups flour or as needed; not too stiff. Let rise 1 hr. or so just according to how fast it will rise, then work out and let rise. You can use this recipe for rolls, too.

Elizabeth Stutzman
Union City, PA

Snap judgement has a way
Of becoming unfastened

TASTY AIR BUNS

1 cup warm water
2 pkg. yeast
2 t. sugar
Let stand 10 min.
Mix:
7 cups warm water
1 cup sugar
1 cup lard
18 cups flour
2 t. salt

Add yeast to this and 2 T. vinegar. Let rise 2 hrs. and knead. Allow to rise again. Make into buns and let rise 1 1/2-3 hrs. Bake in 375 deg. oven for 30 min. Makes about 92 buns.

Cora Stutzman
Union City, PA

BUNS

3/4 cup warm water
2 pkg. yeast
1 t. sugar
Mix together.
2 cups warm milk
1 T. salt
1 cup sugar
4 eggs
1/2 cup butter
Approximately 7-8 cups flour

Mrs. Raymond S. Weaver
Millersburg, OH

I grumbled because
I had to get up in the morning
Until one morning
I couldn't get up

Beef

MEXICAN HAYSTACK

Put the following items in this order on plates:

crushed saltine crackers
taco chips (crushed)
cooked ground beef (hot)
boiled rice (hot)
shredded carrots
chopped tomatoes
shredded olives

Use your imagination. On top of this pour hot cheese sauce made as follows:

4 T. batter
4 T. flour
1 t. salt
2 cups milk

Add velveeta cheese to your taste. Melt butter in saucepan, add flour and seasoning; stir until well blended. Add cheese.

Fannie S. Miller
Bird-in-Hand, PA

BEEF AND CHEESE

1 lb. ground beef
1 sm. onion
1 1/2 cup spaghetti
1 cup tomatoes
2 T. butter
3 T. flour
2 cups milk
3/4 cup cheese
seasoning to taste

Cook spaghetti until tender. Drain. In a skillet brown the beef and onion in the butter. Add flour, seasoning, and milk. Cook until thickened. Mix 1/2 cup cheese with spaghetti. Place 1/2 of spaghetti mixture in baking dish. Cover with meat mixture, and top with tomatoes. Put on the rest of spaghetti mixture. Top with remaining cheese. Bake at 350 deg. for 30 min.

Naomi Peachy, Little Falls, NY
Catherine Swarey, Belleville, PA

MEAT LOAF

1 1/2 lb. ground beef
2 eggs
3/4 cup oatmeal
1 cup tomato juice
1/4 cup onion, cut fine
salt and pepper to taste

Mix all ingredients and place in casserole. Bake. When half done, mix and spread on top:

2 t. mustard
2 t. flour
1 T. brown sugar
add a little water

When done, remove from oven, let set 5 min. before cutting.

Enos Yoders
Park City, NY

TRAIL BOLOGNA

Use 30 lb. deer or beef meat; chicken meat is good; half in half
Grind in 1 lb. tenderquick

4 T. black pepper
1 T. onion or garlic powder
1 t. mace
1/2 t. salt petre

Mix all together; then add 1/2 gal. water and mix. Put in muslin bags and cook for 90 min. to 2 hrs. in 165 deg. water. Immediately put in cold water. Smoke for 5 or 6 hrs. Use 11x14 in. bag. Don't get water too hot as meat will get too dry. Prick with a fork every now and then. You can put in liquid smoke instead of smoking if you wish. This will keep quite a while if kept where it's cold or in refrigerator.

Clara Hochstetter
Canton, MO

CABBAGE RICE CASSEROLE

Brown 1/4 lb. butter in roast pan. Put 2 cups uncooked rice in butter. Slice 1 medium head cabbage and 6 carrots. Fry 2 lb. hamburger and 1 chopped onion. Mix together meat, cabbage, carrots and 3 t. salt. Put on top of rice. Do not stir. Pour in 1 pt. water and 1 pt. beef broth. Cover with foil and bake at 350 deg. for 1 hr. This is a yummy meal in one dish.

Saloma Petersheim
Mifflintown, PA

MINCE MEAT

3 qts. ground meat
1 1/2 qts. cherries
1 t. salt
1 t. allspice
1 qt. raisins (optional)
1 1/2 qts. diced apples
5 cups sugar
1 t. cinnamon
1 1/2 qt. cider

Cook for 1 1/2 hr.

Bertha Beiler
Loganton, PA

Children have more need
Of models than of critics

YUMESETTS

1 pkg. noodles - cooked
3 lb. hamburger - fried with onion
1 pint peas
2 cans cream of mushroom soup
1 can cream of celery or chicken soup
1 cup sour cream.

Toast 1/2 loaf of bread in butter. Mix with the above ingredients and bake 1 hour. Makes a big roaster full.

Naomi Peachy
Little Falls, NY

CHILI SOUP

2 lbs. cooked beans
2 gal. fresh ground beef
4 qts. tomato juice
3 T. chili powder

Mix meat with onions, garlic, salt and pepper, and roast in oven till it loses its raw color, then add to rest of mixture.

Fannie Gingerich
Ethridge, TN

PORCUPINE MEAT BALLS

1 lb. ground beef
1/2 cup rice
1 t. salt
1 t. pepper
1 onion
1 sm. can tomato soup
1/2 can water

Wash rice. Combine meat, rice, salt, pepper and onion. Shape into small balls. Mix soup and water and pour over meatballs. Cook 30 min. tightly covered.

Sadie Miller
Fort Plain, NY

CORNED BEEF TO CAN

25 lb. beef - cut in small chunks
1 1/4 gal. water
1/2 lb. brown sugar
1 3/4 lb. salt
1/4 oz. salt petre - 1 T.
1/2 oz. soda - 1 T.
1/4 T. pepper
1/2 t. liquid smoke

Bring to a boil; pour over beef chunks. Let stand 4-6 wks; then can 3 hrs. First wash beef chunks in clear water, then let stand 1/2 day in water, cut in small chunks and can.

Esther Marie Fisher
Conneautville, PA

MEXICAN MEAT LOAF

2 cups rice (cooked)
2 lbs. ground beef
2 cans mushroom soup
2 cups cheddar cheese (grated)
1 small onion
1 small green pepper
2 cups taco sauce, mild
corn chips

Brown meat with salt, pepper, onion, green pepper. Drain. Stir in soup. In a greased 9x13 in. pan begin layering ingredients starting with corn chips (enough to cover bottom) then meat, rice, taco sauce and cheese. Continue layering until all ingredients are used. Cover with foil and bake at 350 deg. for 45 min.

Mrs. Wilma Mast
S. Hutchinson, KS

BARBEQUED MEATBALLS

1 cup bread crumbs
1 lb. ground beef
1/2 cup milk
1 t. salt
1/8 t. pepper

Sauce:

3/4 cup ketchup
1 t. worcestershire sauce
small onion (chopped)
3/4 t. salt
1/4 cup vinegar
1 cup water

Mix meat and shape into balls; put in baking dish and pour over the sauce and bake. Bake at 350 deg. for 1 hr.

Esther Fisher
Millersburg, PA

MINCE MEAT

1 cup raisins
3 cups chopped apples
1 cup lean ground beef
pinch salt
enough water to cook

Boil till raisins and apples are soft; then add sugar, cinnamon, cloves and allspice to your taste. Add some apple jell or cider or a little vinegar to improve flavor. This is ready for pies or can be put in jars and seal.

Elizabeth Stutzman
Union City, PA

SLOPPY JOES

1 lb. ground beef
1 lb. can pork and beans
1 cup onions, chopped
2 T. brown sugar
2 T. cooking oil
1 t. prepared mustard
1 cup barbecue sauce

Brown beef in oil. Add onions and saute until tender. Add beans, barbecue sauce, sugar and mustard. Simmer covered for 10 min.

Mary Ann Hilty
Monroe, IN

BEST EVER MEATLOAF

1 can golden mushroom soup
1/2 cup fine dry bread crumbs
1 egg slightly beaten
1/3 cup water
2 lbs. ground beef
1/3 cup finely chopped onions
1 t. salt

Mix thoroughly: 1/2 cup soup, bread crumbs, beef, onion, egg and salt. Shape into loaf (8x4 in.). Place in shallow baking pan. Bake at 375 deg. for 1 hr. and 15 min. Blend remaining soup, water and 2-3 T. drippings; heat; stir occasinally. Serve with loaf.

Elizabeth Mae Raber
Montgomery, IN

THRIFTY MEATBALLS

1 lb. ground beef
1/3 cup milk
1/4 cup chopped onion
1 1/4 t. salt
1 can cream of chicken soup
1/4 cup uncooked rice
1/8 t. pepper
1/4 cup cracker crumbs
2 T. shortening

Combine all ingredients except shortening and soup. Shape in small balls, brown in shortening. Dilute soup with 1 can water, pour over meatballs. Cover and simmer for 1 hr. and 15 min.

Mrs. Ray J. Gingerich
Fillmore, NY

Lamps do not talk
They shine

CONEY SAUCE

3 lbs. hamburger
3 heaping T. quick oats
2 large onions (chopped)
2 T. vinegar
3 T. chili powder
1 cup catsup
1 qt. tomato juice
handful brown sugar

Brown and drain hamburger and onion. Add rest of ingredients and simmer until thickened. You can add up to 40 hot dogs; serve on buns. This sauce freezes well.

Elizabeth Mae Raber
Montgomery, IN

BARBECUED HAMBURGER

Crumble 2 lb.hamburger in a frying pan (10 1/2 in.)
Cut fine 2 onions and add to meat. Let fry till juice disappears. Add enough tomato juice to almost cover meat. Let cook a while. Add:

1 t. mustard
salt and pepper

Add enough rolled oats or flour to thicken for sandwiches.

Mrs. Neal Kauffman
La Plata, MO

MOCK STEAK

For each lb. of hamburger add:

1 cup white crackers (make fine)
1 cup milk

salt, pepper, onions, and garlic salt, and sage powder to suit your taste. Mix together and form on rolls. Let stand overnight - 8-10 hrs. Slice, roll in flour and brown slowly in greased skillet. Put in roaster and pour 1 can creamed mushroom soup. Mix with 1 can milk over top and bake 1 hr. For extra goodness, top each piece with velveeta cheese and let melt.

Joe Borntreger
Cashton, WI

MOCK TURKEY

3 lb. hamburger, fried
1 can celery soup
1 qt. milk
1 can cream of chicken soup
1 can cream of mushroom soup
1 loaf bread, cut in cubes

Put all in roaster. Mix well with soups and milk. Bake at 350 deg. for 1 hr.

Louella Borntrager
Sugar Creek, OH

PIGS IN A BLANKET

1 head of cabbage
2 lb. rice
1 lb. or more fresh hamburger
1 med. onion, finely chopped
1/2 cup lard
salt and pepper to taste

Cut core out of cabbage. Cook in salt water until leaves start loosening. Put them in covered dish. (Peel off part of thick ribs or leaves) Boil rice until 1/2 done; put through strainer and wash in cold water. Drain. Mix into fresh hamburger. Fry onion in at least 1/2 cup lard. Add to hamburger mixture. Mix well; add salt and pepper. Put a heaping tablespoon of this mixture in each leaf. Roll snugly. Put in roast pan and pour tomato juice with some beef broth. Bake 2-3 hrs. in fairly hot oven.

Saloma Petersheim
Mifflintown, PA

POOR MAN'S STEAK

1 lb. hamburger
1 cup milk
1 cup cracker crumbs
1 small onion, chopped
1 t. salt
1/4 t. pepper

Mix well and shape in a narrow loaf. Let set for at least 8 hrs. or overnight is best. Slice and fry in skillet on both sides till brown. Put slices in roaster and spread mushroom soup on each piece; use 1 can for this amount. Bake 1 hr. at 325 deg.

Ella Hershberger
Oakland, MD

PORKY PIE

4 med. sweet potatoes
1 1/2 t. salt
2 T. butter
1 1/2 t. cinnamon sugar
1 lb. ground pork
1 1/2 cups water
2 T. flour
dash of pepper

Cook potatoes in salt water and peel. Mash slightly and add butter, 1/2 t. salt and cinnamon sugar. Add a little milk if necessary. Brown pork patties and drain. (Canned pork works fine too) Make a gravy with water, flour and pork broth. Pour on patties in a shallow baking pan. Spread sweet potatoes over top. Bake at 400 deg. for 20 min.

Sadie Miller
Fort Plain, NY

HAMBURGERS WITH SAUCE

1 lb. hamburgers 1 cup cracker crumbs
onions, salt, pepper and a little milk and make a roll - let stand overnight.

Sauce:

1 can mushroom soup 1 chopped onion
3 T. ketchup 2 T. worcestershire sauce
enough water to make sauce.
Pour over hamburger and bake 50-60 min.

Esther Marie Fisher
Conneautville, PA

HEARTY HAMBURGER SOUP

1 lb. hamburger 1 cup chopped onions
1 cup diced carrots 1/2 cup green peppers (opt.)
2 cups tomatoe juice 1 cup diced potatoes
1 1/2 t. salt 1/8 t. pepper
Fry hamburger and onions together. Have carrots, potatoes and celery cooked; then combine this all together and heat and serve with crackers.

Ella Hershberger
Oakland, MD

YUM-A-ZETTI

1 pkg. noodles cooked in salt water 3 lb. hamburger fried with onion
1 pt. peas 2 cans mushroom soup
1 cup milk 1/2 loaf bread toasted in butter
Mix soup and milk together; pour over other ingredients which have been put in a roaster. Mix. Bake at 350 deg. for 1 hr.

Louella Borntrager
Sugar Creek, OH

Chicken

KENTUCKY FRIED CHICKEN

2 cups stale bread crumbs grated or substitute cracker crumbs
3/4 cup grated parmesan cheese
1 clove garlic, crushed
1/4 cup chopped parsley
2 t. salt
1/8 t. pepper
1 or 2 fryers, cut up
1 cup melted butter or margarine

Mix bread or cracker crumbs, cheese, garlic, parsley, salt and pepper. Dip chicken pieces in butter, then in crumb mixture, coating well. Arrange in open shallow pan. Pour remaining butter over all. Bake at 350 deg. for 1 hr. or until tender when pricked with a fork. Baste frequently with drippings.

Mrs. Jacob Stutzman
Jeromesville, OH

PAPRIKA CHICKEN

1/2 cup flour
2 t. paprika
1 t. pepper
1/4 t. dry mustard
3 t. salt

Mix together ingredients, roll cut up raw chicken in mixture. Bake at 350 deg. for 1 1/2 hr.

Esther Marie Fisher
Conneautville, PA

CHICKEN CASSEROLE

Fill bottom of casserole with broken bread
4 cups cooled chicken
1 cup cream of mushroom
1/4 cup melted butter
1/2 cup salad dressing
4 eggs, well beaten
2 cups milk
1 t. salt and pepper and celery salt
engough cheese to cover
2 cans celery soup

Bake 350 deg. for 1 1/4 hr.

Esther Marie Fisher
Conneautville, PA

Whenever you're angry pretend you are a bird
Sing just a little, but don't say a word

CHICKEN CROQUETTES

2 T. butter
2 1/2 T. flour
1 cup milk
2 cups minced cooked chicken
1 t. salt
1/4 t. onion juice
1/8 t. pepper
2 T. minced parsley or celery
2 eggs (beaten)
1 cup diced bread crumbs

Melt butter in saucepan, add flour and seasoning; then slowly add milk till a paste is formed. Add chicken and seasoning. Cool thoroughly, roll in crumbs, then beaten eggs and crumbs again. Deep fry.

Fannie Miller
Bird-in-Hand, PA

BAKED CHICKEN

1/2 cup flour
2 t. paprika
1 t. pepper
3 t. salt
1 cut up broiler or young chicken

Mix dry ingredients well in plastic bag and then dust cut up chicken parts. In cake pan melt 1/4 lb. butter. Place in pan chicken parts, not crowding. Bake at 350 deg. for 1 1/2-2 hrs. or until done.

Sadie Miller
Fort Plain, NY

Life for most of us
Is a continuous process
Of getting used to things
We hadn't expected

SHAKE AND BAKE

3/4 cup cornflake crumbs
2 t. salt
1 t. paprika
1/4 t. dry mustard
1/4 t. black pepper
1 - 4 or 5 lb. fryer.

Coat meat with crumbs and put in roast pan. You can put 2 layers in. Add a little water, cover and bake at 375 deg. for 2 1/2 hrs. or until done.

Lydia Stoltzfus
Bloomsburg, PA

GOLDEN EMBER SAUCE FOR BARBECUE CHICKEN ON GRILL

6 cups butter or margarine
1 3/4 cups lemon juice
1/2 cup prepared mustard
1 cup brown sugar
9 T. salt
2 T. paprika
1 3/4 t. pepper
1 T. worcestershire sauce
2 cups ketchup
1/2 bottle tabasco sauce

This recipe is for 50 chicken halves.

Aaron Brubacker
Liverpool, PA

CRISP GOLDEN CHICKEN

Mix together:

1 egg
1/2 cup water

Mix the following ingredients:

1 cup flour
2 t. salt
1 t. baking powder
2 t. paprika
a little pepper

Dip chicken into egg mixture, then into flour. Place chicken on cookie sheet in which 1/4 lb. butter has been melted. Do not place chicken pieces on top of each other. Bake for 1 1/2 hrs. in 350 deg. oven. Bake on one side 45 min. and then turn and bake on other side 45 min. longer.

Joni H. Shrock
Middlefield, OH

IMPOSSIBLE PIE

The cooked meat of 1 chicken
2 t. salt
1 cup cheese
1 (6 oz.) can tomato paste
1 t. oregano
1/2 t. basil leaves
1/2 cup small curd cottage cheese
2/3 cup bisquick
1 cup milk
2 eggs
1/4 t. pepper

Combine all ingredients and bake at 350 deg. for approx. 30 min.

Saloma Petersheim
Mifflintown, PA

Happiness is not perfected until it is shared

CHICKEN STIR-FRY

1 lb. chicken or turkey breast
medium head broccoli
1/4 head cabbage
2 small carrots
2 stalks celery
other vegetables optional(onion, mushrooms, canned water chestnuts, sugar snap peas, chinese cabbage)

Slice chicken into thin strips. Chop vegetables coarsely. Heat 2 T. oil in nonstick skillet. Slightly brown chicken strips before adding vegetables. Stir fry vegetables until tender-crisp.

Sauce:
1 cup chicken broth
3 T. soy sauce

Thicken with 2 T. cornstarch. Pour over stir-fried vegetables. Serve with hot rice, additional soy sauce and chow mein noodles.

Mrs. Wilma Mast
S. Hutchinson, KS

CHICKEN BAR-B-Q SAUCE

1 onion (finely chopped)
1/2 cup ketchup
2 T. brown sugar
2 T. vinegar
2 T. prepared mustard
1 T. worcestershire sauce
1 t. salt
dash of pepper

Simmer 10 minutes. To use with young chicken; roll meat in flour. Put in roaster. Add 1/2 in. of water and cover with sauce. Bake 1 hr. at 350 deg. For older chicken, cook until tender. Put in roaster. Bake 1/2 hr. at 350 deg.

Catherine Swarey
Belleville, PA

OVEN FRIED CHICKEN

Young frying chicken, cut up
Mix together:
2 cups crushed cornflakes
1/4 cup parmesan cheese
1 t. paprika
1 t. dry mustard
1 t. salt
1/2 t. pepper

Melt 2 T. butter in baking dish; dust chicken with flour, dip in a mixture of 2 beaten eggs and 1/2 cup cream. Roll in crumb mixture, coat well. Lay skin side down in baking dish. Bake at 375 deg. for 1 1/2 hr. or until done.

Esther Fisher
Millersburg, PA

CHICKEN CROQUETTES

2 T. margarine
2 1/2 T. flour
1 cup milk
Make a white sauce and add:
2 cups chopped chicken or turkey
1 t. salt
a little pepper
2 eggs, beaten
crushed cracker crumbs

Cool thoroughly. Shape into croquettes, dip in cracker crumbs, then into eggs, then in cracker crumbs again. Fry in vegetable oil.

Esther Fisher
Millersburg, PA

FINGER LICKING GOOD CHICKEN

Fry chicken as usual, then dip in a mixture of:
1/2 cup vinegar
1/2 cup water
1/2 cup melted oleo
1 t. worcestershire sauce
Put on tray or cookie sheets and bake 1/2 hr. or until done.

CORN CRISP CHICKEN

1 broiler, cut in pieces
1 cup cornflake crumbs
1 1/2 t. salt
1/8 t. pepper
1/2 cup milk

Combine cornflake crumbs with salt and pepper. Dip chicken in milk, then in crumbs; put foil on cookie sheet, then chicken (only one layer). Bake 1 1/2 hr. Don't turn meat while roasting; leave uncovered.

Mrs. Raymond S. Miller
Millersburg, OH

SAVORY CHICKEN DUMPLINGS

4 lb. stewing chicken, cut up
4 cups water
1 T. salt
Thicken with:
3/4 cup flour
1 cup water
2 t. savory

Cook chicken till tender. Remove pieces and thicken with flour and water. Bring to a boil and simmer while preparing batter for dumplings.

1 cup sifted flour
1 1/2 t. baking powder
1/2 t. salt
2 T. butter
4 t. parsley flakes
1 beaten egg
1/4 - 1/2 cup milk

Mix dry ingredients. Chop in butter and blend to make crumbs. Blend in milk and beaten egg mixed stirring as little as possible to mix for light dumplings. Drop into chicken mixture by tblsp. and simmer covered 15 min., then uncovered 5 min. Serve as soon as possible. Diced potatoes, carrots, celery and onions may be added to chicken broth.

Lydiann J. Bricker
Panama, NY

MARY Z'S BAKED CHICKEN

Cut up chicken
Rolled soda cracker crumbs
Salad oil
Seasoned salt

Grease pan to bake with. Dip chicken in oil, then in cracker crumbs. Sprinkle on seasoned salt. Lay in prepared pan, 1 layer in depth. Bake in moderate oven 375-400 deg. for about 1 hr. or till tender and brown.

When two men in a business always agree
One of them is not needed

Ham

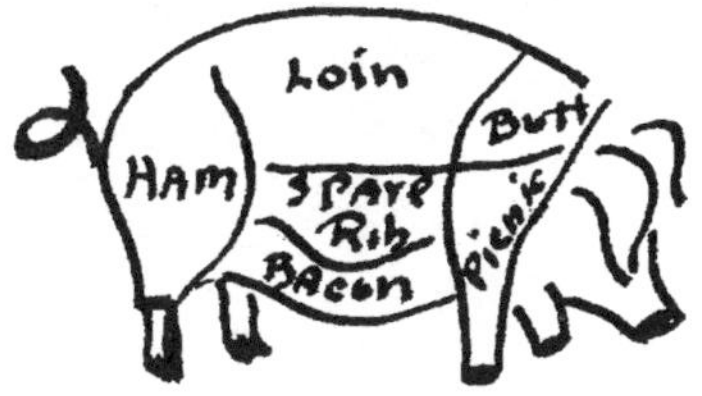

PORK AND BEANS

8 lb. beans
1 1/2 lb. bacon
1 lb. sugar
1/2 t. red pepper
1 cup dried mustard
1/3 cup salt or suit taste
4 qt. tomatoe juice
1 cup molasses
1 t. cinnamon

Soak beans overnight; add 2 qt. water to tomatoes, sugar, molasses, salt, pepper, cinnamon, and mustard together, cook beans until nearly tender, slice bacon fine and divide in cans after they are filled. Put a little cornstarch in each can, seal and pressure can 1/2 hr. at 10 lb. pressure.

Clara Hochstetter
Canton, MO

SUGAR CURE FOR HAM

2 cups salt
2 T. black pepper
3 T. brown sugar
1 T. red pepper

Mix and rub on ham.

Mattie Borntreger
Cashton, WI

SPAMBURGER

Grind 1 can Spam
1 med. onion
2 t. catsup
2 T. milk
1/2 lb. white American cheese
Then add:
3 t. mayonnaise

Spread a generous amount on slices of bread and broil in broiler.

Fannie Miller
Bird-in-Hand, PA

Whatever you choose to give away
Always be sure to keep your temper

SOUTHERN BAKED HAM

3/4 cup flour
1/4 t. powdered mustard
1/4 cup brown sugar
3-4 lb. pre-cooked ham
1 cup coffee cream or milnot

Slice ham 1/3" thick. Roll each slice in mixture of flour, brown sugar and mustard. Place in a baking dish. Pour cream over meat and bake 1 1/2 hrs. at 350 deg. Time will vary, depending whether meat is pre-cooked.

Mary Ann Hilty
Monroe, IN

A man who boasts
Of his ancestors
Is like a potato
The only good
Is under the ground

CHALUPA

3 lb. pork roast
1 1/2-2 lbs. dry pinto beans
1 med. can green chiles, chopped
2 cloves garlic
pepper to taste
2 T. chili powder
1 T. cummin
1 t. oregano
1 T. salt

Cover roast with water. Add washed beans and rest of ingredients. Cook very slowly for 6-7 hrs. Shred roast with a fork. Serve in layers: chips (tortillas), meat mix, shredded lettuce, diced tomatoes, green onions, taco sauce, shredded cheese, sour cream.

Mrs. Wilma Mast
S. Hutchinson, KS

TO SALT SAUSAGE

1 pt. salt
1 cup brown sugar
2 heaping T. pepper
1 t. red pepper

Mix together. Add 1 lb. salt mixture to 50 lb. sausage, before stuffing.

Mrs. Vernon E. Bontrager
Iowa City, IA

SAUSAGE

50 lbs. meat
12 oz. salt
2 oz. black pepper
1 T. red pepper
4 T. sage
2 handfuls brown sugar

Mix real good.

Emma Hershberger
Dover, DE

SCRAPPLE

12 qts. pork stock and broth
2 T. salt
1 T. red pepper
7 T. sage
2 1/4 cups wheat flour
4 1/2 cups corn meal

Boil the stock and broth; then add the rest of the ingredients. Pour into bread pans and freeze.

Emma Hershberger
Dover, DE

MOCK TURKEY

2 lb. hamburger
1 can cream of chicken soup
1 can cream of mushroom soup
1 can cream of celery soup
3 cups milk
1 large pkg. bread stuffing or 1 loaf bread, cubed

Brown hamburger; add salt and pepper to taste. Add soups, milk, toasted bread crumbs or cubes; put in pan. Bake at 350 deg. for 45 min.

Ida Schrock
Haven, KS

Seafood

TUNA SUPPER DISH

1/2 cup butter
1/2 cup flour
3 cup milk
1 can tuna
2 cups peas cooked & drained
Salt & pepper to taste

Melt butter in heavy pan. Blend flour into butter and allow to simmer for one full minute. The trick here is to remove pan from heat to add the cold milk. Bring pan back to medium heat and stir sauce until it begins to bubble. Salt and pepper to taste. Add drained tuna and peas. Bring to boiling and serve immediately over hot cooked rice or buttered toast.

Mrs. Wilma Mast
S. Hutchinson, KS

SALMON CARBONDRA

1 cup salmon
1/4 cup hot melted oleo
1 cup grated cheese
1/4 cup chopped parsley
8 oz. noodles
2 eggs beaten
Salt & pepper to taste

Drain salmon, break into large chunks, set aside, cook noodles and drain; immediately pour in hot oleo, tossing to coat evenly. Add eggs, cheese, parsley, salt and pepper, stir again. Sprinkle salmon chunks on top and toss lightly, so chunks won't break up. Serve with additional cheese if desired.

Mrs. Ray J. Gingerich
Fillmore, NY

FISH LOG

Combine: 2 cans tuna
1-8 oz. package cream cheese
2 T. grated onion
1 T. lemon juice
Dash of Liquid Smoke
1 tsp. prepared horseradish
1/4 tsp. salt

Shape into a log. Wrap in aluminum foil. Chill. Roll in 1/2 cup chopped parsley and pecans. Serve with crackers.

Mrs. Wilma Mast
South Hutchinson, KS

BAKED FISH A LA PRESTON

2 lbs. haddock
2-3 cups bread crumbs
2-2 1/2 oz. jars sliced mushrooms
2 cups melted oleo
1-2 cans evaporated milk

Grease bottom of a 3 qt. casserole, sprinkle with a light coating of bread crumbs. Cut haddock into serving size pieces. Place half the fish on the bottom of casserole. Mix the remaining bread crumbs, mushrooms, and melted oleo. Spread half the mixture on top of fish. Add the balance of the fish and top with the rest of the crumb mixture. Pour milk over all and bake at 380 degrees for 30 minutes. Makes 6-8 servings. You can use frozen fillets and use milk only half of strength if wanted. Is best using whole evaporated milk.

Mrs. Joe J. Miller
Apple Creek, OH

The way most
fisherman catch fish
Is by the tale

HOW TO SELECT FRESH FISH

In buying whole fish look for the following:
Eyes: bright, clear, full and bulging
Gills: reddish pink, free from slime or odor
Scales: adhering tightly to the skin, bright colored with characteristic sheen
Flesh: firm and elastic, springing back when pressed, not separated from bones
Odor: fresh, free from objectionable odors

Pancakes & Cereals

FEATHERLIGHT PANCAKES

Sift together:
2 cups flour
3/4 t. salt
1 t. soda
3 T. sugar
Combine:
2 beaten eggs
1 3/4 cups sweet milk
1/2 cup vinegar
1/2 cup melted shortening

Mix well and add to dry ingredients, stir until smooth. Bake at once. Ladle into griddle, brown and turn. Yield 20 pancakes.

Mrs. Jacob Stutzman
Jeromesville, OH

FAMILY LIFE CEREAL

12 cups oatmeal
6 cups wheat germ
2 cups sugar
6 cups coconut
Mix well and add:
1 cup vegetable oil

Mix well. Put in cake pans and bake till light brown and crisp. Low heat.

Mrs. Neal Kauffman
La Plata, MO

CEREAL

12 cups oatmeal
6 cups coconut
1 cup oil or butter
6 cups wheat germ meal
3 cups brown sugar
1 1/2 t. salt

Mix all together and toast in oven until coconut is brown. Serve as breakfast cereal.

Joe Borntreger
Cashton, WI

Sometimes one pays most
For the things one gets for nothing

FEATHER WEIGHT PANCAKES

2 cups sifted flour
1 t. soda
3 T. sugar
3/4 t. salt
2 eggs, well beaten
1/4 cup vinegar
1 3/4 cups sweet milk
1/4 cup shortening (melted)

Sift flour, baking soda, sugar and salt together. Combine eggs, vinegar, milk and shortening and mix well. Add to dry ingredients and stir only until smooth. Pour into hot frying pan. When edge has formed a crust, turn.

Clara Hochstetter
Canton, MO

CRUNCHY CORN

12 cups oatmeal
6 cups coconut
6 cups wheat germ
3 cups brown sugar
1 cup lard
pinch of salt

Mix dry things together before adding lard. Roast in oven. Makes 2 gal.

Mrs. Joe J. Yoder
Lawrenceburg, TN

GRANOLA

8 cups oatmeal
4 cups wheat germ
2 cups bran
1 1/2 cups coconut
1 cup nuts or sunflower seeds

Pour 1 cup honey and 1 cup oil over ingredients. Bake 1 hr. at 200-225 deg., stirring often.

Fannie Miller
Bird-in-Hand, PA

GRAPE NUTS BREAKFAST CEREAL

8 lb. whole wheat flour
5 lb. brown sugar
1 1/4 t. salt
2 T. soda
2 T. vanilla
2 T. maple
3/4 lb. oleo (melted)
2 1/2 qt. buttermilk or sour milk

Put together in order given, adding flour last. Put in greased cake pans and bake 30-40 min. till done in 350 deg. oven. Cool overnight. Put through shredder and bake them again in a slow oven until nice and brown. Seal in tight jars to keep.

Sue Wickey
Norfolk, NY

COLD BREAKFAST CEREAL

12 cups rolled oats
6 cups wheat germ
1 cup brown sugar or
1 cup honey mixed with 1 cup veg. oil or melted oleo or butter
1 1/2 t. salt
3 cups coconuts and 3 cups nuts

Mix all together and pour in cake pans. Toast in oven until coconut turns brown. Stir often while toasting at 325 deg.

Sue Wickey
Norfolk, NY

PANCAKE MIX

Mix:
10 cups flour
3 T. soda
3 T. salt
5 heaping T. baking powder
1/4 cup sugar
2 cups oatmeal (quick)
3 cups whole wheat flour
3 cups crushed corn flakes

Mix thoroughly and store until used.

To make batter, use:
1 cup mix
1 cup milk
1 egg
1 T. shortening

Mrs. Philip Yoder
Fairbank, IA

The best place to find a helping hand
Is at the end of your arm

TASTY PANCAKES

2 beaten eggs
2 cups sour milk
1 t. soda
2 1/4 cups flour
2 t. baking powder
1 t. salt
4 T. melted butter
2 T. sugar

(If sweet milk is used,omit the soda and increase baking powder to 3 t.)

Beat eggs until fluffy. Add milk. Sift flour, baking powder, soda, salt and sugar. Beat flour mixture into egg mixture. Mix well. Add melted butter and beat until smooth.

Saloma Petersheim
Mifflintown, PA

PANCAKE MIX

8 cups sifted white flour
4 cups buckwheat flour
8 T. salt
3/4 cup baking powder
3/4 cup sugar

Mix all ingredients well and store in airtight container. For each 1 1/2 cup mix use 1 egg beaten, 1 cup milk and 2 T. shortening. Mix well. Fry on hot griddle.

Saloma J. Byler
Dewittville, NY

GRAPENUTS

3 qt. brown sugar (slightly packed)
5 qt. whole wheat flour
1 1/4 T. salt
2 T. soda
2 T. vanilla
1 1/2 t. maple flavor
3/4 lb. oleo
2 1/2 qt. buttermilk

Put dry ingredients in bowl except soda which should be added to milk. Last add melted oleo and flavor. Dough should be fairly thick. Bake at 350 deg. Makes about 15 lbs.

Mrs. Noah Wengerd, Jr.
Conewango Valley, NY

TASTY PANCAKES

2 beaten eggs
2 cups sour milk
Add 2 T. vinegar if sweet milk is used
2 t. sugar
2 1/4 cups flour
2 t. baking powder
1 t. salt
4 T. melted butter or oil

Beat eggs till light. Add milk. Sift flour with baking powder, salt and sugar. Beat flour mixture into egg mixture. Add melted butter. Beat until smooth.

Sadie Miller
Fort Plain, NY

PANCAKE SYRUP

1 cup sugar
2 cups water

Bring to boil; add 1 level T. cornstarch. Mix with a little water, bring to a full rolling boil, add 1 t. maple flavor and 1/2 t. vanilla.

Sadie Miller
Fort Plain, NY

WAFFLES

3 cups sifted flour
3 1/2 t. baking powder
3/4 t. salt
3/4 cup Crisco
3 egg yolks, beaten
2 cups milk
3 egg whites - stiffly beaten, add last
To bake in waffle iron

Esther Marie Fisher
Conneautville, PA

PANCAKE RECIPE

2 well beaten eggs
5 T. salad oil or melted butter
2 cups milk
3 t. baking powder
1/2 cup sugar
1 t. salt
2 1/4 cups flour

Stir together sugar, salt, flour, and baking powder. Add eggs, oil or butter, and milk.

Mrs. Samuel D. Beachy
Clark, MO

POTATO PANCAKES

2 cups grated raw potatoes
2 T. milk
4 T. flour
1 t. baking powder
1 egg beaten
2 T. butter
1 t. salt

Mix all together, drop by spoonfuls into skillet, fry in mixed butter and lard until brown and crispy.

Louella Borntrager
Sugar Creek, OH

HOMEMADE CEREAL

12 cups rolled oats
6 cups wheat germ
1 cup melted shortening
add a little cinnamon
6 cups coconut
3 cups brown sugar, more or less
1 t. salt

Mix all together and brown lightly in oven. Cool and store in airtight container. Serve with milk and honey.

Mrs. Joseph Schrock
Agusta, WI

GOOD GRAPENUTS

7 cups wheat flour
3 cups brown sugar
4 cups sour milk
2 t. soda
2 t. salt
1/2 cup melted oleo
2 t. vanilla
2 t. maple flavoring

Bake as a loaf cake. Crumble and toast. Instead of 4 cups sour milk, use part cream or buttermilk.

Mrs. Joseph Schrock
Agusta, WI

BREAKFAST CEREAL

2 cups rolled oats
1 cup brown sugar
1 t. salt
1/2 cup coconut
2 cups wheat flour
1 t. soda
1/2 cup butter

Mix into crumbs; then put on cookie sheet and roast in oven at 400 deg.

Mrs. Leroy J. Byler
Fredericktown, OH

WHOLE WHEAT PANCAKES

2 cups whole wheat flour
4 t. baking powder
1/2 t. salt
1 1/2 cups milk
1 T. melted butter
2 eggs beaten

Sift together dry ingredients, add milk, butter and eggs. Beat until blended. Bake on slightly greased hot griddle.

Elizabeth Mae Raber
Montgomery, IN

A man should never be ashamed
To confess he failed
It is but another way
Of saying he is wiser
Than he was yesterday

Pies

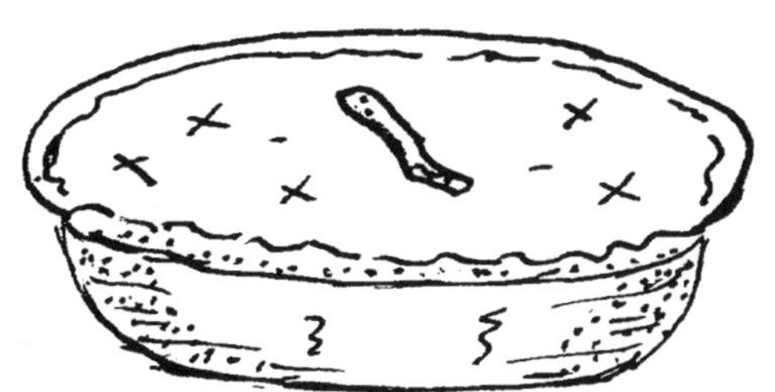

MULBERRY PIE

Fill unbaked pie shell with mulberries.
Mix together:
3 T. flour
1 cup sugar
1 T. vinegar
Cook with 1 cup water; pour over berries in crust and put crust on top and bake.

Ida Schrock
Haven, Kansas

FISH PIE

2 cups brown sugar
3/4 cup lard (scant)
1 cup sour milk
flour to roll as pie dough
1 t. soda
1 t. baking powder
Filling:
1 cup molasses
1/2 cup sugar
3 T. flour
1 pt. water
1 t. vanilla
Boil till thick. Put 1 crust in pie pan; fill with filling and a top crust without any holes in it. Bake at 350 deg. for1 hr. (The natives said they used to put a fish design on top, hence it got its name; we think it tastes somewhat like vanilla pie, which they didn't know anything about.)

Esther Fisher
Millersburg, PA

TOLL HOUSE PIE

1 - 6oz. pkg. (1 cup) Nestle's Toll House or semi-sweet chocolate morsels
2 eggs
1/2 cup flour
1/2 cup white sugar
1/2 cup brown sugar, firmly packed
1 cup butter, melted and cooled
1 cup chopped walnuts
1 - 9 in. unbaked pie shell
whipped cream or ice cream (optional)
Preheat oven to 325 deg. In a large bowl, beat eggs until foamy. Add flour, sugar and brown sugar; beat until well blended. Blend in melted butter. Stir in Nestle's Toll House or semi-sweet chocolate morsels and walnuts. Pour into pie shell. Bake for 1 hr. Serve warm with whipped cream or ice cream.

Mrs. J. David Byler
Punaxsutawney, PA

PIE PASTRY MIX

4 cups flour
1 3/4 cups lard or 2 cups Crisco
1 T. baking powder
1 1/2 t. salt
Cut in shortening. Mix together and add:
1/2 cup water
1 T. vinegar
1 beaten egg
This crust will not soak like usual dough.

Mrs. Philip Yoder
Fairbank, IA

DELICIOUS APPLE PIE

Fill an unbaked pie crust about 3/4 full of raw, coarsely chopped apples. Then mix the following:
1 cup brown sugar
1/2 T. flour
1 cup sweet cream
1/2 t. cinnamon
Pour over apples and bake till brown.

Mrs. Philip Yoder
Fairbank, IA

POTATO PIE

Pie Crust (regular pie crust) in bottom of deep pie pan. Slice potatoes thick and put a layer in pan. Add a layer of ham, cut in cubes; then another layer of potatoes; then ham until pan is full; add salt and pepper to taste and water. Put a crust on top and bake until done. Eat it with milk or gravy. (Other meat can be used instead of ham.)

Mrs. Philip Yoder
Fairbank, IA

MOCK MINCE PIE

2 eggs
2 1/2 cups sugar
1/2 cup oleo
2 cups hot water
1 cup raisins
1 cup bread crumbs
2 T. vinegar
1/4 t. all spice
1 t. cinnamon
1/4 t. nutmeg
Pour hot water over raisins. Add oleo and bread crumbs to raisins and water. In a large bowl, beat the eggs and add sugar. Add vinegar and spices to egg mixture after oleo is melted. Pour in unbaked pie shell and top with crust. Bake in hot oven until browned. Makes 2 pies.

Miss Sara Shetler
Glasgow, KY

BUTTERSCOTCH PIE FILLING

1st part:

3/4 cup brown sugar
1/4 cup hot water
oleo, size of small egg
1/2 t. vanilla
pinch of salt

Boil together for 5-10 min.

2nd part:

1 1/4 T. flour
1 1/4 T. cornstarch
1/2 cup white sugar
2 egg yolks

Mix with milk to a smooth paste. Add 1 1/2 cups milk and heat to boiling point. Then add 1st part and bring to boiling. Makes 1 pie.

Miss Sara Shetler
Glasgow, KY

A well informed person
Is one who has opinions just like yours

EGG CUSTARD PIE

3 eggs
1/2 cup sugar
2 cups milk

Bring to a boil.
Add egg yolks and sugar and beat a little.
Add boiling milk, 1 t. vanilla, 1/4 t. salt.
Add beaten egg whites
Bake at 450 deg. for 50 min. 400 deg. for 10 min. or more.

Eva Kauffman
Newburg, PA

PIE CRUST

Blend 6 cups flour and 2 cups lard to coarse crumbs. In a cup combine 1 egg and 1 t. vinegar and 1 t. salt; beat together. Add water to fill the cup. Combine all the ingredients with a fork or hands. This is always flaky and never fails.

Mrs. Samuel D. Beachy
Clark, MO

RAISIN CRUMB PIE

3/4 cup raisins
2 cups water
2/3 cup brown sugar
1 T. vinegar (scant)
2 T. cornstarch or clear jell
Pinch of salt

Bring to a boil water with raisins, brown sugar, vinegar and salt. Mix cornstarck or clear jell with enough water to make a smooth mixture and add to above. Bring to a boil. When cold, pour into unbaked pie shell. Top with the following crumbs and bake in hot oven till browned.

1 cup flour
1/2 cup brown sugar
1/2 t. soda
1/4 cup shortening

Mrs. Samuel D. Beachy
Clark, MO

CHOCOLATE PIE FILLING

1 qt. sweet milk or water
1 cup sugar
2 T. cornstarch
2 T. flour
1 T. cocoa
3 eggs
Flavor

Cook; pour in shells. Makes 2 pies.

Mrs. Samuel D. Beachy
Clark, MO

MOCK APPLE PIE

30 soda crackers broken in fourths
1 1/2 cups water
1 1/2 cups sugar
1 1/2 t. cream of tartar
1 t. cinammon
1 t. nutmeg
1 T. butter or oleo

Put cracker in unbaked crust; put rest in saucepan and bring to boil. Pour over crackers. Put crust on top. Bake at 400 deg. for 35 min. or till brown.

Ida Schrock
Haven, KS

The man who has never made a mistake
Will never make anything else

BUTTERMILK COCONUT PIE

1 1/2 cups sugar
3 eggs beaten
1/2 cup buttermilk
1 cup coconut
2 T. flour
1/2 cup butter or margarine
1 t. vanilla

Combine sugar and flour in a large bowl. Add butter, eggs, buttermilk, vanilla and 2/3 cup coconut. Mix well. Pour mixture into pastry shell. Sprinkle with remaining coconut. Bake at 325 deg.

Mrs. Samuel D. Beachy
Clark, MO

APPLE PIE

Put 2 cups shredded apples in unbaked pie shell.
Mix:
1 cup sugar
2 T. flour
1 1/2 cups sweet cream
cinnamon and salt to taste

Pour this over apples and bake.

Mrs. Samuel D. Beachy
Clark, MO

POT PIE

1 cup sugar
1 cup water or milk
2 cups flour
2 T. butter
pinch of salt
2 t. baking powder

Cream sugar and butter; sift flour, baking powder and salt. Add alternately with water or milk to creamed mixture. Pour over any fruit desired and bake. Serve with milk.

Mrs. Samuel D. Beachy
Clark, MO

Wherever you wander
Wherever you roam
Be healthy and happy
And Glad to come home

SPAGHETTI PIE

6 oz. spaghetti
2 T. butter or margarine
1/3 cup grated parmesan cheese
2 well beaten eggs
1 cup cottage cheese (8 oz.)
1 pound ground beef or bulk pork sausage
1/2 cup chopped onion
1/4 cup chopped green pepper
1 - 8 oz. can (1 cup) tomatoes, cut up
1 - 6 oz. can tomato paste
1 t. sugar
1 t. dried oregano, crushed
1/2 t. garlic salt
1/2 cup shredded mozzarella cheese (2 oz.)

Cook the spaghetti according to package directions, drain (should have 3 cups spaghetti). Stir butter or margarine into hot spaghetti. Stir in parmesan cheese and eggs. Form spaghetti mixture in a "crust" in a buttered 10 in. pie plate. Spread cottage cheese over bottom of spaghetti crust.

In skillet cook ground beef or pork sausage, onion and green pepper till vegetables are tender and meat is browned. Drain off excess fat. Stir in undrained tomatoes, tomato paste, sugar, oregano, and garlic salt; heat through.

Turn meat mixture into spaghetti crust. Bake uncovered in 350 deg. oven for 20 min. Sprinkle the mozzarella cheese on top. Bake 5 min. longer or till cheese melts. Makes 6 servings.

Joni H. Schrock
Middlefield, OH

MILNOT PUMPKIN PIE

1 cup brown sugar
1/4 t. cinnamon
1/4 t. nutmeg
1 cup cooked pumpkin
1 can milnot or 1 2/3 cups rich milk
1/2 t. salt
2 eggs, slightly beaten
2 T. flour

Mix sugar, spices, salt and flour together and stir into pumpkin. Add milnot and eggs. Pour into 9" unbaked pie shell and bake in a hot oven, 450 deg., for the first 10 min. Reduce heat to 350 deg. and continue baking for another 25-30 min. or until filling is firm.

Lucinda Hilty
Monroe, IN

NEVER FAIL PIE DOUGH

4 cups flour
2 t. salt
1 t. baking powder
Put in a sifter and sift into a bowl.
Add 1 1/2 cups lard or 1 3/4 cups vegetable shortening. Work together.
Then add:
1 egg
1 T. vinegar
1/2 cup milk
Beat together and mix well. Roll out. Makes 4 crusts.

Joe Borntreger
Cashton, WI

BEST EVER PIE CRUST

5 cups flour
1 1/2 cups lard (hard)
1/2 t. salt
1/2 t. baking powder
2 eggs
1 cup water
Combine flour, salt and baking powder. Cut lard into flour mixture. Do not overmix; these are sufficiently blended when particles are the size of peas. Mix water and eggs together. Add to flour mixture. Mix till soft and smooth.

Aaron Brubacker
Liverpool, PA

Find the thankless heart
And you will also find an unhappy one

CHERRY CRUMB PIE

1 qt. fresh or canned sour cherries
2 cups sugar
2 T. clear jell
Crumbs:
1 cup flour
1 cup sugar
4 T. butter
pinch of salt
Cook cherries, sugar and clear jel until thick. Cool slightly. Pour into unbaked pie shell; sprinkle with crumbs and bake in hot oven till crumbs are brown.

Aaron Brubacker
Liverpool, PA

IMPOSSIBLE COCONUT PIE

1 egg
1 cup sugar
1 cup milk
1/4 cup flour
1/2 t. vanilla
pinch of salt
1/4 t. baking powder
1/4 cup oleo (melted)
1 cup coconut

Beat all together. Bake at 350 deg. 30-35 min. Needs no crust - check with knife blade for doneness or when golden brown.

Mrs. Emma Stutzman
Bronson, MI

FRENCH CHERRY PIE

1 - 3 oz. Philadelphia cream cheese
1/2 cup powdered sugar
1 cup whipping cream (whipped)
1/2 t. vanilla
1 can prepared cherry pie filling

Cream the cheese, sugar and vanilla. Fold in whipped cream. Pour into baked pie shell. Spread evenly over the bottom of pie shell, then spread cherry pie mix over the top of cheese mixture. Chill and serve.

Mrs. Emma Stutzman
Bronson, MI

FAVORITE PEACH PIE

4 1/4 cups water
1 1/2 cups sugar
2/3 cup clear jel
1 box Royal jello peach
pinch of salt
2 T. butter

Bring to boiling point, then add 4 cups peach slices. Cool 1 min. longer. Makes 3 pies.

Louella Borntrager
Sugar Creek, OH

BEST PUMPKIN PIE

1 cup white sugar
1 cup brown sugar
2 round T. flour
1/2 t. cinnamon

Mix well, then add 4 round T. pumpkin, 2 egg yolks and 3 cups milk (may be heated). Beat the whites stiff and fold in last. Makes 2 pies. Bake at 325 deg. for 1 hr.

Louella Borntrager
Sugar Creek, OH

SODA CRACKER PIE

14 soda crackers, rolled fine
1 cup sugar
1/2 t. baking powder
3 egg whites
1 1/2 t. vanilla
1/2 cup chopped walnuts

Beat egg whites until frothy. Start adding sugar gradually, and beat until mixture stands in stiff peaks. Fold in vanilla, crackers, baking powder and walnuts. Spread evenly in well greased 9" pie pan and bake at 325 deg. for 45 min. Cool.

Topping:
Beat 1 cup whipping cream until stiff. Fold in one (10 oz.) pkg. Flav-O-Rite frozen strawberries (well drained). Spread over pie and refrigerate 4 hr. or more. Serves 6 or 8.

Ida Miller
Medford, WI

CARAMEL OATMEAL PIE

3 eggs (slightly beaten)
3/4 cup Karo syrup
pinch of salt
1/2 cup oatmeal
1 cup brown sugar
1 T. butter
2 T. water

Pour into unbaked pie shell. Bake.

Mrs. Daniel C. Borntreger
Riceville, IA

RAISIN CRUMB PIE

3/4 cup raisins
2 cups water
1/4 t. salt
1 cup brown sugar
1 t. vinegar
1 T. clear jell

Bring raisins, sugar, water, vinegar and salt to a boil. Mix clear jell with a little water and add to hot mixture. Put in unbaked pie shell. Top with the following crumbs and bake in a hot oven.

Crumbs:
1 cup flour
1/2 cup brown sugar
1/2 t. soda
1/4 cup margarine

Mrs. Daniel C. Borntreger
Riceville, IA

SHOE STRING APPLE PIE

2 1/2 cups sugar
3 eggs well beaten
4 cups shredded apples
2 T. flour
4 T. water
pinch of salt

Mix all together and put in 2 unbaked pie shells. Sprinkle cinnamon on top and bake at 325 deg. until well done.

Mrs. Vernon E. Bontrager
Iowa City, IA

BUTTERSCOTCH PIE

1 cup brown sugar
1/2 t. salt
2 rounded T. flour

Mix together. Stir 1/2 cup to 1 cup milk into this mixture to make a smooth paste. Now add 2 egg yolks (save whites for meringue for the pies). Add butter the size of a walnut, then slowly stir and add enough boiling water for 1 pie (1-1 1/2 cups water). 1 t. vanilla added last when cooked, cook till thick like pudding. Now it is ready to be put in a baked pie shell and top with meringue.

Sue Wickey
Norfolk, NY

Why look for trouble
It's something you don't want

QUEEN OF PIES

(Strawberry Pie)

1 qt. fresh strawberries
1 1/2 T. cornstarch
2 baked pie shells (8 in.)
1/2 cup sugar
1 cup whipped cream

Crush slightly half of the strawberries in a saucepan and cook until soft, about 10 min. Add combined sugar and cornstarch. Cook over low heat until transparent and thick, stirring constantly. Cool. Chill. When ready to serve, place whole berries in chilled, baked pie shell. Top with boiled strawberry mixture and whipped cream.

Ida Miller
Medford, WI

CHOCOLATE CHIP PIE

24 marshmallows
1/2 cup milk
1 cup whipping cream
1/2 t. vanilla
2 squares semi-sweet chocolate (grated)

Heat marshmallows with milk until dissolved. Cool. Fold in whipping cream, vanilla and chocolate. Let stand a few minutes, then pour into a graham cracker crust. Let set a few hours before serving.

Mrs. Daniel C. Borntreger
Riceville, IA

GROUND CHERRY PIE

1 cup ground cherries
2 cups water
1 cup sugar
1 T. real lemon
pinch of salt

Boil and thicken with 4 T. clear jel mixed with water. Boil slowly for 7 min. Remove from heat. Add 1 T. butter, 1 t. lemon flavoring. Cool. Pour into pastry-lined pan and top with pastry. Brush top with milk or sprinkle with sugar. Bake at 400 deg. till golden brown.

Lydiann J. Bricker
Panama, NY

WALNUT PIE

4 eggs (separated)
5 cups milk
5 t. flour
1 cup syrup
1 1/2 cups sugar
1 cup walnut meats

Mix ingredients together, folding in beaten egg whites last. Pour into 3 unbaked pie shells. Bake in a moderate oven.

Mrs. Daniel C. Borntreger
Riceville, IA

COCONUT CUSTARD PIE

2 eggs beaten
1 cup molasses (white or dark)
1 cup milk
1 t. vanilla
1/2 cup sugar
1 T. flour
2 T. melted butter
1 cup coconut

Mix all together and pour into unbaked pie shell.

Naomi Peachey
Little Falls, NY

PEANUT BUTTER PIE (UNBAKED)

1/4 cup butter or margarine
3/4 cup sugar
1/2 cup peanut butter
2 eggs
1 t. vanilla

Cream sugar and butter; add peanut butter. Stir until smooth. Add eggs one at a time, beating 3 min. after each one. Add vanilla. Put in a rice krispie crust and top with whipped cream.

Rice Krispie Crust:
1/4 cup margarine
20 lg. marshmallows or 2 cups miniature
2 1/2 cups rice krispies

Melt margarine in double boiler, add marshmallows and stir until melted and well blended. Remove from head. Add rice krispies. Stir until well coated. Press mixture into 9" pie pan.

Catherine Swarey
Belleville, PA

BOSTON CREAM PIE

4 egg yolks
9 T. water
1 1/2 cups sugar
2 cups flour
3 t. baking powder

Beat egg yolks and water till stiff; add sugar slowly and beat well; add blour and baking powder slowly. Beat egg whites and 1 t. salt till stiff and add to mixture.

Filling:
3 cups scalded milk
1 cup sugar
1 T. cornstarch
1 T. flour
1 egg
1 t. vanilla
pinch of salt

Crumbs for topping
3 cups brown sugar
1 1/2 cups flour
3 T. butter
cinnamon

Bake cake 350 deg. - 10 min. then put crumbs on top of layer.

Fannie Miller
Bird-in-Hand, PA

PECAN OR RICE KRISPIE PIE

2 cups molasses — 1 cup sugar
6 eggs beaten — 1/2 t. salt
2 t. vanilla — 6 T. butter
1 cup pecans or krispies

Place pecans or krispies in crust before pouring the syrup in. Makes 2 pies. Bake 325 deg. - 50 min.

Bertha Beiler
Loganton, PA

FRENCH RHUBARB PIE

Bottom:
1 egg — 1 cup sugar
1 t. vanilla — 2 cups diced rhubarb
1 T. flour — 1 T. tapioca

Topping:
1 cup flour — 1/2 cup brown sugar
scant 1/3 cup margarine — 1/4 cup oatmeal

Soak rhubarb in water several hours or overnite. Then drain well. Bake 400 deg. - 10 min., 350 deg. - 30 min. or until done.

Bertha Beiler
Loganton, PA

SHOO-FLY PIE

Bottom Mix:
1 qt. water — 1 qt. molasses
8 eggs — 1 cup brown sugar
1 t. soda — 1 t. salt
1 T. vanilla

Crumbs:
3 qt. flour — 6 cups brown sugar
3 cups lard — 3 t. soda
1 1/2 t. salt

Mix 7 1/2 cups crumbs in syrup, then rest of crumbs for top. Makes 12 pies.

Bertha Beiler
Loganton, PA

VANILLA CRUMB PIE

Boil:
3 pt. water
2 cups sugar
4 T. cornstarch
2 eggs, well beaten
2 cups white syrup
Cool, add 4 t. vanilla. Pour in 4 unbaked pie crusts.
Crumbs:
2 cups flour
1/2 cup oleo
1 t. cream of tartar
1/2 cup sugar
1 t. soda
Sprinkle on pies and bake till nice and brown.

Martha Mast
Revere, MO

LEMON SPONGE PIE

Sift together:
9 T. flour
2 1/2 cups sugar
Cream in 5 T. oleo
Mix:
6 egg yolks
7 cups sweet milk
Add to creamed mixture. Add 6 T. lemon juice or 3 T. flavoring, and well beaten egg whites. Bake in 375-400 deg. Makes 3 pies.

Martha Mast
Revere, MO

SQUASH OR PUMPKIN PIE

For each pie take:
1 T. flour
2 eggs
1/2 t. salt
1 cup cooked squash
3/4 cup sugar (half brown and half white)
1 t. vanilla
1 cup milk - a little more milk may be added
sprinkle of cinnamon
Beat the eggs, milk, salt, cinn. vanilla, flour and sugar real good, then add cooked, mashed up squash or pumpkin. Mox and pour into unbaked pie crust. Bake 45 min. in 350-400 deg. oven or until done.

Sue Wickey
Norfolk, NY

COCOANUT PIE

3/4 cup sugar
2 large cups whole milk
2 egg yolks
2 T. flour
1 cup cocoanut
1 t. salt

Mix real good; pour into unbaked pie shells and bake in 375-400 deg. oven for 30-40 min. until done.

Sue Wickey
Norfolk, NY

MEAT 'N POTATO PIE

1 can cream of mushroom soup
1/4 cup onion - finely chopped
1/4 cup dry bread crumbs
1/4 t. salt
1/4 cup milk cheese (shredded)
1 lb. ground beef
1 egg (slightly beaten)
2 T. parsley
2 cups mashed or prepared potatoes

Mix thoroughly 1/2 can soup, meat, onion, egg, crumbs, parsley and seasoning. Firmly pres into 9" pan. Bake 25 min., pour off fat. Frost with potatoes - top with remaining soup and cheese. Bake 10 min. more. Garnish with cooked bacon if desired.

Bertha Beiler
Loganton, PA

APPLE PIE FILLING

9 cups apples, peeled and cut fine
3 1/2 cups sugar
1/2 cup tapioca - fine
pinch of cinnamon and salt

Add water and cook 1 min. Makes 4 pies.

Mrs. Joe J. Yoder
Lawrenceburg, TN

Young people on the way up the ladder
Should never forget those at the bottom
Holding it steady for them

PEANUT BUTTER CREAM PIE

Filling:
1/3 cup white sugar
1 1/2 T. cornstarch
2 egg yolks
pinch of salt
1 1/2 cups milk
1 1/2 T. flour
1 t. butter

Crumbs:
1/3 cup powdered sugar
1/2 cup peanut butter

Mix together and set aside.

Heat sugar and 1 cup milk to boiling point. Use other 1/2 cup milk to mix with thickening and egg yolks. Add butter, vanilla and salt after pudding is removed from heat. Use egg whites on top of pie. Take a baked pie shell, put some crumbs in bottom and on top of egg whites.

Mrs. Joe J. Yoder
Lawrenceburg, TN

Very few people
Have carved their way to success
By cutting remarks

BUTTERSCOTCH PIE

4 T. butter
1/2 cup milk
1 cup sugar
3 T. white syrup

Cook till brown. Then add 1 cup milk and 1/2 cup water. Stir till smooth.

Mix:
1/2 t. salt
2 egg yolks
4 T. cornstarch or flour
1/2 cup water

Slowly add to above mixture to avoid lumps. Cook till smooth and thick, add 1 t. vanilla; pour in baked pie shell. May spread with meringue of egg whites and 4 T. sugar and brown in hot oven.

Martha Mast
Revere, MO

TAMALE PIE

1 can whole corn
1 pt. tomatoes
1/2 lb. ground beef
1/4 lb. ground pork
1 small onion
1 1/2 T. butter
1 1/2 t. salt
1/2 to 1 T. chili powder
1/2 garlic bud (optional)

Boil all together for 15 minutes. Remove from heat. Add:

3/4 cup milk
1 cup granulated corn meal
1 egg beaten

Mix well. Pour into buttered casserole. Bake 1 hr. at 325 deg.

Saloma Petersheim
Mifflintown, PA

CHOCOLATE CREAM CHEESE PIE

1 - 8 oz. pkg. cream cheese
6 - 6 oz. pkg. chocolate chips
3/4 cup brown sugar
1/8 t. vanilla
2 eggs, separated
1 cup heavy whipping cream

Melt chocolate over heat in a double boiler. Cool. Blend cheese, 1/2 of the sugar, salt and vanilla. Beat in egg yolks. Add chocolate and blend in. Beat egg whites until stiff. Slowly beat in 1/4 cup sugar. Beat till very stiff. Fold into chocolate mixture. Fold in whipped cream. Pour into one baked pie crust and chill.

Barbara Schrock
Spartansburg, PA

GRASSHOPPER PIE

1 pkg. marshmallows
1 1/2 cups milk

Melt together; cool and stir in 2 cups whipped cream, 1 t. peppermint flavor and green food coloring. Put on top of crushed oreo cookies. It takes from 10-12 cookies for 1 pie. Add 1/2 cup melted butter to crushed cookies and press in pie pan. Grind them in a nut grinder or other grinder. Makes 2 pies.

Mrs. Ammon A. Troyer
Ashland, OH

CARAMEL PECAN PIE

3 eggs
3/4 cup karo syrup
pinch of salt
1 cup pecans (don't chop)
1 unbaked pie shell
1 cup brown sugar
1 T. melted butter
2 T. water
2 T. flour

Mix in order given. Bake.

Mrs. Ammon A. Troyer
Ashland, OH

BAKED BUTTERSCOTCH PIE

1 cup brown sugar
1 T. flour
1/4 t. salt
1 1/4 cups milk
1/2 cup white sugar
butter size of walnut
2 egg yolks
1 t. vanilla

Combine all ingredients. Add beaten egg whites and pour into unbaked shell. Bake at 400 deg. until it rises. Makes a delicious pie with minimum of effort.

Mrs. Ammon A. Troyer
Ashland, OH

RASPBERRY BISCUIT PIE

Thicken black raspberries same as for regular pie, maybe a bit thicker. Make biscuit dough as follows:

2 cups flour
1/2 t. salt
3/4 cup milk (sweet or water)
4 t. baking powder
2 T. shortening

roll and line a pie pan with 1/2 of dough. Roll remainder dough for cover. Bake till brown, 20 min. or so. Serve warm with milk.

Cora Stutzman
Union City, PA

A Long face and a broad mind
Are rarely found under the same hat

BANANA CHOCOLATE MALLOW PIE

16 marshmallows
1/2 cup milk
1 t. vanilla
ripe bananas
2 T. sugar
2 T. cocoa
1/4 t. salt
1 (8 in.) baked pie crust
1 cup chilled whipping cream

Combine chocolate, milk, and salt in double boiler. Heat over simmering water until marshmallows and chocolate are melted, stirring occasionally. Remove from heat. Let stand until cool, but not set. Cover bottom of pie shell with slices of ripe bananas. Beat whipping cream to medium consistency. Sweeten with sugar, add vanilla. Fold whipped cream into cooled marshmallow chocolate mixture. Turn filling into pie shell pouring over bananas. Put pie in refrigerator to set.

Mose E. Helmuth
Edgewood, IA

RHUBARB CREAM PIE

2 eggs, well beaten
2 cups cubed rhubarb
1 1/2 cups sugar
5 T. water
2 T. flour

Stir all together and pour in unbaked pie crust. Dot with butter and sprinkle with cinnamon.

Mrs. J. David Byler
Punxutawney, PA

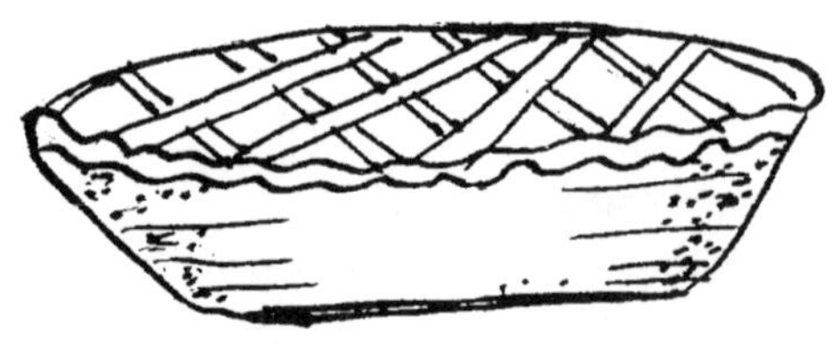

WHITE CHRISTMAS PIE

Soak:

1 T. knox gelatin
1/4 cup cold water

Mix in a saucepan:

1/2 cup sugar
4 T. flour
1/2 t. salt
1 1/2 cups milk

Cook over low heat, stirring until it boils. Boil 1 min; remove from heat. Stir in softened gelatin. Cool. When partially set, beat with beater until smooth.

Blend in:

3/4 t. vanilla
1/4 t. almond extract
1/2 cup whipping cream, whipped until stiff
3 egg whites, beaten
1/2 cup sugar
1/4 t. cream of tartar

Beat egg whites, add cream of tartar, beat until stiff. Beat in sugar until soft peaks form.

Fold everything together; fold in 1 cup coconut. Makes filling for 2 small pies.

Mary Ann Hilty
Monroe, IN

PUMPKIN CHIFFON PIE

1 envelope unflavored gelatine
3/4 cup brown sugar
1/2 t. salt
1/2 t. nutmet
1 t. cinnamon
1/2 cup milk
1/4 cup water
3 egg yolks
1 1/2 cups cooked pumpkins
1/2 cup coconut

Mix all the above together and put over medium heat for 10 min., stirring constantly. Remove from heat and cool. Beat 3 egg whites until stiff. Add 1/4 cup sugar and beat into pumpkin mixture. Pour in a 9 in. baked pie shell. Top with whipped cream before serving.

Aaron Brubacker
Liverpool, PA

Gossips were running people down
Long before the automobile was invented

PUMPKIN PIE

1/2 cup white sugar
1/2 cup brown sugar
1 T. flour
pinch of salt
1 can evaporated milk
1/2 t. cinnamon
1/4 t. nutmeg
1/2 cup pumpkin
1 egg separated

Mix together dry ingredients, add pumpkin, beat egg yolks and add. Stir in milk, last add beaten egg whites, pour in unbaked pie shell. Bake at 400 deg. for 10 min., then at 325 deg. for 30-40 min.

Ella Hershberger
Oakland, MD

CHOCOLATE PIE

Make meringue as follows:
2 egg whites
1/4 t. cinnamon
1/4 t. salt
1/2 cup sugar

Spread on baked pie shell and bake.
Cool and put in filling:
2 egg yolks, slightly beaten
1/4 cup water
1/2 cup chocolate bits, melted

Pour half of this mixture on baked meringue.
Combine:
1/4 cup sugar
1 cup cream (whipped)
1/2 t. cinnamon

Whip cream. Put 1/2 of cream on top. Combine other half with remaining chocolate mixture. Fill pie.

Saloma Petersheim
Mifflintown, A

RICE KRISPIE PIE

Beat 2 eggs.
Add:
2/3 cup brown sugar
1/2 cup molasses
1/4 t. salt
1 t. vanilla
1 T. flour
1/2 cup milk
3 T. melted butter
1 cup rice krispies (heaping)
1/2 cup chopped pecans

Esther Marie Fisher
Conneautville, PA

PECAN PIE

3 eggs beaten
1/2 cup sugar
1 T. flour
2 T. melted butter
1/4 t. salt
1 cup molasses (white and dark)
1 cup milk
1 cup chopped pecans

Bake at 350 deg. for 45 min.

Esther Marie Fisher
Conneautville, PA

VANILLA TARTS

1 1/4 cups sugar
1 cup cold water
1 1/4 cups molasses

Divide into four crusts

2 cups sugar
1/2 cup lard
1 t. soda
1 t. vanilla
1 cup buttermilk
1 egg
3 cups flour

Enos Yoders
Park City, KY

LEMON PIE

1 T. butter
3 egg yolks
1/2 t. salt
1 1/2 cups boiling water
2 T. vinegar
1 cup sugar
4 T. cornstarch
1 1/2-2 t. lemon flavor

Mix sugar, salt, cornstarch and vinegar and slowly stir in the boiling water. Cook until clear. Add butter, beaten egg yolks and flavor; pour into baked crust. Top with white egg beaten stiff with some sugar and flavor; put in oven to brown on top.

Joe Borntreger
Cashton, WI

CAKE PIE

1 1/4 cups sifted flour
1 t. baking powder
1/4 t. salt
3/4 cup sugar
3 T. chopped nuts and coconut for top
1/4 cup shorteing
1/2 cup milk
1 t. vanilla
1 egg unbeaten

Sauce:
1/4 cup sugar
1/2 cup sugar
1 cup water
1/2 T. flour

Make thin sauce, cook first.

Measure into sifter flour, baking powder, salt and sugar. Place shortening in bowl, sift dry ingredients. Add milk, vanilla. Mix until all flour is wet. Beat 2 min. or 30 strokes. Add egg and beat 1 min. or 150 strokes. Pour batter into pastry lined pie plate. Pour lukewarm sauce gently over batter; sprinkle with nuts or coconut. Bake at 350 deg. for 50-55 min.

RHUBARB PIE

1 1/2 cups diced rhubarb
1 cup sugar
2 T. flour
1 egg beaten
pinch of salt

Mix together well. Put in unbaked pie crust.

For topping, blend:
1/2 cup brown sugar
2 T. flour
2 T. butter

Joe Borntreger
Cashton, WI

KARO PECAN PIE

2 eggs beaten
1 cup syrup
1/8 t. salt
1 cup pecan meats
1 t. vanilla
1 cup sugar
2 T. melted butter

Mix ingredients together, adding pecan last. Bake in hot oven 400 deg. for 15 min.; reduce heat to moderate 350 deg., bake 30-35 min. or longer or until a silver knife inserted in center of filling comes out clean. For oatmeal, put in 1 cup cream yet. It's also good to add cream anyways.

Joe Borntreger
Cashton, WI

COCONUT OR CUSTARD PIE

4 eggs beaten
3/4 cup sugar
2 cups milk or rich milk

Bake in a crust, put coconut on top, if you wish. Bake at 350 deg. slowly.

Joe Borntreger
Cashton, WI

DUTCH APPLE PIE

3 cups apples (sliced)
1 cup sugar
1/2 t. cinnamon
1 T. flour
2 T. butter
2 T. cream

Mix together and put in unbaked pie shell. Put crumbs on top and bake at 450 deg.

Crumbs:
1/2 cup sugar
1/3 cup butter
3/4 cup flour

Cathryn Schmucker
Litchfield, MI

PEACH PIE

7 fresh peaches (peeled)
1 cup sugar
1/2 cup water
3 T. cornstarch

Crush 3 peaches and add sugar, water and cornstarch. Cook until mixture is thick and clear. Slice remaining peaches into a baked pie shell. Pour the cooled mixture over the sliced peaches and chill. Serve with whipped topping.

Mrs. Wilma Mast
S. Hutchinson, KS

RHUBARB CUSTARD PIE

2 cups rhubarb (cut)
1 1/4 cups sugar
1 T. flour
2 eggs
1 cup milk

Cut rhubarb in small pieces; put in pie shell. Mix rest of ingredients and pour over rhubarb. Sprinkle top with nutmeg. Bake at 400 deg. for 10 min., then at 375 deg. till set.

Cathryn Schmucker
Litchfield, MI

GRACE'S PECAN PIE

Beat 3 large eggs until light and creamy.
Add:
1/2 cup granulated sugar
1 cup karo
1 cup pecan nut meats
1 t. vanilla
Bake 50 min. at 350 deg.

Louella Borntrager
Sugar Creek, OH

ROYAL APPLE PIE FILLING

1 cup brown sugar
1/4 cup flour
3/4 cup water
3 cups sliced apples
1/4 t. salt
1 t. vanilla
1 T. vinegar
2 T. butter

Mix sugar, flour, salt. Add water and vinegar. Cook until thick, stirring constantly. Remove from fire, add butter and vanilla. Pour this syrup over apples in a 9 in. unbaked pie shell. Bake at 400 deg. for 40 min.

Louella Borntrager
Sugar Creek, OH

CRUMB PIE

1 cup brown sugar
2 T. flour
1 cup light corn syrup
2 cups hot water
1 t. vanilla

Boil together and pour into 2 unbaked pie shells. Cover with crumbs. Bake in a slow oven.

Crumbs:
2 cups flour
1 t. soda
1 t. cream of tartar
1 cup brown sugar
1/2 cup butter

Mrs. Daniel C. Borntreger, Riceville, IA
Ella Hershberger, Oakland, MD

Houses are made of brick or stone
Homes are made of love alone

THANK-YOU (PIE FILLING TO CAN)

4 cups sugar
8 cups water
2 t. salt
8 T. lemon juice

Heat the above ingredients.

Paste made of 2 cups clear jell and 4 cups water. Stir in heated ingredients and boil. Remove from heat and add 4 cups karo, 16 cups fruit of finely cut apples or blueberries or whatever you like. Cold pack this 10 or 15 min.

Ella Hershberger
Oakland, MD

If I do not believe as you believe
It proves you do not believe as I believe
And that is all it proves

LEMON PIE

1 cup white sugar
1/2 t. salt
juice of one large lemon
1 T. butter
2 egg yolks
1 1/2 cups water
1 t. lemon rind
1/2 cup flour

Cook in double boiler. Makes 1 pie.

Meringue for pie:
2 egg whites
3 T. sugar

Put this filling in a baked pie shell.

Ella Hershberger
Oakland, MD

APPLE JESS PIE

1 1/2 cups chopped apples
2 eggs
1 1/2 cups milk
1 t. cinnamon
1 stick margarine
1/2 cup butter

Mix eggs, sugar, margarine and cinnamon. Then add apples; mix. Pour in unbaked pie shell. Bake.

Fannie Gingerich
Ethridge, TN

OATMEAL PIE

6 eggs, well beaten
2 cups light brown sugar
2 cups light corn syrup
1 cup butter
2 1/2 cups oatmeal
1 cup coconut
3/4 cup milk

Mix all together. Put into unbaked pie shell. Bake 40 min. at 350 deg. Makes 4 pies.

Fannie Gingerich, Ethridge, TN
Mrs. Ammon A. Troyer, Ashland, OH

STRAWBERRY PIE

Fill baked crust with fresh sliced strawberries; cover with following syrup:

1 cup sugar
1/2 cup fresh strawberries

Cook about 5 min. and strain. Add 2 T. cornstarch mixed with a little water. Cook until thick. Lower heat and cook until transparent. Pour over berries. Jello can be used instead of berries in syrup. Top with whipped cream.

Fannie Gingerich
Ethridge, TN

PIE CRUST

1 cup shortening
1/2 cup water
1/2 t. salt (a pinch of salt)

Enough flour to make a dough - 2 cups or so - mix together like regular pie dough. The trimmings will not stiffen when rolled out again.

Sue Wickey
Norfolk, NY

RHUBARB CUSTARD PIE

2 cups rhubarb
1 t. butter
3/4 cup cream
2 eggs - separated
1 t. vanilla
2 T. flour mixed with 1 cup sugar

Beat egg yolks, sugar, flour cream and vanilla together. Add rhubarb. Pour mixture in crust and dot with butter. Bake at 375 deg. for 45 min. Cover with meringue made of 3 egg whites beaten stiff and 1/4 cup sugar. Bake until meringue is nice and brown.

Mrs. Ray J. Gingerich
Fillmore, NY

NO CRUST COCONUT PIE

3 1/2 cups sugar
8 eggs
1 cup flour
1/2 cup melted oleo
4 cups milk
3 cups coconut
2 t. vanilla
pinch of salt

Pour into greased pie pans and bake at 350 deg. for 45 min. or until golden brown. Makes 3 pies.

Mrs. Ray J. Gingerich
Fillmore, NY

PIE CRUST

Mix:
1/2 cup cold water
1 t. vinegar
3/4 cup lard
Add:
1/4 t. salt
flour to make a very soft dough.
Makes 2 pies with tops or 3 crusts.

Martha Mast
Revere, MO

PIE CRUST MIX

12 cups flour
4 cups cold lard
4 t. salt

Mix well till crumbly. Store in cool place. Use 2 cups mix to 2-3 T. water, and blend well (do not overwork).

Mrs. Neal Kauffman
LaPlata, MO

PECAN PIE

3 eggs well beaten
1/2 cup white syrup
1/2 cup brown sugar
1/4 cup melted oleo
1 t. vanilla
1 cup chopped nuts

Mix all together and pour in unbaked pie crust. Bake at 400 deg. for about 45 min. or until done.

Elizabeth Mae Raber
Montgomery, IN

LEMON BANANA CHIFFON PIE

1 1/2 t. unflavored gelatin
3 T. flour
1/4 cup sugar
1 cup milk
2 egg whites
3 T. lemon juice
2 beaten egg yolks
1/2 cup sugar
1 T. oleo
2 sliced bananas

Soften gelatin in lemon juice. Mix next 2 ingredients, stir in milk. Coof over medium heat, stirring constantly until thick. Slowly stir a bit of hot mixture into yolks; return to saucepan; cook a few min., stir often. Mix in oleo and gelatin; cool. Beat egg whites until soft peaks form; slowly add 1/4 cup sugar, beating till stiff peaks form; fold into cooled mixture. Pour in a baked pie crust, chill until set.

Elizabeth Mae Raber
Montgomery, IN

To succeed, wɔrk your tongue little,
Your hands much, and your brains most

RHUBARB PIE

4 eggs
1/2 t. salt
1 t. vanilla
2/3 cup white sugar
2 2/3 cups hot milk

Beat above ingredients, then add 1 cup cut rhubarb. Pour into unbaked pie shell. Bake 400 deg. approx. 30 min.

Saloma J. Byler
Dewittville, NY

COCONUT MACAROON PIE

1 1/2 cup white sugar
1/2 cup butter
pinch of salt
1 1/2 cups shredded coconut
2 eggs
3/4 cup rich milk
1/4 cup flour

Beat eggs, add sugar and salt; beat until lemon color; add soft butter, blour and blend well. Add 1 cup coconut and pour in unbaked pie shell; save 1/2 cup coconut for top. Bake at 350 deg.

Mrs. Ammon A. Troyer
Ashland, OH

PILGRIM PIE

2 eggs
2 oz. margarine
1 t. vanilla
1 cup rolled oatmeal
1 cup sugar
1 cup corn syrup
1 cup coconut
1/2 t. salt

Cream margarine and sugar; add remaining ingredients. Bake in unbaked pie shell for 10 min. at 450 deg. and 30 min. at 350 deg. Don't make pans too full. Quick to make; delicious to eat.

Mrs. Ammon A. Troyer
Ashland, OH

PEACH CREAM PIE

Mix:
1 cup cream
2 T. cornstarch
1 cup brown sugar

Put in an unbaked pie shell lined with peaches. Sprinkle top with cinnamon; add milk till pan is full. Bake in moderate oven till custard is set.

Mrs. Jacob Stutzman
Jeromesville, OH

COCONUT CUSTARD PIE

3/4 cup white sugar
2 eggs
2 cups milk and cream mixed
1 T. flour
1/2 cup coconut
1 t. vanilla

Last put in whites of eggs, well beaten. Bake in moderate oven until set. Makes 1 pie.

Mrs. Jacob Stutzman
Jeromesville, OH

BEATLENUT PIE

3 eggs beaten
1/4 cup soft margarine or butter
1 t. vanilla
1/2 cup chopped nuts
1/4 cup quick oats
3/4 cup sugar
1 cup milk
3/4 cup maple flavored syrup
1/2 cup coconut
3 T. flour

Combine all ingredients except oatmeal, nuts and coconut. Beat well, then add oatmeal, nuts and coconut. Bake in 312 deg. oven 15 min.

Mrs. Jacob Stutzman
Jeromesville, OH

STRUESEL PIE

Bake 2 pie shells. Take 2/3 cup peanut butter, 1 1/2 cup powdered sugar. Blend together until mealy. Sprinkle 2/3 over shells, save 1/3 for top. Combine:

1 cup white sugar
2/3 cup cornstarch
1/4 t. salt
4 cups milk
6 egg yolks

And cook, add 1/4 cup butter and 2 t. vanilla; let cool. Pour into shells. Beat 6 egg whites until stiff. Beat in 1/2 t. cream of tartar, 1 cup white sugar mixed with 2 t. cornstarch. Beat until stiff and pour on pies. Sprinkle peanut butter mixture on top. Put in hot oven till brown. Makes 3 small pies.

Mrs. Ammon A. Troyer
Ashland, OH

EASY SHOO-FLY PIE

1 cup brown sugar
1 cup flour
1 t. soda (scant)
2 T. oleo soft
1 t. vanilla
1 cup molasses
1 cup warm water
1 egg beaten

Mix well all ingredients. Mixture will divide while baking; pour into unbaked pie shell. Bake at 350 deg. for about 35 min.

Martha Hostetler
Fort Plain, NY

RAISIN PIE

3/4 cup raisins
1 cup brown sugar
3 pints water
1 T. vinegar
2 T. clear jell
salt

Top Crumbs:

1 1/2 cups flour
1 cup brown sugar
2/3 cup margarine

Makes 2 pies.

Mrs. Noah Wengerd, Jr.
Conewango Valley, NY

COLD MINCE PIE

4 slices bread or 1 large cup (crumbed)
1 cup raisins
2 cups boiling water
Stir and let set until cool.
Add:
3 cups sugar
1 t. cinnamon
1 t. cloves and nutmeg mixed
Mix together, then add to first part and also add:
1/2 cup vinegar
1/2 cup butter or oleo
2 beaten eggs

A little pudding may be added if desired. This makes 3 or 4 pies according to the size of the pan. Mixture will be thin but it will thicken as it bakes. This is very delicious.

Mary A. Kinsinger
Meyersdale, PA

WHIPPED TOPPING

1/4 cup boiling water
1/2 t. cream of tartar
1 egg white
3/4 cup white sugar
1 t. vanilla

Beat till it stands in peaks. Can also be used instead of whipped cream to put on pies and puddings.

Mary A. Kinsinger
Meyersdale, PA

LEMON PIE FILLING

2 cups boiling water
3 T. flour
1/2 cup sugar
pinch of salt
2 egg yolks
2 T. Real Lemon juice
1/2 t. lemon extract

Mix together flour, sugar and salt. Add a little water to this to make a paste. Then add egg yolks, Real Lemon and extract. Stir into boiling water and bring to a boil. Add yellow food coloring and 1 t. butter. Add a little more water if mixture is too thick. Pour into baked pie crust and top with meringue.

Mrs. Daniel C. Borntreger
Riceville, IA

ONION PIE

2 cups crushed ritz crackers
10 T. butter
3 cups sliced onions
2 eggs
1 cup milk
1/2 cup cheddar cheese (grated)
salt and pepper to taste

Mix 1 1/2 cups crumbs with 5 T. melted butter. Press into pie plate. Saute onions in 5 T. butter until limp; spoon into pie shell. Mix eggs, milk, salt and pepper. Pour over onions. Add grated cheese and sprinkle with rest of crumbs. Bake at 350 deg. for 30 min.

Fannie S. Miller
Bird-in-Hand, PA

OPEN FACE PEACH PIE

2 T. flour
1 cup sugar (white)
1/2 cup brown sugar

Mix together and put 1/2 of crumbs in unbaked pie shell. Place a layer of fresh peaches (or canned) on crumbs and top with rest of crumbs; pour cream on top enough to fill a pan and bake.

Mrs. Henry Stutzman
Conewango Valley, NY

UNION PIE

3 eggs
1 cup sour cream
1 cup brown sugar
1/2 cup molasses
1 T. flour
1 t. soda
1 t. cinnamon
1 cup sweet milk or 2 cups buttermilk

Put in 2 unbaked pie shells. Bake.

Naomi Peachy
Little Falls, NY

UNION PIE

2 cups sugar
1 cup sour milk
1 cup sour cream
3 T. flour
1/2 t. soda
3 eggs
flavoring to taste
sprinkle cinnamon on top

Pour into unbaked pie shells. Makes 4 pies.

Mrs. Daniel C. Borntreger
Riceville, IA

FAKE PECAN PIE

Cream:

2 T. butter	1 cup sugar

Add:

2 beaten eggs	2 T. flour
1/4 t. salt	1 t. vanilla

Stir well; add:

1 cup rice krispies or corn flakes	1 cup white karo

If not enough for 1 pie add a little water.

Mrs. Ray J. Gingerich
Fillmore, NY

FRESH PEACH PIE

Slice 5 or 6 peaches and soak in a little sugar for a while and then drain. Take the juice and add enough water to make 1 cup. Add 3/4 cup sugar and bring to a boil. Thicken with 2 T. cornstarch or clear jell. Add a little salt, a chunk of butter. Remove from heat and add 2 T. peach jello and stir till dissolved. Add peaches and put in crust. Chill till set. Top with whipped cream.

Mrs. Ray J. Gingerich
Fillmore, NY

COCONUT MACAROON PIE

1 1/2 cups sugar	2 eggs
1/2 cup soft butter	1/2 t. salt
1/4 cup flour	1/2 cup milk
1/2 cup coconut	1/2 t. vanilla

Sprinkle a little coconut on top. Bake in slow oven at 325 deg.

Mrs. Ray J. Gingerich
Fillmore, NY

It balances out with advancing years
We have less hair to comb but more face to wash

PEACH PIE CRUST

6 egg whites - beat until stiff, then gradually add 2 cups sugar and 1/2 t. baking powder.

Fold in:

1 1/2 cups crushed soda crackers
1 cup nuts
1 t. vanilla

Put in 2 greased pie pans, bake at 350 deg. for 20 min. Take out and press down with a greased spoon. Bake till golden brown.

Filling:

5 or 6 peaches sliced and sweetened, then mix with Cool Whip and put in cold crust.

Mrs. Ray J. Gingerich
Fillmore, NY

BOB ANDY PIE

2 cups brown sugar
3 cups milk
2 T. flour
1 t. cinnamon
1/2 t. cream of tartar
3 eggs
butter size of egg

Mix dry ingredients. Add butter, eggs and milk. Bake. Makes 2 pies.

Mary Swartzentruber
Apple Creek, OH

Water falling day by day
Wears the hardest rock away

PUMPKIN PIES

3 cups pumpkin
2 cups brown sugar
3 1/2 cups hot milk
1/2 cup molasses or honey
2 T. flour
1 t. salt
8 eggs - beat whites till stiff and add last

Mix together and pour in unbaked crusts and sprinkle cinnamon on top. Bake at 400 deg. for 10 minutes, then 350 deg. 30 or 35 minutes. Makes 4 pies.

Lydia Stoltzfus
Bloomsburg, PA

STREUSEL CONCORD GRAPE PIE

Unbaked 9" pie shell
4 1/2 cups concord grapes
1 cup white sugar
1/4 cup flour
2 t. lemon juice
1/8 t. salt

Wash grapes, remove skin by pinching at end opposite stem. Reserve skins. Place pulp in saucepan and bring to a boil. Cook a few minutes till soft. Put pulp through strainer. While pulp is hot, mix in skins. Stir in sugar, flour, lemon juice and salt. Pour into pie shell.

Sprinkle with oatmeal streusel:
1/2 cup quick oats
1/2 cup brown sugar
1/4 cup flour
Cut in 1/4 cup oleo

Bake 425 deg., 35-40 min.

Saloma J. Byler
Dewittville, NY

BUTTERSCOTCH PIE

2 cups brown sugar
1/2 t. salt
1/2 cup oleo
3 1/2 cups boiling water
1 t. vanilla

Boil this until the other things are ready.

3 eggs
1 cup white sugar
1 1/2 cups flour
3 cups milk

Mix this and add to the brown sauce and cook until thick. Pour into baked pie crusts.

Mrs. Leroy J. Byler
Fredericktown, OH

STRAWBERRY PIE

Boil for 3 min.
3/4 cup sugar
1 1/2 cups water
1 T. cornstarch

Stir in one small box strawberry jello. Let cool but not set. Put 1 qt. fresh strawberries in baked pie crust. Pour cooled sauce over berries. Top with Cool Whip.

Mrs. Leroy J. Byler
Fredericktown, OH

RICE KRISPIE PIE

3 eggs
1/2 cup brown sugar
1/4 t. salt
1 cup light karo
1 t. vanilla
2 T. butter
1 cup rice krispies

Beat eggs. Add remaining ingred. Pour into unbaked pie crust. Bake at 350 deg.

Mrs. Leroy J. Byler
Fredericktown, OH

STRAWBERRY PIE

4 cups fresh strawberries, sliced
In a cause pan cook:
1/2 cup water
3/4 cup sugar
2 T. cornstarch

Let come to a boil, stirring constantly. Cook over low heat 2 min. Add 1 pkg - 3 oz. - strawberry gelatin. Stir until gelatin is dissolved. Put strawberries in a baked pie shell, pour mixture over berries, and chill. If desired, put whipped cream on top.

Alma Yoder
Lovington, IL

Relish & Pickles

RED BEETS

3/4 pint vinegar filled up with water
1 cup red beet juice
2 1/2 cups white sugar
1 T. salt
Enough juice for 8 pints beets.

Mrs. Noah Wengerd, Jr.
Conewango Valley, NY

BREAD AND BUTTER PICKLES

25 med. pickles
4 onions
1/2 cup salt
Soak 3 hrs. in 6 cups cold water; drain.
Put in:
4 cups vinegar
2 cups sugar
1 t. celery seed
1 t. mustard seed
1 t. tumeric

Enos Yoders
Park City, KY

SWEET LIME PICKLES

Slice 7 lbs. picles, soak 24 hrs. in 2 gal. water in which 2 cups hydrated lime has been dissolved. Then wash good till about clear in cold water. Then soak in water for 3 hrs. Drain. Mix 1 qt. vinegar, 1 1/2 qt. water, 5 lbs. white sugar, 1 T. salt and 1 T. mix pickle spice. Boil this mixture and pour over pickles. Let stand overnight. Next day bring pickles to a boil. Boil hard for 35 min. Can and seal.

Mrs. Noah Wengerd, Jr.
Conewango, NY

MRS. DAVID'S LIME PICKLES

1 gal. sliced cucumbers
(1 cup slaked lime mixed in1 gal. of water)
Soak cucumbers slices in lime water for 24 hrs.; then drain and wash cucumbers in clear water and cover with cold water. Let stand 24 hrs.
Then mix:
3 qt. vinegar (a little water can be added if vinegar is too strong)
6 cups sugar 3 T. salt
1/2 box pickling spice
Add cucumber slices; simmer gently for 3 1/2 hrs. Pack into jars and seal. (Good crisp pickles.)

Sue Wickey
Norfolk, NY

Manhood often grows in the soil of hardship

SWEET DILL PICKLES

Slice pickles thin and put in jars. Add a small onion and a small bud of dill or 1 t. dill seed on top.
Heat and pour the following over pickles:
2 cups vinegar 2 cups water
3 cups sugar 2 T. salt
Cold pack 5 min. after they come to a hard boil. Liquid for 3 1/2 qt.

Bertha Beiler
Loganton, PA

SWEET DILL PICKLES

Chunk or slice pickles; put in jars cold. Add 1 small clove garlic, 1 sprig dill or 1 heaping t. dill seed, to each quart of pickles.
Heat:
1 1/2 cups sugar 1 cup vinegar
5 cups water 1 T. salt
Pour over pickles and seal. Set jars in hot water and bring to a boil. Uncover and let set till cool. Brine makes about 3 qts. pickles.

Martha Hostetler
Fort Plain, NY

BANANA PICKLES

Pare large pickles, cut long way and take out seeds.
Mix:
1 cup vinegar
1 cup water
3 cups sugar
1 t. mustrad seed
1 t. tumeric
1 t. celery seed
Bring syrup to a boil. Pack pickles in jars. Pour syrup over pickles and seal. Cold pack 10 min. Makes 3 qts.

Saloma J. Byler
Dewittville, NY

HOT DOG RELISH

3 carrots
3 sweet red peppers
2 qt. cucumbers
2 qt. green tomatoes
2 qt. onions (pared)
1/2 T. salt
1 1/2 cups sugar
1 1/2 cups vinegar
1/2 t. cayenne pepper
2 T. mixed pickle spice
Chop or grind vegetables. Place in bowl, sprinkle with salt and allow to stand overnight. Nest morning drain, then add sugar, vinegar and cayenne pepper. Add spice (tied in cheesecloth). Simmer 45 min. Put in jars and seal. Makes 6 pt. (good on any meat.)

Saloma J. Byler
Dewittville, NY

MUSTARD PICKLES

Clean pickles and put in glass gallon jar.
Mix brine of:
2 qt. vinegar
1/4 cup salt
3 T. dry mustard
Mix with vinegar to make a paste
1/2 cup horse radish
1/2 t. each of cinnamon, allspice and cloves
2 t. alum
1 t. saccharin
These keep for months. Keep where cool. Dill can be added on top of pickles if wanted.

Martha Hostetler
Fort Plain, NY

FALL PICKLES (UNCANNED)

7 cups thinly sliced pickles
2 cups sugar
1 cup sliced peppers
2 heads dill
1 cup vinegar
1 cup sliced onions
1 T. salt celery seed
1 clove garlic

Mix and keep where cool.

Martha Hostetler
Fort Plain, NY

MUSTARD PICKLES

4 qt. vinegar
4 cups sugar or to suit taste
6 oz. jar French's mustard
1 pkg. saccharin
3/4 cup salt

Pack pickles in jars. Bring syrup to a boil and pour over pickles. Seal. Put jars in a canner. Bring to a boiling point.

Saloma J. Byler
Dewittville, NY

MILLION DOLLAR PICKLES

6 qt. sliced pickles
6 medium onions, sliced or chopped
1/2 cup salt

Cover with water, let set overnight. Next morning drain and add the following:

3 cups vinegar
1 T. mustard seeds
6 cups sugar (part brown)
2 cups water
1 T celery seeds

Fix like other pickles. Bring to a boil and put in jars.

Clara Hochstetter
Canton, MO

DILL PICKLES

Makes 7 qts.

2 qts. water
1 1/2 cups vinegar
1/2 cup salt (scant)

Peel, slice and pack pickles in jars with onions and dill to taste. Use a medium head dill, one small onion, several cloves, garlic per qt. Pickles can be sliced lengthwise or crosswise. Cold pack, heat to boiling point, then set out to cool and seal.

Clara Hochstetter
Canton, MO

RELISH

Pickle Relish for hot dogs, etc.
Grind enough of each to make 4 cups:

green peppers
onions
green tomatoes
pickles

Add 1/2 cup salt and let stand overnight.
Rinse and drain - make a brine:

5 cups sugar
2 T. mustard seed
1 T. celery seed
1 T. tumeric
2 1/2 cups vinegar
1 1/4 cups water

Bring to a boil, add relish and cook for 3 min. Put in jars and seal.

Esther Marie Fisher
Conneautville, PA

EASY CUCUMBER PICKLES

150 small cucumbers
1 cup salt

Dissolve salt in 2 qts. hot water and pour over pickles. Let stand overnight. Drain and rinse with cold water.
Combine:

2 cups vinegar
3 T. pickling spices
3 cups sugar
1 qt. water

Fill jars with pickles and add 1/4 t. alum to each jar. Heat juice to boiling and add pickles. Fill jars with hot juice and pickles.

Lydia Stoltzfus
Bloomsburg, PA

ZUCCHINI RELISH

10 cups grated peeled zucchini (use cabbage grater)
3 or 4 cups onions
2 large red peppers
1 T. salt
1 1/2 cups vinegar
1 cup water
1/2 t. celery seed
4 1/2 cups sugar
2 T. cornstarch
1 t. dry mustard
1 t. nutmeg
1 t. tumeric

Boil together in kettle 30 minutes. Makes about 7 pints. You can use this same recipe with pickles instead of zucchini.

Lydia Stoltzfus
Bloomsburg, PA

JUICE FOR MIXED PICKLE

2 cups pure vinegar
4 cups water
5 cups sugar
2 T. celery seed
salt to taste
1 t. tumeric
1 T. clear jel

Bring to boiling point; then pour over your vegetables that have all been cooked soft, then cold pack 1/2 hr. For stainless steel dishpan-full of vegetables, it takes a double bath of juice.

Louella Borntrager
Sugar Creek, OH

AUNT MATTIE'S MIXED PICKLES

2 qt. onions small
2 qt. lima beans
2 qt. small pickles
2 qt. green tomatoes
2 bunches celery
2 hd. cabbage
2 qt. pod beans
2 1/2 qt. weakened vinegar
4 cups sugar
2 T. flour
1 T. dry mustard
1 t. tumeric powder
salt to taste

Pour pickles and green tomatoes in salt water and leave set overnite or for an hr. or so. Boil everything separate till about ready except pickles and tomatoes. Mix all together and put in hot vinegar and boil. Put in cans. You can substitute a pt. of carrots and a pt. of red peppers for color.

Mrs. Joe J. Miller
Apple Creek, OH

MOM'S SWEET PICKLES

1 t. celery seed
1 t. mustard seed
1 t. salt
Pickles, sliced or chunked
3 cups water
3 cups vinegar
6 cups sugar
1 t. tumeric

Put first 3 ingredients in bottom of each qt. jar. Add pickles. Heat water, vinegar, sugar and tumeric into a syrup. Pour into jars and cold pack for 5 min.

Mrs. Joe J. Miller
Apple Creek, OH

CASSIA BUD PICKLES

1 peck or 75 cucumbers 3 or 4 in. long
1 pt. salt dissolved in 1 gal. hot water
Pour over cucumbers and let stand for a week. Drain, then add 1 gal. boiling water and 1 T. alum, let stand 24 hr. Drain again, cut pickles lengthwise, cover with boiling water, let stand for 24 hr. Drain and make a syrup of:
6 cups white sugar
5 pt. vinegar and water about half and half
1/2 oz. celery seed
1 oz. or 1/4 cup cassia buds
Boil together and pour over pickles. Let stand 24 hr. for 3 mornings pour off liquid and heat again. Add 1 cup sugar each morning or according to taste.

Elizabeth Stutzman
Union City, PA

HOT DILL PICKLES

3 cups water — 1 cup vinegar
1/4 t. red pepper — 2 T. pickling salt
2 t. dill weed — 2 cloves garlic (crushed)

Pack small cucumbers in jars. Cover with above mixture. Process in hot water bath 10 min. Makes 4 pints.

Mrs. Wilma Mast
S. Hutchinson, KS

KOSHER DILL PICKLES

Wash pickles, slice lengthwise, put in jars. To each qt. add:
2 heads fresh dill — 1/8 t. alum
1/8 t. tumeric — A clove of garlic
1 pk. sweet and low — 1/8 t. red hot pepper

Mix and fill jars with:
2 cups vinegar — 1/2 cup salt
6 cups hot water

Put in canner and bring to a boil. Then take off immediately so pickles won't get mushy. If you use barn salt, don't put that much in.

Mrs. J. David Byler
Punxsutawney, PA

GARLIC DILL PICKLES

Heat syrup of:

2 cups vinegar
2 cups water
3 cups sugar
2 T. salt

Fill jars with sliced cucumbers. Add 1 head dill and 3 garlic buds to each jar. Add syrup in hot water. Bring to boil and remove.

Mrs. Samuel D. Beachy
Clark, MO

CHURCH PICKLES

7 cups cucumbers
7 cups green peppers
1 cup onion rings
2 T. salt

Wash (do not peel) cucumbers, slice thin. Put in mixing bowl and set at least an hr. Then rinse and squeeze out moisture. Make the following syrup and pour over cucumber mix:

1 cup cider vinegar
2 cups sugar
1 t. celery seed

Good fresh for church or may be put in jars and bring to a boil to seal.

Mrs. Philip Yoder
Fairbank, IA

LUNCH PICKLES

5 qt. cucumbers (cut up)
2 onions (cut)
1/3 cup salt

Soak in water overnight. Drain in morning.

Bring to a boil:

1 1/2 cups vinegar
1 t. mustard seed
1/2 t. tumeric
1 1/2 cups water
1 t. celery seed
5 cups sugar

Add cucumbers and onions; reheat until it begins to simmer; put into jars and seal.

Mose E. Helmuth
Edgewood, IA

FREEZER COLE SLAW

2 heads shredded cabbage
shredded carrots
red and green peppers cut up fine
1 T. salt
Mix and let stand 1 hr. Meanwhile mix:
1 1/2 cups granulated sugar
3/4 cup vinegar
1/4 cup water
1 t. celery seed
1 t. mustard seed
Put in a saucepan, bring to a boil, let cool and pour over cabbage; put in freezer containers and freezer.

Esther Fisher
Millersburg, PA

RED BEETS

6 cups water from beets
6 cups vinegar
7 t. salt
14 cups white sugar
Mixed pickling spice as desired.

Mrs. Leroy J. Byler
Fredericktown, OH

CURRY PICKLES

6 qt. sliced cucumbers with peel
1 qt. vinegar
1 t. mixed spice
1 t. curry powder
1 t. tumeric
1 t. mustard seed
1 t. celery seed
6 large onions or 12 small ones
Slice onions, soak cucumbers and onions in salt water 3 hrs. Drain. Heat vinegar and spices. Add cucumbers and onions. Boil 1/2 hr. put in cans and seal. By omitting tumeric you have what they call bread and butter pickles.

Alma Yoder
Lovington, IL

When fear knocks at the door
Send faith to answer it and
You will find no one is

Salads & Dressings

DRESSING FOR POTATO SALAD

2 cups sugar
5 T. vinegar
1 1/2 t. celery seeds
3 cups salad dressing
2 T. prepared mustard

Mix and store in a cool place.

Clara Hochstetter
Canton, MO

CREAMY BACON DRESSING FOR LETTUCE SALAD

3 T. cream or top milk
1/4 cup sugar
2 T. vinegar
1 T. parsley
2 T. bacon bits
1 cup salad dressing
1/2 t. salt
1 T. lemon juice
1 T. minced onion bits

Esther Marie Fisher
Conneautville, PA

ORANGE SALAD

2 pkg. dream whip or 1 large cool whip
1 cup commercial sour cream
1/2 pkg. miniature marshmallows
1 - 20 oz. can crushed pineapples (drained)
1 - 17 oz. can fruit cocktail (drained)
1 - 3 oz. box jello

Mix dream whip or cool whip. Add sour cream and stir in dry jello. Fold in fruit and marshmallows.

Mrs. Leroy J. Byler
Fredericktown, OH

COTTAGE CHEESE SALAD

1 pt. small curd cottage cheese
1 small box orange jello (dry)
1 - 9 oz. Cool Whip
1 small can crushed pineapples (drained)
1 can mandarine oranges (drained)

Mix together and chill.

Mrs. Leroy J. Byler
Fredericktown, OH

RIBBON SALAD

First Layer:

2 pkg. lime gelatin — 4 cups water

Put in oblong dish and let harden.

Second Layer:

1 pkg. lemon gelatin — 1 cup hot water
1 pkg. marshmallow — 1/4-1 large pkg. cream cheese
1 or 2 cans crushed pineapple — 1 cup whipping cream

Dissolve cream cheese and marshmallows in hot gelatin. Add pineapple. When starting to set, add whipping cream. Pour on set lime gelatin.

Third Layer:

2 pkg. cherry gelatin — 4 cups water

When starting to set, pour on set second layer. To serve, cut in squares and place on lettuce leaf.

Mrs. Ammon A. Troyer
Ashland, OH

CAULIFLOWER SALAD

Take a flat container - put in a layer of lettuce, then a layer of cauliflower, then a thin layer of dressing. Add fried bacon and cheese and mix. Add onion bits if you like.

Dressing for cauliflower salad:

1 qt. miracle whip — 2 cups sugar
celery seed

Esther Marie Fisher
Conneautville, PA

HOME-STYLE DRESSING MIX

2 t. instant minced onion — 1/2 t. salt
1/8 t. garlic powder — 1 T. parsley flakes
1 cup mayonnaise — 1 cup buttermilk

Combine ingredients in a glass jar. Shake until well blended. Chill before serving.

Mrs. Wilma Mast
S. Hutchinson, KS

GERMAN POTATO SALAD

6 slices bacon
1/2 cup chopped onions
2 T. flour
2 T. sugar
1 1/2 t. salt
1 t. celery seed
dash of pepper
1 cup water
1/2 cup vinegar
6 cups sliced cooked potatoes

Cook bacon till crisp; drain and crumble, reserving 1/2 cup drippings. cook onion in reserved drippings till tender. Blend in flour, sugar, salt, celery seed and pepper. Add water and vinegar, cook and stir till thickened and bubbly. Add bacon and potatoes, tossing lightly. Heat thoroughly, about 10 min.

Joni H. Shrock
Middlefield, OH

COTTAGE CHEESE SALAD

1 lb. marshmallows
1/2 cup milk

Melt the above, then add 1 large pkg. cream cheese; stir until melted and cool.

Add:
1 (No. 2) can drained crushed pineapple
1 cup whipped cream

Fold in:
1/2 cup chopped nuts
1 qt. cottage cheese

Makes 3 qts.

Mary Ann Hilty
Monroe, IN

KOUNTRY KITCHEN POTATOE SALAD

4 cups diced and cooked potatoes
4 hard boiled eggs, diced
1/4 medium onion, diced
3/4 cup diced celery

Mix together:
1 cup salad dressing
1 T. mustard (prepared)
1 1/4 T. vinegar
1 1/4 t. salt
dab of milk
3/4 cup sugar

Blend well and add to above ingredients, mixing just enough to cover.

Miss Sara Shetler
Glasgow, KY

SANDWICH SPREAD

6 onions
6 green tomatoes
6 pickles
6 green peppers
6 red peppers

Grind this together, put 1 large handful salt in and let stand 2 hr. Drain, add 2 qts. water and boil 15 min. Add 1 pt. prepared mustard, 5 cups white sugar, 1 pt. vinegar, 1 t. tumeric. Mix and cook 5 min. longer.

Fannie Gingerich
Ethridge, TN

FROZEN SLAW

1 med. head cabbage, cut
1 green pepper, chopped fine
1 large carrot, grated
1 small onion, chopped

Add 1 t. salt to cabbage and let stand 1 hr. Squeeze juice from cabbage and add carrot, pepper and onion. While cabbage is standing, make a syrup of:

2 cups sugar
1 cup vinegar
1/2 cup water
1 t. celery seed
1 t. mustard seed

Boil for 1 min. Let stand until lukewarm, then pour over the cabbage mixture and cool completely. Package and freeze.

Esther Marie Fisher
Conneautville, PA

Bad habits are at first a caller
Then a guest and at last a master

PISTACHIO SALAD

1 - 20 oz. can crushed pineapples
1 small pkg. pistachio pudding
1 cup miniature marshmallows
19 oz. Cool Whip
1/2 cup milk

Mix together and chill.

Cathryn Schmucker
Litchfield, MI

PINEAPPLE MOLDED SALAD

2 - 3 oz. pkg. lime jello
2 cups liquid
16 large marshmallows
4 oz. cream cheese
1/4 cup salad dressing 1 - 2 lb. can crushed pineapples
1/2 pt. whipping cream

Dissolve marshmallows in hot gelatin. Beat when jelly. Add salad dressing, cream cheese and pineapple to whipped jello. Add whipped cream and mold.

Cathryn Smucker
Litchfield, MI

SWEET & SOUR DRESSING FOR LETTUCE

8 cups Miracle Whip salad dressing
4 cups white sugar
1/2 cup Wesson oil
1/2 cup mustard
1 1/2 t. celery seed

Mix well; makes approx. 1 gal.

Mrs. Leroy Stutzman
Sugar Creek, OH

FRENCH DRESSING FOR SALADS

2 cups white sugar
2 cups Wesson Oil
3/4 cups catsup
1/3 cup vinegar
2 t. Worcestershire sauce
1/2 cup onion (optional)
1 cup salad dressing
pinch of salt

Mrs. Leroy Stutzman
Sugar Creek, OH

LIME PARTY SALAD

Melt in top of a double boiler:
1/4 lb. marshmallows (about 16)
1 cup milk
Pour hot mixture over:
1 small box lime jello

Stire until dissolved, then stir in 1 - 3 oz. pkg. cream cheese. Add No. 2 can undrained crushed pineapple. Cool. Blend in 1 cup whipped cream, 2/3 cup mayonnaise. Chill until firm. Makes 12 servings.

Mary Ann Hilty
Monroe, IN

ZUCCHINI PRESERVES

3 cups zucchini (grated)
1/2 cup bottled lemon juice
2/3 cup sugar
1 pkg. gelatin (any flavor)

Boil grated zucchini, lemon juice and sugar together 30 min. Add gelatin and remove from heat. Pour in jars and seal.

Clara Hochstetter
Canton, MO

The man who always says what he thinks
Is brave and friendless

CHRISTMAS SALAD

2 - 3 oz. pkg. or 3/4 cup lime jello
1 can crushed drained pineapples
2 cups boiling water
1 1/2 cups cold water

Mix lime jello with water and add pineapples. Chill overnight.

1 cup pineapple juice
1 1/2 T. or 1 1/2 pkgs. unflavored gelatin dissolved in 3/4 cup cold water
1 1/2 cups whipped cream
4 oz. cream cheese

Heat pineapple juice to boil and add gelatin and cream cheese. Cool and add whipped cream (sweetened). Put on top of lime mixture. Let cool several hours.

2 - 3 oz. pkgs. or 3/4 cup strawberry jello
2 cups boiling water
2 cups cold water

Put on 2nd mixture after jello is cold and a little jelled. Chill. Serve.

Lydia Stoltzfus
Bloomsburg, PA

CARROT SALAD

1 box pineapple jello
1 box orange jello
Dissolved in 2 cups hot water
1 can crushed pineapple
2 cups carrots shredded fine

Then add juice of pineapples and enough water to make 2 cups. Mix all together, chill and serve on lettuce or plain.

Louella Borntrager
Sugar Creek, OH

QUICK AND EASY SANDWICHES

1 1/2 lb. hamburger
1 small onion
1 small box velvetta cheese
1 can cream of mushroom soup

Brown hamburger and onion till brown. Add soup and cheese. Stir till melted.

Mrs. Leroy J. Byler
Fredericktown, OH

CHILI SOUP

Brown together:
5 lb. hamburger
2 T. salt
3 cups onions, chopped
1 T. pepper

Add:
2 qt. can tomato juice
1 can water
2 cups ketchup
1/2 gal. kidney beans
1 1/2 t. chili powder
1 T. salt

Put in jars and cold pack 2 hrs.

Mrs. Leroy J. Byler
Fredericktown, OH

DRESSING (FOR TOSSED SALAD OR HOAGIES)

3 cups Wesson oil
1 cup vinegar
6 t. salt
6 t. onion salt
2 t. pepper
2 T. sugar
1 T. garlic powder

Put all ingredients in a jar and shake well.

Catherine Swarey
Belleville, PA

24 HOUR POTATO SALAD

12 cups cooked, diced potatoes
12 eggs, hard-boiled
1/2 onion, chopped
2 cups celery, chopped
3 cups salad dressing
1/2 cup milk
6 T. mustard
2 t. salt
1 1/2 cups white sugar
1/4 cup vinegar

Peel potatoes and eggs and chop. Add onions and celery. Mix other ingred. and pour over potato mixture. Toss. This is best made 2 or 3 days before serving. Makes 1 gal.

Mrs. Joe J. Miller
Apple Creek, OH

24 HR. SALAD

1 can crushed pineapple
1 lb. marshmallows
1 lb. grapes or cherries

Dressing:

juice of 1 can pineapple
2 oranges (juice)
1 lemon (juice)
yolks of 2 eggs
1 T. cornstarch
1/2 cup sugar

Cook this and cool. When cool, fold in:

1/2 pt. whipping cream (whipped)

Put fruit, marshmallows and grapes in after dressing is cold. Let stand 24 hrs. or is also good after standing a few hrs.

Mrs. Joe J. Miller
Apple Creek, OH

Those rare individuals
Who look down on their neighbors
are usually living on a bluff

MACARONI TUNA SALAD

1 lb. elbow macaroni, cooked and cooled
4 hard boiled eggs, chopped
1 family size can tuna, drained
4 slices bacon, fried and crushed
1 med. onion, minced
3 med. carrots, grated
2 stalks celery, chopped

Dressing:

2 1/2 cups mayonnaise
2 T. vinegar
1 cup sugar
3/4-1 cup milk
1/3 cup mustard

Cook macaroni as directed on package until tender. Drain. Add the rest of the ingredients, flaking tuna as you add it. Then add the dressing which has been well blended. Serves 12-15.

Mrs. Joe J. Miller
Apple Creek, OH

TOSSED SALAD

2 heads lettuce torn into bite sized pieces
4 carrots, thinly sliced | 2 stalks celery, sliced or diced
8-10 radishes, thinly sliced | 1 cucumber, sliced thin
Toss with French Dressing. Toss in 2 small cans shoestring potatoes and 2 tomatoes, cut up.

French Dressing:
2 - 10 1/2 oz. cans cream of tomato soup
3 cups granulated sugar | 2 cups salad oil
1 cup vinegar white | 1 T. grated onion
1 t. celery salt | 1 t. salt
1 t. pepper | 1 t. paprika
Chill before serving. Yield 8 cups.

Mrs. Joe J. Miller
Apple Creek, OH

DRESSING (FOR SALAD OR SANDWICHES)

2 cups white sugar | 2 cups Wesson oil
3/4 cup ketchup | 1/3 cup vinegar
2 t. worcestershire sauce | a little onion
pinch of salt | 1 cup Miracle Whip
Whip with an egg beater. A few drops of food coloring may be added.

Catherine Swarey
Belleville, PA

All sunshine makes deserts

BEST FRENCH DRESSING

1 qt. salad dressing | 2 cups sugar
3/4 cups catsup | 1 cup vinegar
3/4 cup cooking oil | 1/4 t. garlic salt
2 t. salt | 1/2 t. paprika
1/4 cup prepared mustard (scant) | dash of pepper
Mix all together real well. Makes 2 qts. It will keep a long time in refrigerator.

Emma Hershberger
Dover, DE

FRENCH DRESSING

2 cups mayonnaise
3 t. sugar
1 t. mustard
1/2 t. garlic
1/4 cup vinegar
1/2 t. salt
1 cup catsup

Naomi Peachy
Little Falls, NY

CARROT OR APPLE SALAD

Soak 3 T. plain gelatin in 1 cup cold water. Dissolve 2 - 3 oz. packages flavored gelatin in 3 cups boiling water. Also add plain gelatin; stir until dissolved. Add 1 cup sugar, 6 cups cold water. Cool till it starts to set, then add 1 qt. chopped carrots or apples, 1 cup pineapples, 1 cup nutmeats. Also may add fine chopped celery.

Martha Mastt
Revere, MO

PINEAPPLE SALAD

1 large can pineapples
24 marshmallows
1 cup whipped cream
2 eggs
2 oranges
1 cup nuts
2 t. flour
1/2 cup sugar

Drain juice from pineapples. Heat juice and add flour, eggs and sugar. Cool and add the rest of ingredients.

Esther Fisher
Millersburg, PA

TARTAR SAUCE

12 large green tomatoes
12 small green peppers
4 medium onions
1 cup prepared mustard
1 cup vinegar
4 t. salt
3 cups sugar
1/2 cup flour
1 qt. salad dressing

Grind tomatoes, peppers and onions until fine and drain. Pour enough boiling water over top mixture to cover and let stand at least 2 min. Heat water mixture then, add mustard, vinegar, sugar and salt; stir well and boil 15 min. Make a paste of water and add flour and add to above mixture. Cook 10 min. While hot, add salad dressing. Stir well and place in glass jars. Seal while hot. Makes 10 pt.

Mrs. Ammon A. Troyer
Ashland, OH

CHEESE SPREAD

2 - 8 oz. pkg. cream cheese
1 cracker barrel - sharp
1 medium onion
1 medium green pepper

Cream, cream cheese with shredded cheese barrel, onion and pepper. Roll in ball and then roll in chopped nuts.

Barbara Schrock
Spartansburg, PA

APPLE SALAD

8 apples, drained and diced
2 bananas, diced
1/2 cup chopped celery
1/2 cup raisins
juice of 1 1/2 lemons
1/4 cup coconut
1/2 cup nuts

Dressing:

1 cup water
1 t. vinegar
1/4 t. salt
1 cup sugar
pineapple juice
1 T. cornstarch or clear jell
1/4 cup cream
1 t. vanilla

Cook; stir till boiling.

Esther Marie Fisher
Conneautville, PA

POTATO SALAD

12 cups potatoes
12 eggs
1/2 cup med. onions
1 1/2 cups fine cut celery
Dressing:
3 cups salad dressing
1/4 cup vinegar
2 1/2 cups white sugar
1/2 cup milk
4 T. mustard
4 t. salt

Cook potatoes not too soft and grad them. Sea shells can be cooked to put in. Can be made a few days ahead.

Mary Swatzentruber
Apple Creek, OH

CRANBERRY SALAD

1 lb. cranberries
1/2 t. soda
1 qt. water
1 t. salt
2 cups sugar
2 - 3 oz. boxes strawberry jello
3 cups miniature marshmallows
1 cup diced apples
1 cup chopped nuts

Put cranberries, water and salt on stove. When starting to boil, add soda and cook 10 min. or until all berries have popped. Add sugar, jello and stir till dissolved. Add marshmallows while hot so they can dissolve. Remove from heat and let cool. Add celery, apples and nuts. This needs to be stirred occasionally until it jells as the ingredients tend to float. Put into container to store; the flavor improves each day.

Mary Ann Hilty
Monroe, IN

LUNCHEON SALAD

6 oz. jello (lime or your choice)
1 cup hot water
When cooled, add:
1 pt. cottage cheese
1 or 2 cans crushed pineapples
1 cup beaten evaporated milk
1 cup chopped walnuts
1 - 8 oz. container Cool Whip

Pour into mold or dish.

Fannie S. Miller
Bird-in-Hand, PA

THREE BEAN SALAD

1 can yellow beans (string)
1 can green beans
1 can red kidney beans
1 cup onions, shredded
1 cup chopped green peppers
1 cup sugar
1/2 cup wine vinegar (regular can be used)
1/2 cup white vinegar (" " " ")

Wash and drain the canned beans; then marrinate overnight in rest of mixture. Can also be canned; cold pack 15 min.

Fannie S. Miller
Bird-in-Hand, PA

COLE SLAW

1 med. head cabbage
1 diced celery
1/2 cup chopped onion
1/2 cup green pepper
2 cups sugar
1/2 cup vinegar
2 t. salt
1 t. celery seed
2 t. mustard seed

Mix all together. Can be refrigerated or canned. Cold pack to boiling. Let set covered until cooled.

Lydiann J. Bricker
Panama, NY

TOSSED TACO SALAD

1 head lettuce
1 bunch green onions, chopped
4 tomatoes, chopped
1 pkg. - 5 1/2 oz. - taco chips
1 lb. ground beef
1 bottle - 8 oz. - thousand island dressing
1 can red kidney beans, drained
12 oz. cheese, grated

Mix first six ingredients together. Brown ground beef and drain. Add to salad, toss with dressing. Makes a large salad.

Mrs. Emma Stutzman
Bronson, MI

It may be true that life begins at 40
But everthing else starts to wear out,
Fall out, or spread out

GOLDEN CREAM SOUP

3 cups cubed potatoes
1 cup water
1/2 cup celery (cut up)
1 chicken boullion cube or 1 1/2 t. chicken flavor soup base
1/2 cup carrots (small cubes)
1/4 cup onion chopped (optional)

Cover and simmer 15 min. or until tender. When tender, add this mixture:

Salt to suit taste
2 1/2 T. flour
2 cups milk

Stir well and cook till thickened. Top with toasted bread cubes and velveeta cheese when finished.

Mose E. Helmuth
Edgewood, IA

A smile is alight in the window of the face
Showing the heart is at home

PEACH PARTY SALAD

2 pkg. orange jello
2 cups boiling water
1 - 30 oz. can crushed pineapples
1 1/2 cups pineapple juice
2 cups drained sliced peaches
1/2 cup sugar
1 egg
1 cup marshmallows
1 1/2 cups shredded cheese
1 cup cream (whipped)

Dissolve jello in water. Drain pineapple. Add water to make 1 1/2 cups liquid. Add 3/4 cup liquid to jello. Chill until syrupy. Spread peaches in 9" square pan. Add jello. Chill till firm. Combine sugar, flour, remaining 3/4 cup pineapple juice and egg. Cook over low heat, stirring until thick and smooth. Let mixture cool. Fold pineapple, marshmallows, 1 cup of cheese and whipped cream into cooked mixture. Spread over jello. sprinkle with remaining cheese. Cover, chill overnight.

Mrs. Wilma Mast
S. Hutchinson, KS

THOUSAND ISLAND DRESSING

1 1/2 qt. salad dressing
3/4 cup pickle relish
3/4 cup catsup
1 1/2 t. salt
1/4 cup sugar

Mix by hand or with mixer. Makes approximately 2 qt.

Mrs. Emma Stutzman
Bronson, MI

Soups & Sandwiches

MAIDRITE SANDWICHES

Put in top of double boiler:

2 lb. hamburger
2 onions (diced)
1 t. chili
1 cup catsup
1 t. prepared mustard
salt to taste

Cook 1 hr. Serve hot for sandwiches or bread or buns.

Mrs. Clarence Miller
Medford, WI

CHUNKY BEEF SOUP

2 1/2 gal. water
2 large cans beef - College Inn
1 cup each white and brown sugar
1 stick butter
1 1/4 cups beef soup mix
4 qts. tomatoe juice
1/4 cup salt

Take approx. 2 qts. flour and add water to make a smooth paste to thicken soup; heat to boiling point, then mix in vegetables which have been cooked and salted separate.

4 qts. carrots, cut up fine
4 qts. peas
4 qts. hamburger or chunk beef.
4 qts. potatoes, cut in small pieces
2 large onions

Brown hamburger and onions together. Makes 21 qts. Cokd pack 2 hrs.

Louella Borntrager
Sugar Creek, OH

CHEDDAR CHEESE SOUP

2 cups water
1/2 cup diced carrots
1/4 cup chopped onion
1/4 t. pepper
2 cups diced potatoes
1/2 cup diced celery
1 t. salt

White Sauce:

1/4 cup butter
2 cups milk
1 cup cubed ham
1/4 cup flour
2 cups cheddar cheese, grated

Combine water, vegetables and seasonings in large kettle. Boil 10 min. In small saucepan make white sauce by melting butter, add flour, stir till smooth. Slowly add milk; add white sauce, cheese and ham to vegetables that have not been drained. Heat thoroughly. Serve with crackers.

Cathryn Schmucker
Litchfield, MI

CHICKEN AND DUMPLING SOUP

Chicken Broth:

1 fryer chicken, 2 1/2 lb. cut up
6 cups cold water
3 chicken bouillon cubes

Soup Base:

1 can chicken broth (10 3/4 oz.)
1 can cream of chicken soup (10 3/4 oz.)
1 can cream of mushroom soup (10 3/4 oz.)
1 cup chopped celery
1 1/2 cups chopped carrots
1/4 cup chopped onions
1 cup chopped potatoes
1 cup fresh or frozen peas

Cook fryer, cut in pieces, reserved chicken broth and 1 t. seasoned salt.

Feather Dumplings:

2 cups flour
1 t. salt
1/4 t. pepper
4 t. baking powder
1 egg
2 T. butter
2/3 cup milk

Place fryer, water and bouillon in kettle and bring to boil. Let simmer until chicken is tender. Cut up chicken in bite size pieces - set aside. Strain chicken broth. Put chicken and broth in large kettle, add rest of soup base ingredients, simmer soup on low heat until vegetables are tender. Mix up feather dumplings by sifting dry ingredients together. Add butter, egg, and milk to moist stiff batter. Drop by t. into boiling liquid. Cook covered and without "peeking" for 20 min.

Cathryn Schmucker
Litchfield, MI

CHILI SOUP

2 lb. beans
1 gal. ground beef
4 qts. tomatoe juice

Garlic, red pepper, grind garlic to beef, put in baking pan in hot oven, stir often to keep from caking. When hot, put in a large dish pan. Add cooked beans and tomatoe juice, chili, pepper, red pepper and salt. Bring to a boil, put in jars and pressure can for 1 hr. at 10 lb.

Clara Hochstetter
Canton, MO

POTATO SOUP

Cooked shredded potatoes
Salt and pepper to taste
Parsley and butter
Add small pieces of ham, and rich milk. Serve with crackers.

Mrs. Raymond S. Miller
Millersburg, OH

CHURCH SPREAD

2 cups white sugar
2 cups light karo
2 cups brown sugar
2 cups green label karo

Boil 2 min. When cook, but not cold, add 5 egg whites beaten stiff and stir until cold.

Mrs. Leroy J. Byler
Fredericktown, OH

CHICKEN NOODLE SOUP

1 gal. diced potatoes
1 gal. diced celery
1 gal. diced carrots
1 gal. fine noodles
8 chickens, cooked and diced
parsley, salt and pepper to taste

Boil each vegetable separately till half done. Save water from vegetables for juice. Add water if too thick. Add 4 boxes lipton noodle soup. Cold pack 2 1/2-3 hrs.

Saloma J. Byler
Dewittville, NY

CHILLA SOUP

4 lb. hamburg (fry in butter)
3 qt. strained tomatoes
1 qt. red kidney beans
12 small onions
2 red peppers
chilla powder to taste

Cook each separate, then mix and cook 1/2 hr.

Naomi Peachy, Little Falls, NY
Saloma J. Byler, Dewittville, NY

The little pitcher with big ears
Is likely to have a big spout too

BARBECUED SANDWICHES

1 lb. chipped ham or 1 lb. chipped or thinly sliced bologna
1 small onion, diced fine (opt.) 1/2 cup catsup
1 T. mustard 1-3 T. brown sugar

Combine above ingredients. Place a layer of meat, then a layer of sauce in a casserole - finished with sauce on top. Bake at 300 deg. for 1 hr. or instead of baking, add 1/2 cup water to sauce and cook everything but meat on top of stove for 20 min., add meat and heat thoroughly until done. Toss it with a fork instead of a spoon while stirring.

Mrs. Joe J. Miller
Apple Creek, OH

Muttonchop sideburns
Aren't worn only
by the young
You also see them
On Old Goats

SANDWICH SPREAD

First Part:
6 large green tomatoes 6 red peppers
6 onions 6 green peppers

Grind through a food chopper. Sprinkle with a handful of salt and let set 2 hrs. Drain 30 min. Then pour 2 pt. vinegar over this and cook 15 min.

Second Part:
1 cup flour 1 t. tumeric
1 pt. mustard 1 pt. vinegar
5 cups sugar

Mix this together and stir in 1st part like for any thickening and cook 15 min. Put in jars and seal. May be sealed with parafin.

Mrs. Joseph Schrock
Agusta, WI

MINESTRONE SOUP

1 lb. ground beef
1 cup diced onion
1 cup cubed raw potatoes
1 cup sliced carrots
1/2 cup diced celery
1 cup shredded cabbage
1-2 cans tomatoes
1/4 cup rice
1 small can
bay leaf crushed
1/2 t. thyme
1 leaf basil
4 t. salt
1/8 t. pepper
1 1/2 qts. water

Brown ground beef and onion in a large pan. Add next five ingredients, bring to a bil. Sprinkle rice into mixture. Add remaining ingredients, cover and simmer 1 hr. Serve as a main dish topped with shredded cheese. Serves 6.

Mrs. Joe J. Miller
Apple Creek, OH

CHILI SOUP

1 qt. tomatoes
1 qt. hamburger
1 qt. kidney beans
2 cups macaroni
1 large onion (chopped)
1 t. chili powder

Cook macaroni and beans. Fry onions good and brown. Chop hamburger and add all together and heat. Add salt and brown sugar to taste. Seal in jars and pressure cook one half hr. at 10 lbs.

Mrs. Joseph Schrock
Agusta, WI

One pound of learning requires
10 pounds of common sense to apply it

SUGAR SPREAD

1 cup water
5 cups white sugar
5 cups brown sugar
1 gal. white syrup

Cook all together for 5 min. Stir occasionally. Cool, and stir while cooling to prevent sugaring. Let set a while, then add 8 egg whites, beaten stiff. Mix till smooth. Add vanilla or maple flavor.

Mrs. Joseph Schrock
Agusta, WI

CREAM OF MUSHROOM SOUP

Pick and clean any good variety of mushrooms. Chop 2 cups of mushrooms and add 7 heaping tblsp. flour in 1 cup oleo or butter. Brown, then add some cold water and milk to desired thickness. Add salt and pepper to suit taste. Makes approximately 6 qts.

Mrs. ray J. gingerich
Fillmore, NY

BROCCOLI SOUP

1 - 10 oz. frozen broccoli frozen or 2 1/2 cups fresh
1 qt. half cream and half water
1/2 lb. velveeta
1/2 cup grated carrots
1/2 cup flour
1/4 cup butter
2 chicken bouillion cubes

Cook broccoli and carrots; add cream and flour. Best if shaken together. Add remaining ingredients, stir until melted. Great with crackers and sandwiches.

Alma Yoder
Lovington, IL

Misc

BUTTERSCOTCH DIP FOR ICE CREAM

1 1/2 cups brown sugar
3 T. white karo
1/3 cup cream
4 T. oleo

Boil together, stirring constantly, approximately 3 min. once it boils.

Mrs. Ray J. Gingerich
Fillmore, NY

HOT CHOCOLATE MIX

8 cups non-fat dry milk
1 cup sugar
11 oz. non-dairy creamer
1 1/2 lbs. Nestle's Quick

Combine all ingredients. Store in tight containers. Add 1/4 cup mix to 1 cup of hot water.

Emma Hershberger
Dover, DE

SIMPLE PIZZA DOUGH

2 cups bread flour
2 t. baking powder
1 t. salt
1/4 cup Wesson oil
2/3 cup milk

Mix flour, baking powder and salt. Add oil and milk; roll out on cookie sheet. Put pizza sauce on top. Can also put cut up sausages or weiners on. Put grated cheese on top. Bake at 375 deg. for 25 min.

Rebecca Byler
Newburg, PA

PLANT FOOD FOR FLOWERS

1 t. cream of tartar
1 t. saltpetre
1 t. ammonia
1 t. epsom salts

Mix into 7 gallons warm water. Feed to plants once a month.

Fannie S. Miller
Bird-in-Hand, PA

BOILED SOAP

16 lbs. lard
4 boxes lye
1 lb. Borax
9 gal. water

Stir while adding the water or the lye gets hard lumps sometimes. Don't add all the water right away, only 6 or 7 gals. It says boil fast 2 hrs. or slowly for 8 hrs., but I boil it till it is soap. (Add more water if you need more.)

Joe Borntreger
Cashton, WI

BOILING SOAP

6 gals. crackling & tallow
6 boxes lye
6 buckets of water or as needed

Put 2 buckets of water in kettle first, then add all the cracklings and lye; let cook till cracklings are cooked up; then add more water as needed.

Joe Borntreger
Cashton, WI

MISS SAGE SOAP

Dissolve one can of lye in 3 qts. of cold water in crockery or enamel container. Add 3/4 cup of borax and when dissolved, slowly add 9 cups of melted fat—any clean fat will do. Stir constantly with wooden stick or spoon 10-15 min., then occasionally the next 24-36 hrs. It will be white granulate and easy to handle for all purposes. The secret is lots of stirring even if the mixture separates, stirring will take care of that.

Mattie Borntreger
Cashton, WI

CORNMEAL MUSH

8 cups water
3 1/2 cups cornmeal
2 heaping T. flour
Water to mix

Cook over medium heat about 30-40 min.

Esther Marie Fisher
Conneautville, PA

A BLIGHT CONTROL

1 t. salt petre
1 t. baking powder
1 t. epsom salt
1 t. Bo-peep

To 1 gal. water and put on plants, every 2 weeks.

Mary Swartzentruber
Apple Creek, OH

CHOCOLATE DIP

Melt milk chocolate and use 1 cup (keep in double boiler) and add milk till the right thickening. If you don't add enough, it will just get hard, but be careful you don't add too much!

Mrs. Ray J. Gingerich
Fillmore, NY

EASY CHOCOLATE DIP

Take 1 cup Nestle's Quick and add just a little hot water and mix, then add approximately 2 cups white Karo syrup and mix well.

Mrs. Ray J. Gingerich
Fillmore, NY

HEALTH TEA

1 gallon water
From 8-12 clover flowers
Boil 10-15 min.
Cool and add 3/4 cup vinegar
3/4 cup sugar
2 big T. honey

Enos Yoders
Park City, KY

MIRACLE WHIP

Cook together 1 cup water and 1/2 cup flour, 1/4 cup sugar and 1/4 cup vinegar. Mix together 1 egg, plus enough water to make 1/2 cup, 1 T. lemon juice, 1/2 t. dry mustard, 1/4 cup cooking oil, 1 t. salt. Drop first mixture in part 2 by spoonfuls and beat with egg beater till smooth.

Fannie Gingerich
Ethridge, TN

BLOOD CLEANER

Slice one lemon to 1 qt. of boiling water and 1/4 t. cream of tartar. Drink 2 cups daily with meals at 1 cup for breakfast and 1 cup for noon meal till you have used 3 lemons.

Mattie Borntreger
Cashton, WI

APPLE BUTTER

4 gal. apples, snitzed and unpeeled
1/2 gal. syrup
6 lb. granulated sugar

Put snitz in cold packer, then add syrup and sugar, and put cover on. Next morn don't lift lid, cook for 4 hr. slowly over low heat. Put through a sieve or food mill and can.

Fannie Gingerich
Ethridge, TN

GRAHAM CRACKERS

2 cups brown sugar
1 cup milk
4 cups graham flour
1 cup lard or 3/4 cup lard and 1/4 cup butter
2 cups pastry flour
1 t. soda
1 t. vanilla
1 t. baking powder
1 t. salt

Then roll out thin and cut into squares and prick with a fork. Bake in a hot oven till real brown.

Enos Yoders
Park City, KY

SWEET POTATOE SYRUP

2 qts. brown sugar
1 lb. butter
2 qts. molasses
4 cups water

Makes approx. 3/4 gal. syrup.

Bertha Beiler
Loganton, PA

The bond of matrimony are no good
Unless the interest is kept up

HOME MAKE SOAP

Mix the following in stone crock or iron kettle in the following order:

10 cups cold water
9 cups melted grease
1/2 cup ammonia
3 T. borax
1 can lye

Sprinkle lye in last and let stand 5-10 min., then stir frequently for the first 1 1/2 hr.; after that once every hr. throughout the day. Avoid inhaling fumes. Let set for a few days, then put in tight containers so it will not dry out. This gets crumbly and will readily melt in water.

Mrs. Noah Wengerd, Jr.
Conewango Valley, NY

HOMEMADE CRUMB SOAP

9 cups melted lard
10 cups water
1/2 cup borax
1/2 cup ammonia
1 can lye

Mix together in order given. Stir for 15 min. until lye is dissolved. Set aside and let cool, then stir every 20 min. throughout the day. Let set in crock for a couple days, then put in tight containers, so it will not dry out.

Clara Hochstetter
Canton, MO

MARSHMALLOW CREME

2 cups sugar
1 cup water
2 1/2 cups corn syrup

Cook 15 min. or cook till soft balls. While this is cooking, place the following in a bowl:

1/2 cup warm white syrup
7/8 cup egg whites or 7 egg whites

Beat slowly until mixed, then beat hard until light and fluffy. Beat in first mixture in a fine stream (with a spoon). When all is mixed, beat hard for 3 min. Add 1 t. vanilla. Store in jars, don't cover till it's cold.

Joe Borntreger
Cashton, WI

HOMEMADE GRANULATED SOAP

1 can lye
3/4 cup borax
3 qts. cold water
4 1/2 lbs. melted fat

Use part tallow and part lard. Dissolve lye in cold water in a crock or stainless bowls using wooden spoon to stir. When dissolved, add borax. Slowly add melted fat (have fat good and warm) stirring slowly for 10-15 min. Continue to stir off and on for 24 hrs. The soap will be white and granulated. Spread out onto a pasteboard box and let dry at leat a month. Store in tight containers.

Mrs. Joseph Schrock
Agusta, WI

PEAR BUTTER

1 gal. pears
1 qt. canned apricots
8 lb. sugar
1 T. salt

Cook 1 1/2 hours. Put pears and apricots through food mil, then add sugar and salt.

Bertha Beiler
Loganton, PA

CHOCOLATE SYRUP

2 cups sugar
1/2 cup cocoa
1 cup cold water
1/2 t. salt
vanilla

Stir sugar, cocoa, and 1/2 cup cold water until smooth. Add remaining water. Cook, stirring until thick and smooth. Then cook 3 min. Add salt and vanilla. Good on ice cream.

Mrs. Daniel Borntreger
Riceville, IA

HOME MADE NOODLES

1 qt. egg yolks
1 qt. water
2 T. salt
Flour to make a stiff dough.

Makes 8 1/2 lb. noodles.

Saloma J. Byler
Dewittville, NY

MARSHMALLOW TOPPING

2 cups white sugar
2 1/2 cups light karo
1 cup water

Boil this to a firm ball stage; remove from heat; set aside for 5 min. Beat 7/8 cup egg whites until foamy. Then add 1/2 cup karo and beat some more. Add mixture and beat well. Add 1 t. vanilla. Makes about 1 gal. topping. Stir your jam in the topping or whatever you wish.

Mrs. Joe J. Yoder
Lawrenceburg, TN

GRAHAM CRACKERS

4 cups graham flour
1 cup brown sugar
1 t. soda
1 heaping t. baking powder
2 cups white flour
1 cup butter or lard
1 t. salt
1 cup sweet milk

Roll thin, bake at 475 deg.

Mrs. Joe J. Yoder
Lawrenceburg, TN

KETCHUP

3 qt. tomato juice
1 t. salt
3 drops cinnamon oil
1 1/2 qt. sugar
4 T. dry mustard
a little pepper
1 pt. vinegar

Mix and boil together till thick. Can also use a little clear jell to help thicken it.

Esther Fisher
Millersburg, PA

PIZZA SAUCE

3 qts. tomato juice
1/2 t. pepper
2 t. celery seed
1 t. cinnamon
1/2 cup chopped onions
2 T. salt
a cup vinegar
1/4 t. cloves
1 T. dry mustard
1 1/2 cups sugar

Boil 30 min. and thicken with clear jell.

Lydia Stoltzfus
Bloomsburg, PA

Trying times are times for trying

EASY HOMEMADE PIZZA

In a bowl combine:

4 cups flour
6 t. baking powder
1 t. salt

Combine:

1 1/3 cups milk
2/3 cups Wesson oil

Pour all at once over flour mixture. Mix with fork then shape into ball. Knead until smooth. Roll out for about 3 - 12 in. sheets. Place on greased cookie sheets.

Pizza Sauce

Combine:

4 - 6 oz. cans tomato paste
2/3 cup water
2/3 cup Wesson oil
2 t. oregano
2 t. garlic powder
1 t. salt
1/2 t. pepper

Put on top of dough. Add hamburger, cheese or sausage, onions or green peppers. Bake at 400 deg. for 20-25 min. Tomato juice may be thickened and used as a substitute for tomato paste.

Aaron Brubacker
Liverpool, PA

FRIED CORN MEAL MUSH

3 cups yellow cornmeal
2 qts. boiling water
1 t. salt
1/2 cup white flour

Bring water to a boil. Sift together cornmeal, salt and flour. Slowly add dry ingredients to boiling water, stirring constantly to prevent lump. Cook till done, pour into flat pans to mold. Let stand overnight. Cut slices 1/4 in. thick and fry on both sides till golden brown. Delicious with tomato gravy, hot maple syrup or apple butter.

Martha I. Shetler
Glasgow, KY

FRIED EGGPLANT

2 medium-sized eggplants
2 eggs
1 t. salt
1 cup cracker crumbs
a little pepper

Pare eggplant and slice 1/4 in. thick. Beat eggs, salt and pepper together. Dip eggplants in egg mixture and roll in cracker crumbs. Fry in hot fat until golden brown on both sides.

Tastes a lot like fish!

Martha I. Shetler
Glasgow, KY

Everytime you turn green with envy
You are ripe for trouble

ROACH POISON

1 cup flour
16 oz. boric acid
1 small chopped onion
1/4 cup shortening or oil

Enough water to form a stiff dough. Shape into small balls and place where you think roaches hide, etc. Make sure no children or pets get these as are poisonous.

Martha I. Shetler
Glasgow, KY

BLOOD POISON SALVE

1/2 lb. white Rosin
1/2 lb. bees wax
1/2 lb. mutton tallow or sheep lard
4 oz. gum camphor
6 oz. soft soap (dish wash soap)

Put first three ingredients in a pan to dissolve, add rest while cooling. Cut camphor fine before putting it in jars. Use for a drawing salve.

Martha I. Shetler
Glasgow, KY

UNSTIRRED APPLE BUTTER

5 gal. apples
10 lb. sugar
1 t. cinnamon
1/4 t. cloves
1 cup vinegar

Cut up apples (unpeeled) in quarters; put apples, sugar and spices in large cooker. Cover tightly and place over low or simmer overnight. Do not lift lid; in morning add 1 cup vinegar, simmer 6 hrs. more over low heat without removing lid. Then put through victoria strainer or food mill. May be used for snitz pies, putting in desired flavor.

Esther Fisher
Millersburg, PA

PIZZA DOUGH

1 1/2 cups flour
1/2 T. yeast
1/4 t. salt
1/2 cup water
1 1/2 T. Wesson oil

Enough for 1 cookie sheet.

Esther Fisher
Millersburg, PA

COOKED APPLE BUTTER

1 qt. white karo
1 cup white sugar
1 qt. applesauce

Cook this to heavy jam, then add:

1 pt. apple butter from store
1/2 box strawberry jello

Mrs. Raymond S. Miller
Millersburg, OH

ZUCCHINI BUTTER

"A mock apple butter"

4 cups cooked and blended zucchini (remove seeds)
4 T. vinegar
1 t. lemon juice
2 cups sugar
1 t. cinnamon
1/8 t. all spice
1/2 cup red hots candy (if desired)

Put in crockpot or in oven and cook to the desired thickness. We like this better than apple butter and it's cheaper.

Mary A. Kinsinger
Meyersdale, PA

PIZZA DOUGH

1 T. yeast dissolved in 3/4 cup warm water
1 T. oil
2 cups pie flour
1 t. sugar
1 t. salt

Combine flour, sugar and salt. Add oil to yeast and water mixture. Combine with flour. Knead until smooth. Let rise 20-30 min. Spread dough on pizza pan and spread pizza sauce, meat and cheese and seasoning as desired. Let it rest 10 min. Bake at 500 deg 10-15 min.

Bertha Beiler
Loganton, PA

SUMMER IN JUG WINE

Use fresh picked blackberries

Crush 1 gal. of black, add 1 qt. boiling water; let stand 1 day; strain and add 3 qts. of water and 2 pounds brown sugar. Mix and put in jugs with loose cork. Put in cool place - ready about October. Use for flu and colds.

Mrs. Joe J. Yoder
Lawrenceburg, TN

WHOOPING COUGH TEA

1 cup flax seed
1 sliced lemon
1 qt. water

Simmer 4 hrs. Steam 2 oz. honey. Take 1 T. full 3 times a day or after each cough spell.

Mrs. Joe J. Yoder
Lawrenceburg, TN

SOAP MAKING FROM LYE CAN

1 can lye
2 1/2 pints cold water
6 lb. or 9 pints fat and tallow lard (melted)

This makes 9 lb. soap. Stir it together when lukewarm. Stir till thick. Cut it before it bets too hard.

Mattie Borntreger
Cashton, WI

PLAY DOUGH

1 cup flour 1/2 cup salt
2 t. cream of tartar 1 cup water
1 T. cooking oil

Mix all together. Cook 3 min. or until it pulls away from side of pan. Knead. Divide dough for different colors. Use food color.

Lydiann J. Bricker
Panama, NY

KNOX BLOX

3 envelopes knox gelatin 3 cups boiling water
3 (3 oz.) pkg. strawberry jello

Mix together the gelatin and jello. Add the boiling water, stir until completely dissolved. Chill and cut into sqaures or cutt with cookie cutters to make attractive shapes for different occasions.

Colleen Headings
Hutchinson, KS

MARSHMALLOW CREAM

2 cups sugar 2 1/2 cups corn syrup
1 cup water

Cook to 240 deg. While this is cooling, place the following in mixing bowl:

1/2 cup corn syrup 1/2 cup egg whites

Beat slowly until mixed, then beat hard until light and fluffy. Beat in first mixture in a fine stream. When all mixed, beat hard 3 min. Add 1 t. vanilla or maple flavr. Store in can or jar. Stir until cold.

Mrs. Jacob Stutzman
Jeromesville, OH

PLAY DOUGH

2 1/2 cups flour 1/2 cup salt
3 T. corn oil 1 T. alum
2 cups boiling water cake coloring

Stir together. Keep in covered container. Nice for children to play with.

Mrs. Vernon E. Bontrager

DEEP DISH TACO SQUARES

1 lb. ground beef
1 cup sour cream
2/3 cup mayonnaise
2-3 medium tomatoes, thinly sliced
2 T. chopped onions
2 cups buttermilk baking mix
1 cup chopped green pepper
1 cup shredded sharp cheddar cheese

Fry beef, with salt and pepper until born; drain. Mix sour cream, mayonnaise, cheese, and onion and reserve. Mix baking mix and 1/2 cup water until soft dough forms. Pat into 9x13 in. greased pan, pressing dough at least 1/2 in. up sides. Layer beef, tomatoes and green peppers in pan; spoon sour cream mixture over top. Sprinkle with paprika if desired. Bake in 375 deg. oven until edges of dough are light brown, about 30-40 min.

Joni H. Shrock
Middlefield, OH

SNACK CRACKERS

1 lb. oyster crackers
3/4 cup oil

Pour oil over crackers and stir well.
Mix together and put on crackers:

1 t. garlic powder
1 t. dill seeds
1 t. lemon pepper
1 pkg. dry (Hidden Ranch Valley salad dressing mix)

Put in low oven and heat for 30 min., stirring occasionally.

Fannie S. Miller
Bird-in-Hand, PA

PUPPY CHOW (CHEX SNACKS)

1 stick oleo
1 cup peanut butter
1 lb. chocolate chips

Melt together over low heat. Put one box of Chex cereal in dishpan. Pour hot mixture over chex cereal. Stir real good, then dump 2 cups powdered sugar in large tupperware bowl and put cereal mixture in bowl and put lid on and shake real good. Put on cookie sheet till cold.

Lucinda Hilty
Monroe, IN

TACO SHELLS

1 1/2 cups water
1 cup white flour
1/2 cup cornmeal
dash of salt
Roll out and bake.

Esther Marie Fisher
Conneautville, PA

OYSTER CRACKER SNACK

Mix:
1 1/2 cups vegetable oil
1 1/2 t. lemon pepper
1 pkg. ranch dressing
1/2 t. garlic powder
Pour over 2 pkgs. small dainty oyster crackers. Bake at 200 deg. for 1 hr. Stir every 15 min.

Cathryn Schmucker
Litchfield, MI

PEANUT BUTTER POPCORN

Melt together:
1/4 cup oleo
2 T. peanut butter
3 T. white sugar
Pour over 3 qt. lightly salted popcorn.

Martha Maste
Revere, MO

PEANUT BUTTER CORN

1 cup white corn syrup
1 - 12 oz. jar peanut butter
1 cup flaked coconut
1 cup granulated sugar
4 1/2 cups corn flakes
Combine sugar and corn syrup. Bring to a boil. Remove from heat and stir in peanut butter. Pour this mixture over the cornflakes and coconut. Mix well. Drop by t. on wax paper.

Martha I. Shetler
Glasgow, KY

When we are willing to do what we can
We shall be surprised at how much we can do

SOFT PRETZELS

2 pkg. dry yeast
1 cup lukewarm water
2 cups milk, scalded
2 T. sugar
2 t. salt
7 1/2 cups sifted flour

For Boiling:

2 qt. water
1 T. soda

For Brushing Top:

1 egg, beaten
1 T. water

Dissolve yeast in water. Add scalded milk to sugar and salt. Cool. Add flour and yeast. Let rise till doubled. Roll out and form pretzels. Let rise 1/2 hr. Boil 1 minute in soda water. Brush with egg water and sprinkle with coarse salt. Bake 18 min. or till brown on greased baking sheet. Delicious!

Saloma Petersheim
Mifflintown, PA

ICE CREAM SANDWICHES

2 cups sugar
1 cup shortening
2 eggs
1 t. vanilla
1 cup sour cream
pinch of salt
2 t. soda
4 or 5 cups flour
6 T. cocoa
1 t. cinnamon (can omit)
1/2 t. ginger

Make dough to handle. Chill several hours. Roll 1/4 in. thick. Prick with fork and cut in squares. Put on cookie sheet and bake. Let cool on sheet. Spread with your favorite ice cream. Delicious.

Emma Hershberger
Dover, DE

BURFI (MILK FUDGE)

3 1/2 pt. whole milk
7 oz. sugar
2 T. butter

Put milk in heavy bottom kettle and stir as fast as you can for 45 min. to 1 hr. until milk is so thick it rolls into a ball. Stove should be quite hot. When milk becomes paste-like, and the spatula leaves a momentary trail, add sugar and butter. Continue cooking and stirring (till you think you can't stir anymore!) then let it cook a few minutes longer. Pour into buttered pie plate.

Saloma Petersheim
Mifflintown, PA

POPCORN BALLS

1 cup sugar
1/3 cup corn syrup (light or dark)
1/3 cup water
1/4 cup butter or margarine
3/4 t. salt
3/4 t. vanilla
3 qt. popped corn (keep warm)

Stir and cook sugar, corn syrup, water, butter and salt until sugar is dissolved. Continue cooking without stirring until syrup forms a soft ball in cold water. Add vanilla. Pour syrup slowly over popcorn. Mix well to caot every kernel. Grease hands with butter before shaping. Makes 12 medium sized balls

Catherine Swarey
Belleville, PA

OPERA CREAMS

1 1/2 cups sugar
1 cup cream
butter, size of a walnut
1 t. vanilla
2 t. cocoa
(For a vanilla flavored candy, omit cocoa)

Mix. Cook until a soft ball. Let cook without stirring. When cool, stir until very light in color. Drop on waxed paper with a teaspoon.

Catherine Swarey
Belleville, PA

CRISPY CARMEL CORN

7 qts. popped corn
1 cup peanuts
2 cups brown sugar
1/2 cup white corn syrup
1 t. salt
1 t. vanilla
1/2 t. soda
1 cup margarine

Measure into a saucepan the brown sugar, margarine, corn syrup and salt. Bring to a boil and boil 5 min. Remove from heat and stir in vanilla and soda. Pour over the freshly popped corn and peanuts which has been measured into a large container. Mix well and turn out into two large cake pans. Put into a 250 deg. oven for one hr. Stir corn occasionally while in oven. When corn is removed from oven and cool enough to handle, the kernels can easily be separated and stored in a covered container.

Aaron Brubacker
Liverpool, PA

PARTY MIX

Mix together:

1/2 box Cheerios
1/2 box Corn Chex
1/2 box Rice Chex
2 boxes pretzels
peanuts or cashews

Stir in 1/2 lb. melted margarine and 2 T. Worcestershire sauce. Bake in 350 deg. oven for 30 min., stirring often.

Then mix:

2 t. celery salt,
2 t. seasoned salt
1 t. sour cream and onion

Sprinkle over party mix and return to oven for 15 min. or more.

Bertha Beiler
Loganton, PA

CRACKER JACK

2 cups brown sugar
4 T. molasses
1/2 pt. water
Butter, size of an egg

Put in butter pan with 1 t. cream of tartar. Boil until spins a thread, remove from heat and stir in 1/2 t. soda. Then pour syrup over popcorn. Stir and dry in oven.

Mrs. Joe J. Yoder
Lawrenceburg, TN

The human body is quite sensitive
Pat a person on the back and
The head often swells immediately

OVEN CARMEL CORN

15 cups popped popcorn
1/4 cup light corn syrup
1/2 t. salt
1/2 cup oleo
1 cup brown sugar
1/2 t. soda

Combine oleo, brown sugar, corn syrup and salt. When it starts to bubble around the edges, time it for 5 min. Take off of heat and add soda. Stir till foamy, then pour on popcorn. Stir well. Put on cookie sheets and bake until brown, stirring often.

Barbara Schrock
Spartansburg, PA

EASY POPCORN BALLS

1 cup brown sugar packed
8 cups miniature marshmallows
1 stick margarine
8 qts. popped corn

Melt brown sugar, marshamallows and margarine in saucepan on top of stove. Pour over popcorn. Butter hands and mix to form the size balls you prefer. Place on waxed paper and cool till they aren't sticky anymore. Store in airtight containers.

Barbara Schrock
Spartansburg, PA

JELLO POPSICKLES

1 pkg (3 oz.) jello
2 cups cold water
2 cups boiling water
1 pkg. Kool-Aid
1 cup sugar

Add boiling water to jello, sugar and kool-aid. Then add cold water. Pour into containers and freeze.

Barbara Schrock
Spartansburg, PA

PECAN TASTEES

3 oz. cream cheese
1/4 lb. butter or margarine
1 cup flour

Mix together and form 24 balls, then press into muffin tins.

2 eggs, slightly beaten
1 1/2 cups brown sugar
2 T. melted butter
1/2 t. vanilla
pinch of salt

Put 1/2 t. chopped pecans or other nuts on cream cheese mixture and pour in second mixture. Bake at 350 deg. for 30 min.

Lydia Stoltzfus
Bloomsburg, PA

CRACKER JACKS

1 cup sorghum molasses
1 cup sugar (or less)
pinch of salt
1/2 cup butter
alum (size of a bullet)

Cook in skillet until thick enough. Add 1/2 t. soda. Pour over popcorn and mix.

Mrs. Samuel D. Beachy
Clark, MO

CHOCOLATE LOGS

3 cups powdered sugar
1 1/2 cups peanut butter
1 cup melted butter
3 1/2 cups Rice Krispie cereal
1 cup coconut

Mix butter, peanut butter, sugar. Add Rice Krispies and coconut. Make into two logs. Chill. Dip into coating chocolate.

Saloma J. Byler
Dewittville, NY

Index

D

E

F

G

H

Q

T

U

V

W

Y

Z